Islamic Economics Series – 24

PERSPECTIVES ON MORALITY AND HUMAN WELL-BEING

A Contribution to Islamic Economics

Syed Nawab Haider Naqvi

THE ISLAMIC FOUNDATION

Published by
THE ISLAMIC FOUNDATION
Markfield Conference Centre, Ratby Lane,
Markfield, Leicester LE67 9SY, United Kingdom
Tel: (01530) 244944/5, Fax: (01530) 244946
E-mail: i.foundation@islamic-foundation.org.uk
Web site: www.islamic-foundation.org.uk

QURAN HOUSE, P.O. Box 30611, Nairobi, Kenya

P.M.B. 3193, Kano, Nigeria

British Library Cataloguing-in-Publication Data

Naqvi, Syed Nawab Haider, 1935-
Perspectives on morality and human well-being : a contribution to Islamic economics
1. Islam - Economic aspects 2. Economics - Moral and ethical aspects 3. Economics - Religious aspects - Islam 4. Islamic ethics
I. Title II. Islamic Foundation
297.2'73

ISBN 0 86037 328 2
ISBN 0 86037 387 8 pbk

Typeset and Cover design by: Nasir Cadir

Printed and bound in Great Britain by
Antony Rowe Ltd., Chippenham, Wiltshire

Dedicated

to

my wife *Saeeda;*

our children:

Andalib, Tehmina, Qurrat-ul-ain,
and *Neelofar;*

and grandchildren:

Akbar, Rohina, and *Zara*

Contents

Acknowledgments

In a work of this kind, intellectual indebtedness to people who help grows at an exponential rate. Although it is impossible to mention them all, I am nonetheless deeply indebted to Professor Khurshid Ahmad, Chairman, The Islamic Foundation, who has been a source of unswerving support. I thank him for inviting me to write the present work, and for suggesting invaluable ideas, which have been incorporated into it. I am also especially grateful to Dr. Manazir Ahsan, Director General, The Islamic Foundation, who arranged financial and library support for this project; and to Mr. Khalid Rahman, Executive Director, The Institute of Policy Studies, Islamabad, for making available the necessary facilities. Special thanks are due to Mr. Faisal Khan, a promising lawyer, for his willingness to work 'beyond the call of duty', and for providing highly competent assistance, advice and support. Without his labour of love, this book could not have been completed on time. Also noteworthy is the assistance extended by my daughter, Neelofar Nawab, a lawyer, who suggested some good ideas and made important editorial improvements to the work. I also wish to record my profound appreciation and thanks to Dr. Rehana Siddiqui, Chief of Research, The Institute of Development Economics, Islamabad, for undertaking difficult empirical work which I assigned to her from time to time; to Professor Zafar Ishaq Ansari, Director General, The Islamic

Research Institute, International Islamic University, Islamabad, for granting me unrestricted access to his very rich personal library, and to Professor Alamgir A. Hashmi for a stimulating exchange of views. I also wish to record appreciation of the excellent work done by Dr. Mehmet Asutay, the Head of the Islamic Economics Unit of the Islamic Foundation, Ms. Amrana Arif and Mr. Nasir Cadir, respectively secretary and graphic designer of the Islamic Foundation, and lastly Ms. Suzanne Thackray and Mr. Eric Fox, language editor and proof reader, to prepare this book for final publication. However, no list of acknowledgments can ever be complete without the most prominent mention of my (deceased) parents, (Syed Mohammed, Hasan Fatima and Hameed Fatima); of my uncle and aunt (Syed Mustafa Hasan and Haideri Begum), who very early in my life filled my heart with compassion for the least-privileged in society. I also thank my wife and children, sons-in-law (Imran and Ali Raza) and grandchildren, my sister, Nasim Zehra, and many other noble souls for protecting me from the 'ravages' of time. And yet, while my gratitude to those people noted above is profound, only I bear the responsibility for the views expressed in this book.

Foreword

The fall of the Berlin Wall in 1989, symbolising the collapse of Communism in the former USSR and Eastern Europe, was taken as a turning point in contemporary history, heralding, as claimed by intellectuals like Francis Fukuyama, a 'final victory' for capitalism and liberal democracy – indeed, as the 'end of history'. The euphoria was, however, short-lived. Soon, the capitalist world began to be visited by one crisis after another: the Japanese stagnation after the implosion of its bubble economy, the crescendo in German unemployment and a low growth rate after integration, the Mexican, Argentinian and Brazilian financial debacles, a monetary roller-coaster for France and Great Britain resulting in the latter's exit from the European monetary mechanism, the financial destabilisation of the South East Asian countries, the reversal of the dot.com upswing, the corporate crisis not merely undermining the US economy but also eroding confidence and trust in the key institutions of capitalism and the credibility of captains of economy in the wake of scandals involving Enron (USA), World Com (USA), Xerox Corp. (USA), Vivendi Universal (France) ABB Ltd. (Switzerland), Anderson. And then a decade of long-rising universal protest against globalisation as an instrument for the universalisation of an unjust and exploitative economic order. All these episodes have brought into sharp focus the failings of the capitalist system, only recently eulogised as mankind's final destiny.

Fortunately, the tone and temper of the current intellectual and political debate is changing. Two crucial strands of thought can be clearly discerned: namely, (a) a re-discovery of the critical relevance of morality to economic decision-making, and (b) the incapacity of the market-mechanism alone to ensure economic growth, stability and the well-being of all human beings and national and global economies.

The inherent weakness of the secular, liberal economic model has been exposed. Furthermore, the weakness of an *exclusive* reliance on 'efficiency'/'growth' criterion is being increasingly acknowledged in informed circles. The search for new paradigms that can simultaneously focus on 'efficiency with equity', 'growth with justice', and 'wealth with well-being' goes on.

There is also another dimension to this debate that is equally important. The centrality of the market mechanism is not in dispute. What is unacceptable however is "market fundamentalism", as George Soros one of the icons of capitalism has put it. The market cannot be allowed to be the lone arbiter of economic decision-making. Instead, it must be constrained and guided by moral values and social objectives. Non-market institutions have a role to play as an integral part of the socio-economic matrix. The state too has a positive, although not totalitarian or authoritarian, role to play to ensure not only the efficient working of the market but also the achievement of the moral and social goals of society. The bubble of market fetishism has burst with the crumbling of corporate capitalism and the failure of the Western economic ideology to eliminate poverty, extreme economic inequalities, and gross injustices from human society, both global as well as in developed countries. Within such an intellectual landscape the publication of Professor Syed Nawab Haider Naqvi's book *Perspectives on Morality and Human Well-Being: A Contribution to Islamic Economics* is like a breath of fresh air. It represents an incisive effort to clinch the issues and set the debate in right perspective.

Perspectives on Morality and Human Well-Being goes to the heart of the problem: economic problems, like all human problems, can be equitably solved only with reference to the moral desiderata. The scope of the present study is comprehensive. Prof. Naqvi surveys the moral landscapes of secularism and three major religious traditions: Judaism, Christianity and Islam. Avoiding the brow-beaten track of polemics, he strives to make a rigorous and scientific inquiry into the parameters developed or proposed by these four major cultural and historical movements of human history. Instead of pontificating he leaves judgment to the reader, providing the much needed light to illumine the horizon and facilitate choice. It is the reader who will derive his own conclusion, but the guidelines and lamp-posts are very clear.

Prof. Naqvi has been grappling with the crucial yet generally ignored dimension of the relationship between economics, ethics and religion. His two earlier works *Ethics and Economics: An Islamic Synthesis* (1981), and *Islam, Economics and Society* (1994) were valuable preludes to the present study, which reflects his rendezvous with maturity. No human effort can present the final word, and the present work never assumes to be that chivalrous. But *Perspectives on Morality and Human Well-Being* does represent Professor Naqvi's mature thinking and deserves to be acknowledged as a high water mark in his intellectual journey to Islamic Economics. Three characteristics can be clearly discerned in the present study:

Firstly, he delves, diligently and objectively, into the philosophic premises of contemporary economics and has come up with an honest appraisal of their positive and negative dimensions. He takes economics, and contemporary economic thinking, seriously. As a seasoned researcher he tries to sift the grain from the chaff. He affirms the importance of the economic forces and of the factors that underlie growth. But he is very clear that growth, while necessary, is not enough. And this leads him to bring in the dimensions of justice, sharing and sacrifice as integral to the economic calculus. This becomes possible only in a framework in which ethics and economics are *structurally* integrated, and not merely juxtaposed or at best one acting as a mere appendage to the other.

Secondly, the book focuses on the sources of morality, both secular and religious, and powerfully demonstrates that the religious tradition, particularly the Islamic one, provides an appropriate framework for both private morality and public policy. His exposition of the Islamic moral strategy represents an acceptable and workable formulation in our times. The merit of discussion lies in raising the right questions, surveying the vast landscape of debate and discussion, past and present, and putting forward a formula that can be a basis for further discussion, research and policy formulation. The present work serves that function both ably and effectively.

Thirdly, this work represents a worthwhile shift from simple theoretical discussions and paves the way to evaluating the worth of specific policies on the basis of empirical information. An effort has been made to construct a profile of the contemporary Muslim world in the context of the global situation and to assess its worth in the light of the value-criteria based on the author's formulation of Islamic policy objectives.

In my view Prof. Naqvi has covered fresh ground in all these three areas and as such the present work represents a landmark contribution towards the evolving discipline of Islamic Economics.

I have a couple of observations, however. I place them on record as items for future elaboration. The author's discussion of *Maqāṣid al-Sharī'ah* is relevant and useful, but the question of their re-formulation in the context of contemporary challenges is a very sensitive issue. To deconstruct and reconstruct in fundamental areas of *uṣūl* is a gigantic task. There is no denying the need to build on what the luminaries have achieved in the past. But, as the author himself notes, the process has to be authentic as well as creative. In this context, the role of the Mu'tazilah remains controversial. Their contributions in fields of philosophy, morality and law, although important and path-breaking, remained overtly influenced by aspects of Greek philosopy. As such most of their innovative ideas never received complete acceptence by the Ummah. That is why the real influence on the mainstream Muslim thought remained marginal.

Similarly, the works of some writers like Zia Gokalp, Sir Syed Ahmad Khan *etc.*, lack clarity and erudition, and their command over and understanding of the Qur'ān and the *Sunnah* and the science of Islamic jurisprudence is problematic. The door of *ijtihād* is open and must remain open to ensure the vitality and resilience of the Ummah. But competence and command over the original sources are equally important requirements for this challenging task, along with understanding the problems of the time. True, the forces representing conservatism have not managed to respond creatively to fresh challenges; yet also telling is the failure of the force of liberalism, which lacks vision, a commitment to original sources, and the competence to comprehend the ethos of tradition. Moreover even their understanding of the spirit and challenges of the modern age remains superficial, even somewhat slavish. The middle path then is the right option. Faith, fortitude and loyalty to Divine Principles should go hand in hand with creativity, flexibility and the ability to face the ever-changing intellectual, economic, technological and civilisational challenges. Perhaps what is needed is faith with fortitude, confidence with humility, loyalty with openness, and innovations rooted in tradition. This should be the defining character of the contemporary Islamic debate.

Prof. Naqvi has some strong opinions on some of the issues that emerge from his survey of the intellectual debate of the medieval period of Islamic history as well as the policy prescriptions that, in his opinion, are a logical demand of the empirical profiles based on UN data and definitions. Some of his recommendations (particularly on population policy) may not carry universal support, but that is not needed or even expected. His contribution lies in his painstaking examination of the issues and his bold suggestions to set the Ummah along the path to progress. Most of his observations will be endorsed by a large number of Islamic economists and thinkers. But as he disagrees with some of his colleagues, they too can express their reservations in respect of some of his suggestions and formulations. Therein lies the merit of debate and *shurā*. Islamic Economics is not a body of agreed ideas; it is not a closed system. It represents a new approach to economics and society and is passing through a creative phase of discussion, dialogue, debate and reconstruction of thought and policy. Prof. Naqvi is a key participant in this resounding process. He has broken some new ground, and has shed light on old and new issues in Islamic economics. He has also stepped on some toes. That is part of the game. Yet his positive contributions are enough to assure him a place of distinction in this galaxy of creative writers and thinkers. He has definitely furthered the debate and improved the level of discussion. He has raised some pertinent questions that cannot be ignored. The answers lie in research, discussion and experimentation. Here, it is effort that is its own prize. It is the process that is important, and as long as it moves upwards and onwards, we have enough reason to thank Allah for making us participants in this effort to make the world a better place to live in for all human beings. Let us hope and pray that this intellectual odyssey brings us ever closer to our Lord, perhaps also towards our destiny, both now and in the hereafter.

Islamabad
September 7, 2002 **Prof. Khurshid Ahmad**

Preface

This book marks the culmination of a theme which I have been revisiting, like the ghost of Hamlet's father, since 1978 – namely, the ethical foundations of Islamic economics. The theme is foundational because it explicitly recognises that individual economic well-being has a deep moral basis, which itself is rooted in religious beliefs. However, none of these statements is noncontroversial. The first part of the statement has for long been denied – or contemptuously ignored – by mainstream (i.e., neo-classical) economics, which insists on its secularity and amoral character. It is claimed that individual well-being and social and material prosperity are best looked after by *rational* behaviour, which simply means self-interestedness. The aim of economic activity, which is driven exclusively by selfishness and cupidity is, accordingly, to attain an "unimprovable" Pareto-optimal state in which everyone has a share but no responsibility, because there is nothing for an individual to be responsible for. This state, though distributionally neutral, is *not* regarded as morally reprehensible because it represents the highest feasible collective good. (How can anyone complain about a move from a Pareto-inferior to a Pareto-superior state?) It is, therefore, *not* rational for people to be committed to a cause or to make sacrifices if none are needed – to work for the good of others *means* taking a cut in one's own welfare. Thus, a disregard of social welfare would be regarded as rational, and moral behaviour could be dismissed as irrational. The second part of the statement is even more controversial for its overt non-secularity. It remains unacknowledged even by those (now a rapidly multiplying tribe) who accept the essential morality of economic behaviour. The reason cited, though not always explicitly stated, is that what is morally correct (or incorrect) has been intuitively obvious to men/ women of normal intelligence, even in times before the advent of Religion. Thus, the formation of moral intuition is independent of any particular religious beliefs. And even if religious beliefs are accepted as relevant, then these are *dominated* by secular morality. Therefore, they are redundant as determinants of human well-being.

But, despite the strength of the agnostic positions about its central theme, this work seeks to examine and challenge such positions about the scientific invulnerability of an amoral and a secularist economics. It argues for an economics informed by a deep sense of morality, even one leavened by religious morality. The nature of the spiritual problem hidden behind an apparently amoral economic mechanism is brought out so as to show that economic well-being is guided not by a vague, faceless moral intuition, but by one whose features are honed and chiselled by religious values that individuals hold without question. Not only that; what men/women do for their own well-being and for the collective good, is strongly coloured by the religious beliefs to which human societies subscribe. In the Islamic context, this statement means that the economic behaviour of individuals in a typical Muslim society would *normally* be guided by Islamic morality. No less important is the reverse causation, running *from* economics *to* ethics. One does not have to be a Marxian to believe that a 'living' morality must respond to social and economic challenges – i.e., to the 'unfinished agenda' of human existence – by making life more free, prosperous, and equitable. Indeed, an ethical system that does *not* do so will be overrun by systems that respond to these challenges. These statements, however, should not be construed as an attempt to 'balkanise' economic science into societies and religions, or to deny the universality of *some* of its laws. It is rather a plea to explain human motivation better and more fully. It is also to inform it with a sense of history by taking into account its physical location as well as the moral and religious mainsprings of economic activity.

The present discussion differs from my earlier work, as well as that of others, in Islamic economics in at least two respects: firstly, save a cursory mention towards the end, it omits altogether an analysis of the problems (and prospects) of the abolition of interest and the introduction of Islamic banking in Muslim societies. There are at least two reasons for this omission. (a) The topic has been dealt with at length quite recently [Jarhi and Iqbal (2001); Chapra (2000); Naqvi (2000); Iqbal, Ahmad, and Khan (1998)]; and a modicum of scholarly consensus has been built around *some* of its basic themes. Thus, additional inputs of intellectual effort in this area promise only sharply diminishing returns in knowledge and understanding. (b) My main concern here is with the broader issues of economic growth, distributive justice, poverty reduction, and human deprivation; indeed, with those social elements which are inimical to humane living in real-life Muslim societies. And, contrary to widely-held opinion, the contribution of interest-free banking to the resolution of these issues is tangential at best. On the contrary, it is possible to conceive of situations where an economy-wide substitution of interest for profit may worsen the situation with respect to distributive justice and poverty [Naqvi and Qadir (1986)]! This, however, is *not* an argument for retaining interest in an Islamic economy. Yet it warns against the facile claim that a financial system based on *only* a Profit-and-Loss Sharing (PLS-*only*) arrangement would unlock the door to economic prosperity and personal happiness. The evidence on Islamic banking so far unmistakably shows that PLS instruments have lost out in the process of natural selection, practically vanishing from the Islamic Bank's portfolio. The main reasons are: the rate of return on them has been generally lower than before; and the higher incidence of moral hazard significantly increases the cost of bank loans [Khan and Mirakhor (1992)]. The task ahead is to go beyond procedural puritanism and produce – e.g., through financial engineering – something strikingly original which can win the acknowledgment of the people.

Secondly, also omitted from this analysis are intersystemic comparisons between Islam, capitalism, and socialism. This is because: (a) there is nothing new to add to the many competent treatments of the subject, including my own modest effort [Sayyid Quṭb (2000); Naqvi (1981; 1994); Chapra (1992); Sadr (1982); Taleghani (1982); Ahmad (1981)]. (b) It is tricky territory, where one can easily succumb to the logical error of comparing an *ideal* Islamic economy with the *reality* of capitalism and socialism. Such comparisons seek to prove the superiority of the Islamic system to competing economic systems; but, the plain fact is that, in the absence of a functional Islamic economic system, such 'proof' is, by and large, logically false. The superiority of an Islamic economic system can be convincingly established *only* on the basis of the better actual economic performance of Muslim societies *vis-à-vis* non-Muslim societies. But despite much horn-tooting and waving of flags in the last four decades, Muslim societies have precious little concrete evidence on this count. The Islamisation experience of Pakistan, and especially that of Iran, though most valuable, does not yet provide an adequate basis for meaningful intersystemic comparisons; while others have simply failed to grasp the nettle. We must face the unpleasant reality that, with a few honourable exceptions, Muslim countries might as well have been on the moon, for all the difference they could make to the course of economic events. Indeed, they have generally done *worse* than non-Muslim countries in terms of most indicators of human well-being. True, the economic failure of Muslim societies cannot possibly be blamed on Islamic ethics and economics; but the available empirical evidence also does not entitle us to make general statements about the *a priori* superiority of traditional

Islamic solutions either. As stellar economic achievement still eludes Muslim societies, any self-congratulation would be odd.

Yet, the present discussion of the Islamic economic system is no less urgent for these omissions. There has to be a renewed emphasis on the centrality of having a healthy interaction between religion, ethics, and economics to gain human happiness. I have dealt with this topic elsewhere [Naqvi (1981; 1994)], but here I look at it from a new angle. The central message is that: (a) the Muslim world must give up the dangerous notion of a Muslim society which is challenged by changes and yet remains the same. (b) Moral principles, like the human environment to which they must relate, need to be put under the unblinking gaze of historical evolution to save them from becoming mirror images of a distant past. And they should take into account contemporary Muslim society's demands and aspirations. (c) Expedient measures – i.e., measures which condoned departures from moral ideals to deal with social reality in the Middle Ages – should not be allowed to become permanent moral dilemmas in today's world. Instead, a greater informational base must be built on the foundations of old *and* new knowledge about ethical systems, both secular and religious, to evaluate traditional prescriptions *and* to resolve the social and economic complexities of modern Muslim societies. (d) Reason and science must have a much greater role in Islamic economics, which is chock-full of unyielding anachronisms, not open to intellectual debate or empirical verification. Visiting it, one sometimes feels like cantering 'down the dark defile of a bygone age'. And even when a debate of some kind is conducted, using modern analytical methods, it is simply contrived to reach pre-arranged conclusions, which are invariably nuggets of antediluvian wisdom. Consequently, such exercises, notwithstanding the scientific pretence, do not create *new* knowledge, any more than hanging autumnal leaves back on top of the trees may herald a new spring. What is urgently needed in the Muslim world are bold ventures in the realm of knowledge, beyond empty rhetoric and sterile formalisms.

All this must change to make our discipline relevant to reality. In particular, the deeply ingrained habits of enunciating infallible verities that defy obsolescence must be given up by the students of this difficult but rewarding discipline. The hard fact is that what is intellectually obsolete must be quietly discarded. Rather than staking out a claim about the self-sufficiency of traditional wisdom, the proper attitude should be one of humility – because here, as elsewhere, what we already know is only a small proportion of what we do not know yet. In a milieu of incessant change, a deterministic mindset extinguishes optimism about humankind's capacity to change its condition for the better. The all-enveloping revolution in the realm of ethics and economics must, therefore, be reflected in Islamic economics as well. Its continued vitality and fertility demands a flow of *new* ideas. For want of them, Islamic economics may soon come to resemble "truths", in Aldous Huxley's words which "begin as heresies and end as superstitions".

Fortunately, all is not yet lost. The present work foresees a flourishing future for Islamic economics, if it is delivered from the deadweight of conservatism and if it is allowed to flower in an environment where intellectual freedom is not considered as criminal abuse of the God-given gift of human reason. The key to success lies in the ability to see, in different times and places, the contrast between the extant economic reality and the prevailing religious ethical mores of society, and to design a flexible economic and ethical response to this contrast. This is hard work, but nothing solid can be achieved without it. To this end, I have sought to give a vivid sense of the Islamic moral vision in a logically rigorous manner, and I compare it with self-contained analyses of the secular, Christian, and Jewish moral visions. The aim is to determine the influence of morality in general, and of Islamic morality in particular, on the principal determinants of human well-being, especially those which relate to economic growth, distributive justice, and poverty alleviation; and to recognise that the constraints set by free-riding and assurance problems severely limit what (private) morality *alone* can do to enhance human happiness. However, recognising the latter possibility is *not* a recommendation for launching a vain search for nature-defeating moral perfectibility. It rather opens up a vast fertile territory that an egalitarian *public* policy can productively furrow – to correct the inequities of the existing system of rewards and incentives, and to provide redress to those adversely affected by it. In this context, the need for *explicit* moral guidance is highlighted in cases (e.g., economic growth) where Islamic ethical values are implicit or vague, or where these have fallen prey to gross misinterpretation (e.g., population dynamics, equality between sexes). It is emphasised that what is done in the name of Islamic morality should be seen by the people as *fair* and *just* – i.e., the procedures used to arrive at the principles of justice must be fair and the principles of justice themselves should be just.

To give it an easily recognisable face, and to highlight its originality, the Islamic moral vision is translated into an ethical *system*, which is then factored into four irreducible elements – namely, unity (*tawḥīd*), equilibrium (*al-'adl wa al-iḥsān*), free will (*ikhtiyār*) and responsibility (*farḍ*). These elements (or axioms), in effect, state that all human activities are *vertically* integrated and *horizontally* equilibrated to produce moral, social, political and economic harmony and justice; and that these activities are carried out by a *free* human agency endowed with the powers to make a choice between alternatives as well as being saddled with the *responsibility* for the consequences of its actions. In this broader informational context, bringing ethical values, based on religion, into economic analysis in no way fetters the spirit of scientific inquiry. Instead, doing the former enhances the salience and reach of the latter. It becomes transparent that, as opposed to the limited reach of self-interestedness, a morally charged economic system can accomplish many an objective in one go: promote a high rate of economic development to ensure the equality of social and economic conditions (*not* just the equality of opportunity) for all in terms of their capability to translate material plenitude into the metric of individual happiness; safeguard the freedom to achieve social cohesion and political and social stability; and guarantee effective protection to the poor and the weak against the tyranny of the rich and the powerful.

The aim of this book is *not* to prove the absolute superiority of one ethical system over competing systems; nor is it to show that one or the other system enjoys some kind of an uncontested monopoly over knowledge and wisdom. It is rather to demonstrate that, within the parameters of their inner logic and societal compulsions, all ethical systems stand to gain from what others recommend to maximize human well-being. In other words, the *universal* messages of apparently self-sufficient ethical systems can be enriched by building bridges of understanding between them and learning from each other. With this overarching theme, it is intended to comment on the 'secular' advances in ethical philosophy and delve deep into the diverse historical experiences of Islamic, Christian, and Judaic religions to come up with the many ways in which moral ideals have been (and can be) reconciled with the 'hard' social and economic reality. It this context, worthy of note by Muslim thinkers (and, in particular, the *'ulamā'*) are the intellectual efforts made by the Calvinists and Levellers in Europe, and the Social Gospellers in the United States, to strengthen the processes of industrialisation and economic growth. Their success in abandoning the morally enervating doctrines of predestination, innate human depravity, original sin, and in freeing the mind and the soul from the weight of excessive dogmatism, greatly helped scientific and technological fluorescence in Western societies. The reasons why this has *not* happened in the Muslim world are many, and some beyond its control; but what has contributed most to perpetuate discontent in these societies is that, long ago, they gave up rational thought, ignominiously surrendered before the *un-Islamic* principle of predestination, and forsook the revolutionary concepts of human freedom and individual responsibility. Worse still, with sullen obstinacy, they have clung to statis and inaction when circumstances demand standing up to the difficult social, economic, political, and moral challenges of a fast-changing world. The net result has been to imprison human reason, underrate the power of scientific advance, and undermine economic progress and human development. The tragic reality is that the fabric of Muslim societies is falling apart around a conservative centre that can no longer hold the forces of change.

In a rather optimistic vein, it is argued that, for all their social and economic infirmities, Muslim societies still have it in them to do it better if they mobilise the full force of their moral ideals and translate them into a just and dynamic public policy. This is especially true of the luminous Islamic teachings on distributive justice and poverty reduction. Islam has stated these moral values much more explicitly and emphatically than has been done by Western secular and religious thought. The equality of mankind before Allah and towards each other and the poor having a prior *right* in the wealth of the rich are the two regnant Islamic moral principles which have survived the vicissitudes of Muslim history and wilful misinterpretations to tame the awesome waves of Islamic egalitarianism. By contrast, the tendency in the West to overemphasise unbridled individualism and to substitute public responsibility for individual responsibility has prevented it from satisfactorily resolving the fundamental conflict between the pursuit of self-interest and the commitment to work for collective good, notwithstanding its splendid success in vastly increasing the national wealth. Their dilemma is that collective goals, even when universally accepted, *cannot* be achieved through purely individualistic behaviour, which has a tendency to drift into an incapacitating isolation. In particular, the *dominant* libertarian secular philosophy – that insensitively denies the poor man's right to aid, accepts the rich man's (unlimited) claim to private property, and condescendingly advises the poor to help themselves – is deeply rooted in Western religious ethics. Thus, for instance, Christian thinkers (including religious scholars) have tended to "reverence the attainment of riches as the supreme facility" and "regard the poor as damned in the next world" [Tawney (1937); p. 265]. True, there have been some commendable efforts made in the West to escape from the stranglehold of its traditional religious positions on distributive justice and poverty reduction; but the differences between the old and the new still lie more in the mesmerising appeal of the chosen words and less in substance. Thus, distributive justice is still equated by Christianity and Judaism with the inegalitarian Aristoetlian concept of "commutative justice" – i.e., that which seeks equality in bilateral personal and economic relations – and the *right* of poor peoples and nations in the wealth of the rich is quietly ignored in intellectual debate as well as in policy-making.[1] The superiority of Islamic ethics in this respect comes out clearly in the recent relative economic performance of Muslim and non-Muslim societies. There is evidence that the (poorer) Muslim countries, on average, have done significantly *better* than the (much richer) non-Muslim countries on account of distributive justice. This result, which is decidedly related to their respective ethical heritage, is the more remarkable for all the impediments to distributive justice (e.g., feudalism) which Muslim societies themselves erected – and, unfortunately, sometimes justified in the name of religion. Yet, the manifest originality of the Islamic message in this respect notwithstanding, it is still unwise for Muslim thinkers to become excessively complacent and tradition-bound. 'Secular' moral philosophy would definitely help in articulating the Islamic thinking on the subject more explicitly and cogently as a guide to practical policy. Thus, for instance, the former makes transparent that Muslim countries have come out badly with respect to attempts at poverty reduction, despite the clarity of their moral message, because the unattended moral hazard and assurance problems would not permit private morality alone to address this issue comprehensively. The success in poverty reduction hinges on a proactive public policy that helps sustain high rates of economic growth and human development for decades at a stretch.

The Plan of Work

This work consists of six self-contained, yet logically and thematically connected, chapters. These chapters are developed as follows.

i) Chapter 1 presents an overview of the main theses presented in this study. Chapter 2 argues that an integration of ethics and economics offers a richer view of human motivation and conduct than that provided by value-neutral positivism. The basic premise is that such integration should yield a more accurate explanation of economic and human development strategies to convert material affluence into human happiness. Also, the analysis presented here prominently displays those moral values which quicken the pace of economic progress, help distinguish the better from the worse economic institutions, and emphasise restructuring the latter with a view to producing efficient *and* equitable solutions of economic and social problems. There is a growing body of literature now – known as public-choice theory – which insists that economists cannot sensibly avoid making moral judgements; and that economics would be the more effective for paying explicit attention to ethical concerns.[2]

ii) Chapter 3 demonstrates that the current practice of excluding religion as a source of universally accepted norms of economic behaviour, i.e., truth, honesty, impartiality, individual liberty, justice, equality, rights, fulfilling contracts, etc., has not at all been helpful, even in Western societies. Elaborate non-binding general frameworks of ethical rules and norms are no substitutes for clearly articulated and voluntarily-held ethical mores which flow from the religious beliefs that are accepted voluntarily by believers as binding. True, the former embellish intellectual discourse; but they seldom spill over into concrete action. In sharp contrast, the latter get 'internalised' in individual consciousness. They act as effective sanctions against unethical practices – e.g., 'free-riding', 'moral hazard', 'principal-agency syndrome', 'fraud', etc., – which undermine the efficient working of market-based social and economic institutions. The internalisation of moral values has the entirely wholesome effect of reconciling private interests with collective welfare, at significantly lower 'policing' and regulatory costs than secular economic and social systems normally incur. Indeed, in the latter case, such costs are *not* adequately incurred because they tend to be prohibitively high; but this neglect loosens the moral bindings of the socio-economic fabric. Religious ethical values are now accepted as central to "the functioning of an individualist, contractual economy" [Hirsch (1977); p. 141]; yet this remains a minority opinion in the heavily secularised climate of Western thought.

iii) Chapter 4 asserts that Islamic moral values link the individual to collectivity, by balancing individual freedom with social responsibility; and gives a fairly detailed account of the basics of Islamic morality, especially with reference to central economic issues. Like all religions, Islam can accomplish its social objectives because it does not make excessive demands on the stock of scarce altruistic resources. Performing a morally edifying economic act itself enhances the supply of altruism; and, since it recognises a legitimate role for self-interested objectives (though *not* self-interested behaviour) in the running of a market economy, the demand for altruism remains manageable. An added attraction here is that, contrary to Western (secular) thought where religion is seen mainly, if at all, as an *instrument* to achieving better economic results, Islam regards religion to be *constitutive* of a fuller human life in which material and spiritual urges of humankind coalesce. It then goes on to investigate what *that* means for a smooth functioning of a market economy.

iv) Chapter 5 gives a thorough analysis of the Islamic ethical *system*, and its 'inner' logical structure. It shows that the system can be effectively used to spell out *and* implement Islam's moral vision, and to broaden it by drawing *selectively* on 'alien' philosophies. Chapter 6 attempts to test the implicit hypothesis of the preceding chapter, namely that an ethics-based economic system need not become altogether dysfunctional and that it may even energise economic agents to work for the betterment of society. The supporting empirical evidence, which is presented here for the first time, gives both the strong and the not-so-strong aspects of Muslim practices, and to some extent, of Islamic ethics. The general points that come out are: (a) morality makes a significant impact on an individual's economic and social behaviour; but that the microscopic power of religious morality makes it even more effective than secular morality in achieving social goals. (b) Religious moral values guide *only* if these are explicitly and emphatically stated. (c) They *misguide* if not properly interpreted and if they do not creatively respond to the needs of society. And, finally, (d) a proactive public policy must supplement private morality to maximise collective good.

These are only a few glimpses of the (admittedly modest) effort to make, as Frank Ramsey put it, "a lot of things clearer" (though "nothing absolutely clear") as regards the large number of moral, social, and economic problems that human societies in general, and the Muslim society in particular must face and respond to. To this end, it draws on apparently diverse fields of knowledge (economics, ethics, mathematical logic, and doctrinal history) to weave together a logically valid, Islamically authentic, historically correct – and yet a readable – account of the many ways in which humankind has endeavoured to crown its incessant quest for achieving greater material prosperity – and to have an 'inner' peace – with success. The present work rejects the intentionally vicious doctrine of the "clash of civilisations", which has already consigned the world to the flames of a deep moral crisis, fanned by mutual hatred and total anarchy in international, political and economic relations; and which, above all, has benumbed the individual's sense of compassion and morality. Instead, it seeks to cultivate mutual understanding and trust between peoples, nations, and civilisations. Within the confines of its subject-matter, it proposes an intellectual platform where a minimum inter-religious and inter-cultural consensus can be reached about the relationship between morality and human well-being, while leaving plenty of room for discussion, debate, and dissent. This platform can even become the basis for launching a bigger political agenda to forge unity in diversity, restore harmony to a world in a state of moral disarray, and help bring some cheer to the hearts of the peoples and nations left behind in the race to economic prosperity – all to fulfil the Divine Purpose: "O Men, We created you from a male and female, and formed you into nations and tribes that you may recognise each other" (49:13).[3]

Notes

1. A recent example of Western apathy to the idea of acknowledging the fundamental right of the poor to food, health, and fair wages is their stiff opposition to assume obligations under the United Nations International Covenant on Economic, Social, and Cultural Rights. On this see, *The Economist* (Aug 18-24th, 2001). Muslim countries can take a lead here by fully subscribing to and acting on this Covenant.
2. Public-choice theory is broadly divided into positive and normative theories. The former highlights the *efficiency* aspects of the *non-market* decision-making process, while the latter focuses on the *distributive* aspects of this process. This is in line with Musgrave's (1959) division of government activity between the allocative and redistributive decisions – Musgrave was influenced by Wicksell's (1896) view of the government "as a quid pro quo exchange among citizens" [Mueller (1979); p. 3]. However, these early insights focused on issues relating to allocative efficiency while assuming that the distributive issues have been decided 'before-hand'. See Chapter 2 of this book for details.
3. The English translation of the Qur'ānic verses throughout this book draws on Ahmed Ali (1994). The first number in the parenthesis denotes the Chapter (*Sūrah*) of the Qur'ān, and the second number the verse (*āyah*).

PART I

Religion, Ethics, and Economics

CHAPTER 1

An Overview

I. Introduction

The analysis presented in this book offers three perspectives – i.e., the 'secular-normative', the Judaeo-Christian and the Islamic – on the likely impact of morality on individual behaviour and human well-being. These views are in some respects similar and complementary and in other respects contrasting and competitive. However, the points of similarity between them are no less important than their differences. It may be useful to recount them briefly. (a) Moral values held by individuals in society do make a significant difference to their social, political and economic behaviour, and that without them individuals will live precariously, anxiously and vulnerably. (b) It is *not* at all irrational for individuals to act morally and with regard to the concern of others rather than be utterly self-centred, selfish and insensitive to the collective good. (c) Human well-being is enhanced neither by maximising social welfare in the neo-classical sense of achieving a Pareto-optimal state nor by maximising the sum-total of individual 'utilities'. (d) To elicit the individual's commitment to collective good, it should be possible to evaluate the moral credentials of a society in terms of some noncontroversial, fair, and visible principles of social justice – i.e., an equality of economic, political, and social conditions between members of society, the priority of the needs of the least-privileged in society, and equal capabilities of individuals to convert monetary gains into their happiness and well-being. But beyond these points of similarity, the three perspectives differ, even clash. Thus, the secular analysis would not agree that moral behaviour becomes necessarily more compelling when guided by an internalised sense of obligation which only religion induces in individuals, that human well-being flows both from material and spiritual well-springs, and that material advancements can be consolidated on the foundations of religious spirituality. Furthermore, it would caution against an overemphasis by religious ethical thought on the sufficiency of moral behaviour to generate enough resources for poverty alleviation. The reason is that moral hazard, assurance and coordination problems prevent *voluntary*, altruistic individual behaviour from making a wholesome contribution to his/her well-being. Also, secular moral theories systematically maintain that individual morality (a sense of good and bad) is autonomously determined, independently of religious beliefs; while religious morality would insist that a deepening of the human perception of good and bad has been an integral part of the strengthening of his/her religious consciousness. It is contended in this book that, historically, religious thought has been strengthened, rather than weakened, by the process of secularisation;[1] and that secular morality need not be antithetical to religious moral thinking. What can bring both the ethical systems together is an uncompromising insistence on rational thought, which steers clear of doctrinaire rigidity. To be useful, both should focus on the vital problems of human existence – especially, growth, distributional justice and poverty.

The brief analysis that follows recaptures the highlights of the above-mentioned perspectives on morality and human well-being, which are discussed at length in the ensuing chapters.

II. Ethics and Economics

An economic calculus suffused with some solid ethical concerns should be an attractive alternative to unrepentant self-interest maximisation because "the morality of economic agents influences their behaviour and hence influences economic outcomes" [Hausman and McPherson (1993); p. 673]. Before proceeding further, it would be useful to answer the following question: why has mainstream (neo-classical) economics been so uncompromisingly insistent on keeping economics and ethics separate, indeed divorced, even at the cost of significantly blinkering the economist's moral vision of the economic universe?

i) *The Separation of Economics from Ethics?*

Lionel Robbins (1935) pronounced, without remorse, that economics and ethics are irreconcilably divorced because: "it does not seem logically possible to associate the two studies [economics and ethics] in any form but mere juxtaposition" (p. 148). In particular, economists need not entertain considerations of social justice or be concerned for the poor for the simple reason that doing so would be irrational! Instead, the self-interest principle is advertised as the only one that is "rational". This somewhat counter-intuitive result flows from the efficiency-oriented Pareto-optimality principle – which depicts a situation in which the utility (welfare) of everyone cannot be increased without reducing the utility (welfare) of someone else. The two celebrated fundamental theorems of welfare economics prove that, given some stringent conditions, Pareto-optimality and competitive equilibrium imply each other. Whence follows that the competitive solutions – i.e., those produced by unfettered markets – are "unimprovable". In other words, state intervention is redundant because it cannot improve upon market solutions. Indeed, it is positively harmful because it imposes an avoidable "excess cost" on the economy. No moral problem arises because neo-classical economics does not recognise any conflict between members of a society; and in its 'eyes' the equal and unequal outcomes are equally preferable. Hence, the Pareto-optimality principle is distributionally neutral. It further decrees that the rich could have everything as long as improving the conditions of the poor does *not* require cutting into their pleasures; and that the market solutions need not be equitable or mutually advantageous in any sense of the term. Since only efficiency considerations are deemed "rational", it should not be a matter of concern for economists if observing the Pareto-optimality rule means breaking a few moral principles *because* the broken moral rules must have been "irrational" by definition. Obviously, there is little room in this rarefied world of rationality for maximising social good on logical or moral grounds – except to the extent of holding out the *possibility* of "distortion-free" compensation that is *never* carried out in practice.

This unifocal concentration on efficiency has been bolstered by libertarian moral-right theories [Hayek (1960); Nozick (1974); J. Buchanan (1975; 1985); and many others], which assign priority to individual liberty with such intensity as to exclude any reasonable trade-off between individual liberty and all other socially desirable objectives (e.g., narrowing inequities, reducing poverty and human deprivation) in which normally sane people believe. The reason: state intervention, even to help the poor, invites totalitarianism: "A society in which the position of the individuals was made to correspond to human ideas of moral merit would … be the opposite of a free society" [Hayek (1960); p. 97]. Nozick goes further and lays down that *any* redistribution ("patterning") of income and wealth is an unacceptable encroachment on the individual's virtually unlimited right to private property including those in the means of production, i.e., the property which is acquired by observing the principles of justice in "initial acquisition" and in "transfer". Even for the government to aid the poor (by coercing the rich to do so) would be a violation of moral rights because the poor do *not* have a moral right to aid![2] Hence, the prescription for a minimal government, i.e., that which does no more than safeguard the "negative freedoms" of individuals from encroachment on their right to hold legally acquired private property. In the same vein is Buchanan's valorisation of unfettered markets as providing the best guarantees against the violation of individual liberty because only these (run on the self-interest principle) can diffuse concentration of economic power in any form. Whence follows, that any interference with the working of the free markets is undesirable on moral, political and economic grounds. However, some redistributive activity is allowed at the constitution-making stage in a manner that ensures the *impartiality* of the decisions made at this stage to win *unanimity* about these decisions [Buchanan and Tullock (1962)]. But, on this view, once this deed is done people can go about their business of selfish profit maximisation undisturbed by the distant rumblings of egalitarian reform.

ii) *Uniting Ethics with Economics*

However, notwithstanding the above-mentioned arguments, a strong sentiment for reuniting ethics with economics has now become mainstream. Firstly, there is the plain question of human *survival* in a society devoid of social and personal morality. As Russell (1954) states: "Without civic morality communities perish; without personal morality life has no value" (p. 28). Secondly, treating self-interest and "rational" behaviour as synonymous is hard to defend, even logically. Thirdly, there are two major problems with the view that individuals acting in their self-interest also maximise social welfare. (a) In a large number of real-life cases, e.g., public goods must be provided, or markets are missing or collapse completely [Naqvi (2002)]. (b) This view does not hold in the context of large *groups* within a society. Thus, "even if all members in a large group are rational and self-interested, and would gain if, as a group, they acted to achieve their common interest or objective, they will still not voluntarily act to achieve that common or group interest" [Olson (1971); p. 2].

Fourthly, the superiority (indeed, invincibility) of the self-interest principle cannot be established just by the demonstration that observing moral principles does not maximise individual welfare. For instance, even though it may be in somebody's interest to break one's promises, keeping one's promises will still be regarded by most reasonable people as both moral and rational. Whence follows that while it may not "be at all absurd that maximization of self-interest is not irrational, at least not necessarily so, but to argue that anything other than maximizing self-interest must be irrational seems altogether extra-ordinary" [Sen (1987); p. 15]. In particular, it is illegitimate to dismiss a moral concern for others as irrational behaviour on the ground that only universal selfishness is a sure sign of rationality. In the real world, "the *plurality* of *motivations* is the rule rather than the exception, and one would be hard put to prove that either mere self-interest or pure altruism explains a large enough segment of social or individual action" [Naqvi (2002); p. 180]. Indeed, even historically, linking the spectacular success of capitalism in modern times only to the unrestrained working of the self-interest principle would be a vast underestimation of the role of the so-called *capitalistic ethic*. The fact is that it has always been a symbiosis of self-interest and morality that moved the world. Many empirical studies show that, for instance, in the case of Japan – the most illustrious example of economic success in the post-War era based on a free-enterprise system – qualities like group loyalty, good will, sympathy, respect for others have played at least as much a decisive role as self-interest maximisation may have done [Morishima (1982)].

Fifthly, beyond the libertarian's ubiquitous selfishness, there is a whole world of sane people who recognise that ethical influences do shape human behaviour. Thus, for instance, Harsanyi's (1977) "equiprobability model for moral value judgment", requires individuals to possess not only personal preferences but moral preferences as well. These moral preferences "guide his thinking in those – possibly very rare – moments when he forces a special impersonal and impartial attitude, that is, a moral attitude, upon himself" (p. 635). Rawls (1971; 1999) argues for a wider informational base to measure human happiness than the self-interest principle would demand.

The Justice-as-Fairness and the Difference principles emphasise the need to select those institutions which maximise the supply of "social primary goods" which every individual wants whatever else he/she may want (i.e., "rights and liberties, and opportunities, income and wealth, and bases of self respect") to carry out his/her plans in life, subject to the principle that the needs of the least-privileged in the society are met first" (pp. 78-81). Sen (1992) regards Rawlsian social primary goods as instruments of achieving economic well-being. The real aim is to attain valuable "functionings" (being educated, being healthy, being free, etc.) and the "capability" to achieve them freely. The latter relates to the individual's freedom to convert primary goods and resources into personal happiness, which is the proper "end" of economic activity. The capability approach is capacious enough "to take note of, *inter alia*, utilitarianism's interest in human well-being, the libertarianism's involvement with the processes of choice and the freedom to act and the Rawlsian theory's focus on the individual liberty and on resources needed for substantive freedoms" [Sen (1999b); p. 86]. Sen's approach forms the basis of the UNDP's Human Development Research Programme. The basic moral insight here is that material plenitude need not always translate into human happiness, certainly not to the same extent. To this end, the search for human happiness does not stop when incomes have risen enough; rather, it takes reorganising the structure of property rights on the basis of justice, and making adequate provisions for greater education, healthcare and public goods of various kinds. In a more fundamental sense, the UNDP's research programme goes beyond Pareto-optimality rule's insistence on only distributionally-neutral efficient solutions and the Nozickian exclusive focus on the individual's (unlimited) moral right to private property etc. [see Naqvi (2002)]. It does not need extended ethical lecturing to convince normal people that only a society in which the major social institutions are based on justice and where the needs of the poor and the needy are adequately met is worth supporting. A state of bliss is not reached without sympathy for others (which may be referred to as enlightened self-interest) as well as a moral commitment to help others (which is beyond the reach of self-interest) *even* if that means accepting a cut in one's own welfare.

Finally, an unyielding insistence on self-interest (which implies an unbounded admiration for unfettered markets) is an extraordinary limitation on the economists' moral vision because that means excluding from it a whole range of ethical values – i.e., justice, fair play, and the quest for equality – that have, historically, moved people to action. Also, it prevents the government from doing *anything* about inequality, poverty and an undersupply of 'public goods', within nations and between nations and all that makes social progress illusory. Ill-rooted in facts, such insistence also defies common sense. It is, therefore, best to brush aside libertarianism and accept that an *active* public policy is necessary (though not sufficient) to create the right conditions to maximise the happiness and well-being of a diverse humanity. What is certain is that amoral market solutions produced by self-interest maximisation do not play a central role in a comprehensive agenda for enhancing human well-being.

III. Religion, Ethics, and Economics

Given, then, the ethical underpinnings of economic motivation, the next issues to consider are where to find the ethical principles – e.g., impartiality, justice, a deeply felt sense of commitment and social responsibility, especially to the least-privileged in society (or the "underclass", as Gunnar Myrdal put it) – that command widespread and universal (voluntary) support; and how to operationalise them as major regulators of economic activity? There have been influential economists [e.g., Weber (1905); Tawney (1937); Viner (1978)] who regard Christian ethics to be the driving force of capitalism; and some others [Tinbergen (1985)] who consider it an important force in the development of (Western) socialism. Earlier, Adam Smith's (1776) individualism clearly presumed that the socially beneficial working of self-interest was "subject to built-in restraints derived from morals, religion, custom, and education" [Coats (1971); p. 9]; and John Stuart Mill (1874) regarded religion as "a more cunning sort of police" (p. 415). It has been stressed that religion has, historically, performed a useful (secular) function, whose 'utility' has increased, not diminished, with the passage of time. The fact is that, with the recognition of the ethical connection of economics, it becomes difficult to deny a positive (functional) role to religion – e.g., to improve the working of an individualist economic system like capitalism.

i) *The Functional and Constitutive Roles of Religion*

However, on balance, the economic role of religion has been devalued in the West. The general attitude is that religion, though privately vital, is indifferent, if not altogether irrelevant, when it comes to devising rules for the conduct of economic and social policy. True, ethical behaviour may be vital to producing a greater degree of social cohesion; yet it is asserted that the principles governing it are derivable from reason (even common sense) alone. Secular morality is, therefore, rated higher than religion-based morality. Thus, in the Mill's quote cited above, religion is seen as a useful "supplement to human laws". (Oddly enough, he sees religion as operating mainly through the feeling of self-interest (p. 411).) Russell (1954) forcefully rejects the relevance of religion in the formation of modern ethical philosophy: "the rightness and wrongness of an act depends upon its probable consequences, and not upon its belonging to some class of acts labelled virtuous or sinful without regard to their effects" (p. 138). Joan Robinson (1973) generally asserts the superiority of secular ethical values to religious values. But this view is more of an affirmation of the superiority of secular ethics rather than an assertion of the overriding role of religion in human affairs, or accepting it as a source of ethical values. In particular, this view amounts to a repudiation of the position that religion *per se* has been the dominant force in the evolution of a universally accepted code of ethics. However, there have been some respectable exceptions to this widely held 'secularistic view' of religion. In his account of the rise of capitalism in the West, Tawney (1937) could report that "the line of division between the spheres of religion and secular business...is shifting" (p. 18); and that a crucial factor in the progress of Western capitalism was Calvin's reinterpretation of Christian religious values which ended the "long estrangements" between the duties of religion and the call of business (p. 238). Tinbergen (1985) argues that "new spiritual foundations rooted in religion are required to repair the damage being done by the cultural crisis to human happiness". This is because "far from being an 'opium of the people' religion...is a necessary source of inspiration for developing an individual's spiritual and moral potential" (p. 178). Religion is seen here as *directly* contributing to human happiness by inducing greater spirituality in people, and not only because it may lead to a higher level of economic activity. This view seems to have historical antecedents as well; which is that moral values become decisive in moulding economic behaviour only when these are presented as flowing from religious beliefs. Fogel (2000) attributes "Four Ethical Awakenings" in the United States (from 1730 to the present time) to the work of religious people (the Social Gospellers) who believed that "the value and truth of religion were shown by the capacity to create God's kingdom on earth rather than in the hereafter. The essence of religion became the elimination of poverty and inequality" (p. 121).

ii) *Limits to Voluntarism*

Religion, by virtue of its unique system of reward and punishment which religious (even irreligious) people accept without question, acts as "a solvent for the needs of explicit or internalized social cooperation" [Hirsch (1977); p. 138]; and it encourages self-interested individuals to act for society. The reason is that, without coercion and/or invisible religious sanctions, voluntary cooperation cannot meet society's demands for scarce altruistic resources which will, in turn, raise the "policing cost" to keep the free-riders in check. Also, most ethical values (e.g., honesty, trust, etc.) that help the economy work more efficiently and equitably are public goods that are necessary inputs into much social output. But the former will be undersupplied if the discharge of social obligations is left entirely to the self-interested individual's good sense. To see the nature of the problem, let us consider the feasibility of leaving it all to the individual to discharge his/her social responsibility to aid the poor voluntarily. A moment's reflection should show that the size of the charitable contributions will, at best, be minimal. The source of the problem is the phenomenon of *free-riding* (which, in extreme cases, will break the horse's back) if the required contributions to aid funds are not *enforced* (by the state and out of fear of religious sanctions), and if these efforts are *uncoordinated*. In such situations, the altruistic contributor may find that *either* a sufficient number of people will contribute even if only I do not contribute; *or* that other people will *not* contribute even if I contribute. If all or most contributors reason thus, then, given that charitable giving is a cost, not enough funds will be forthcoming to finance the charity in question. A related phenomenon is the *assurance* problem, which leads to similar results: it is that, even assuming that the contributing individual is *not* a free-rider, he may nevertheless *not* contribute, unless he is reasonably assured that many *will* contribute to charity, on the grounds that doing so is morally and socially irresponsible. It follows, then, that "the laudable desire to be effectively beneficent may be self-defeating, where coercion (secular or religious) is absent. So even in a society of morally upright, altruistic [individuals], the impulse to collective beneficence may be impotent" [Allen Buchanan (1985); p. 73].

IV. Islam, Ethics, and Economics

i) *General Motivation*

Western ideas about the functional and constitutive roles of religion, i.e., its positive contribution to material and spiritual prosperity, are valuable. No less important are the central ethical notions emphasised by (secular) normative public-choice theories: the need to create well-ordered societies based on justice and fairness; the importance of institutions and processes that guarantee the fairness of the basic principles of justice for winning the voluntary support of the people; the necessity to meet the needs of the least-privileged in society on a priority basis, etc. These insights should help formulate the Islamic response to modern social, political and economic challenges. In return, Islam's own highly original contributions should reinforce, even correct, some of these ideas and insights. Most worthy of mention in this context are the following: Islam abolishes the distinction between this-worldly and that-worldly pursuits and concerns and links welfare *(falāḥ)* in this world to that in the hereafter; spiritual ascension is firmly related to doing good to fellow human beings, especially to the poor, the needy and the weak; the act of giving is *not* regarded as charity but the *right* of the poor to receive their share in the wealth of the rich; the individual's right of ownership is only *relative* to Allah's ownership, which is to emphasise that he is only a trustee of his wealth and can spend of it only in prescribed ways.[3] A linkage between religious callings and mundane matters achieve two objectives simultaneously: it strengthens altruism significantly in running efficiently and equitably an essentially individualistic economy, *and* it minimises the free-riding and assurance problems. To some extent the internalisation of moral values which flows from regarding religion as a 'living reality' can be observed in Muslim societies, which are admittedly no more than mere pale shadows of the Islamic ideals. Thus, for instance, Muslims normally give away large amounts of money as *zakāt, khums, ṣadaqāt,* and a lot more to help the poor and the needy, even when they may evade 'secular' taxes. As a result, the differential between the rich and poor is less in Muslim countries than in non-Muslim countries (see Chapter 6). But Islam's contribution to the debate about the role of religion goes well beyond its potential to increase material well-being. The emphasis here is that religion is an internally consistent and a complete way of life that provides guidance about "individual and social, material and moral, economic and political, legal and cultural, national and international challenges that human societies must respond to" [Ahmad (1976); p. 37]. Islam considers religion as *constitutive* of individual well-being and happiness, an *end* to be desired for its own sake. It should strengthen individual's economic and social roles when moral values become deeply internalised in man's consciousness so that both the mind and the soul take on a quiet but magical luminosity. In Islam's unified world-view, religion *defines* man/woman's entire personality as geared to achieving a higher social purpose, of which economic pursuits are only one, though a significant, element. Thus, he/she is given the exalted status of Allah's vicegerent on earth, endowed with a free will (that guarantees human freedom as part of a Divine design) which is informed by a sense of social responsibility that links the individual to the collectivity and encourages him/her to do good to fellow human beings. It may be noted that, in the unified Islamic perspective, social responsibility is not allowed to degenerate into human bondage. Rather it goes with substantive human freedoms, which *increase* by a heightened sense of individual and social commitment, and *decrease* by cupidity and greed. This has a far-reaching policy implication: for Islamic moral values to become a source of social binding, Muslim societies must be reorganised on the basis of human freedom, social justice, and a commitment to help the poor and the needy by *restoring* to them from the wealth of the rich what is morally and legally *theirs* as a matter of right. Thus, in a society where wide inequalities of income and wealth prevail, and in which hunger, starvation and human deprivation is rife, individual freedom and social responsibility lose meaning

– all of which is *ẓulm* and a direct defiance of the Divine principles of *al-'adl wa al-iḥsān*. Even more important, such a defiance is not taken lightly in Islam; instead it is roundly condemned as a denial of faith itself!

The cumulative effect of Islam's 'integrationist' economic-ethical vision is that moral powers – i.e., an overarching sense of justice, freedom and responsibility – come to be shared widely and reinforce each other in a virtuous circle. In it, 'rationality' includes a consideration of our obligations and ideals as well as our interests and advantages so that the demand on scarce altruistic resources does not become unrealistically excessive. The individuals' urge to act out of altruism is extolled, but Islam does *not* envisage a society of only altruistically motivated individuals, in which there are no trade-offs between the conflicting demands on interests, obligations, and passions. At any rate, such would be a morally irrelevant concept because a society in which all, or even most, of its people act *only* out of altruism is *beyond justice*, i.e., one in which, in the absence of injustice, there is no demand for justice![4] But Islam does recognise human greed and love for wealth even though these traits of human nature do not serve as an oriflamme of social and economic forces. In other words, Islam's recognition of self-interest *objectives* does *not* imply a claim about the morality of self-interest *behaviour*. Moral values that entail adverse consequences – inequality, poverty, and social deprivation – cannot form a part of any valid moral philosophy.

ii) *The Principles of Islamic Reform*

There are, at least, four guiding principles of Islamic reform. Firstly, without a proactive public policy, free-riding and assurance problems will choke off the supply of beneficence even in societies of morally upright and altruistic people. But, Islam does *not* envisage that such rightly guided people will be in an overwhelming majority in real-world societies. In other words, voluntary economic behaviour in a morally reformed Muslim society will *not* be radically very different from the very imperfect ones now in existence. Secondly, Islam's comprehensive vision of religion encompasses both its instrumental and constitutive roles: its contribution to human happiness is to restore the balance between the call of the flesh and the beckoning of the soul. That being the case, public policy had better look at these aspects of religion as connected with one another and mutually reinforcing. Thus, for instance, greater political, social and economic individual freedoms enrich human lives and make them aware of their social responsibilities. However, the balancing of human freedom and responsibility implies that: a centrally controlled economy, in which individual freedoms are denied, is contrary to Islamic vision. And so is *laissez faire* capitalism in which economic injustice and poverty are widespread and where the resulting economic unfreedoms greatly compromise the effective use of political and social freedoms by men and women.

Thirdly, the Divine nature of the broad Islamic message does *not* provide any Divine guarantee of the success of the specific implementational strategies designed to address the problems of real-life Muslim societies, but the former does increase the probability of the latter *if* the nature of Islamic reform is correctly understood and efficiently implemented. While it is left to humankind to follow it or not, general Islamic ethical principles provide guidance to the Right Way. Hence the need for an egalitarian public policy which aims to *redress* the inequities of the system of rewards and incentives found in many (unjust) aristocratic, or feudal Muslim societies.

Fourthly, while Islamic ethical principles are universal, the traditional (Islamic) implementational strategies are *not* universal for the simple reason that the latter are limited by the constraints of time, space, the state of development and knowledge. By the same token, such strategies are no less prone to failure than those taken to implement a secular agenda. The general point is that any *Islamic economic system, and the reforms undertaken within its parameters, are going to be as man/woman-made as any other existing economic system (i.e., capitalism, socialism) and as liable to failure*. Its success will not be determined on *a priori* basis by its Divine origin, but will rather be evaluated *empirically* by its success in achieving the Divine purpose – which is to encourage economic and human development by raising the growth rate of per capita income on a sustained basis, universalising literacy and access to health care, minimising poverty, reducing inequalities of income and wealth, and rolling back the tide of human deprivation [Ahmad (1994); Naqvi (1994)]. However, success on this score will require, not a repetitive application of the remedies prescribed by Muslim sages in the distant past, but taking innovative initiatives informed by *new* knowledge. This is a road that Muslim societies have so far not taken, but it is only if they do so that the Islamic economic system will be voluntarily demanded by the Muslims themselves.

Bearing in mind these general principles, the following basic questions must be answered: how to translate Islam's soaring idealism into a set of operational rules for application at theoretical and practical levels. At the theoretical level, it can be demonstrated that an *Islamic economy* (a theoretical construct) can be at least as efficient and equitable as any other economy; and that it can stand its ground as it "opens up, interacts, and competes with other economic systems" [Sirageldin (1995)]. This is the easier part of the problem which has been addressed elsewhere [Naqvi (1997)]. A more difficult task is to find a set of values based on Islam which can serve as a springboard for ethically motivated economic activity in a real-life *Muslim society*. At the practical level, making a choice of specific policies is going to be even more challenging. The answer to this challenge does *not* lie in merely reverting to a set of policies that are labelled *Sharī'ah*-compatible in the traditional sense.[5] The problem is that, because of an informational gap of several centuries, those parts of Islamic Law which deal with social and economic issues have become frigid legal structures which do not vibrate with a sense of reality; nor do they reflect the basic objectives of Islamic Law *(maqāṣid al-Sharī'ah)*, which are the repositories of Islamic ethics.[6] But the problem is even more complicated; it is that these traditional *maqāṣid* too have become totally obsolete and out of touch with the tremendous advances made in the knowledge of ethical principles – especially those relating to the meaning and scope of the ideas of justice. These principles, therefore, must be recast to fill the informational gap noted above. This is especially true of the Islamic position on such vital issues as growth, human freedom, gender equality, etc., where Muslim societies have done exceptionally badly, both in relation to their own lofty ideals and relative to what non-Muslim countries have been able to achieve following *their* ethical ideals. The task of updating the Islamic *Sharīʿah* and the *maqāṣid al-Sharīʿah* and bringing them together into a virtuous circle of evolution is truly monumental; but it must now be taken up systematically.[7]

The central questions which the present study aims to answer, then are: how to create knowledge about the *ends* of an operational Islamic economic system and the *means* to achieve these ends, while keeping in view the modern advancements in economics and ethics; and weaving these diverse elements together in a manner which is logically sound, empirically verifiable, and operationally feasible – and yet religiously authentic? A systematic answer to these questions will help devise a set of rules that can serve as reference points for the creation of knowledge in the realm of Islamic economics, *and* not just for finding new arguments to prove the 'unimprovability' of traditional knowledge about Islamic law, ethics, and economics.

iii) *Rules of Knowledge Creation*

There are two basic rules to create knowledge about Islamic economics: (a) identify an irreducible and logically coherent system of ethical axioms which is an authentic representation of Islam's consequentialist moral philosophy, and which adequately addresses the essential *plurality* of Islamic concerns about the individual's life and society, and predicts new facts and possibilities for an Islamic economy. (b) Focus on understanding the nature of real-life Muslim societies, rather than of some utopian Islamic society, that may have existed in the distant past. This is because the existing Muslim societies, though no more than a pale shadow of their ideals (and which societies are exact replicas of their ideals?), are the *only* places where the Islamic principles can be implemented, even though some of these may have universal relevance as well.

On the basis of these rules we identify *four* fundamental axioms which are authentic representations of Islam's moral vision, giving it concrete form, and providing an overarching analytical framework for deducing empirically *falsifiable* statements about Islamic economics: *tawḥīd* (unity); *al-'adl wa al-iḥsān* (equilibrium); *ikhtiyār* (free will); and *farḍ* (responsibility).[8] The unity axiom acts as a 'unifier' of all the constitutive elements of human life into a mutually consistent and supportive totality, in which economic and ethical aspects of life are inextricably linked with each other. The equilibrium axiom denotes an all-permeating social balance. It fixes the direction of change in the basic socio-economic structure of a society by setting up a just system of rewards and incentives, promotes peace and harmony that decides conflicting claims on economic resources on the basis of fairness and justice. The free will axiom defines (substantive) freedoms *to* make the choices that people have reason to value (e.g., to be literate, to be healthy, to be well-fed, to be politically free, etc.); and it also helps secure freedom *from* self-love, avarice and greed. These freedoms leave maximum space to engage in morally edifying social and economic activities. The responsibility axiom denotes a person's moral *commitment* to improve the quality of social life, especially of the least-privileged in society, who have a prior right in the nation's wealth to ensure that social harmony, rather than discord, flows from freedom. These axioms, in their fullness, generate *new* knowledge about the moral and economic aspects of human life and about the many ways in which the mundane and the spiritual dimensions and human well-being leaven each other to let individual genius flower and enhance social good. The claim is that these axioms illustrate the essentially pluralistic nature of Islamic ethics, and provide an adequate evaluative criteria to judge the working of an Islamic economic system in real-life Muslim societies. Above all, they define the

Islamic moral vision of a good life, and spell out the basic organising principles of a distinct paradigm to organise human experiences and initiatives. There is nothing preordained or deterministic about this moral vision and its consequences. Indeed, it is meliorist in intent: that humankind can change the world for the better by observing the Right Path.

A few assertions can be made about the relevance of some of the (secular) economic and ethical principles briefly discussed in Section II above. Thus, for instance, Benthamite Utilitarianism (which emphasises the maximisation of total utility but does not worry about its distribution) and the Pareto-optimality principle (which rules out the possibility of improving upon competitive market solutions which are efficient, though *not* necessarily equitable) are *not* relevant in conceptualising the workings of the Islamic economic system. The reason being that these principles are *totally* insensitive to distributional problems and leave little room for a reformative public policy to redress distributive inequities, poverty and human deprivation. In particular, the self-interest principle, which neo-classical economics regards as the hallmark of rational behaviour (one that worries only about efficient solutions) will find no more than a faint echo in the Islamic system because the latter defines economic rationality more broadly. In particular, the former's contention that ethical behaviour is a sign of *irrationality* will be flatly denied in the Islamic system – indeed, it would be denied in any real life system that does not regard sanity as a moral crime. In the same vein, the libertarian moral-rights philosophy (which *only* recognises the individual's unlimited moral right to private property and rules out any reformist redistribution of income and wealth, and which rejects the moral right of the poor to aid) is also contrary to the Islamic ethos. In sharp contrast, Islam insists on the prior moral (and legal) *right* of the poor on the wealth of the rich and recommends radical changes in the basic structure of property rights to meet these rights. However, broadly consistent with the Islamic ethical vision are the more reformist moral theories – e.g., the Rawlsian Justice-as-Fairness and the Difference principles and

Sen's Capability Calculus – which insist on social justice, recognise the prior claim of the poor in the wealth of the rich, and recommend a purposive social policy that is impartial with respect to its underlying principles and seeks the voluntary support of the people for its implementation.

Notes

1. It may be instructive to quote from Smith (1962): "In the European historical experience, which itself varied widely, the secularization process coexisted with an intensification of religiosity on the personal and popular levels...Religious beliefs and practice, as faith, intensified rather than declined during the secularization of the state..." (p. 272).
2. Hayek (1960) takes the same position: it is wrong "to suggest that those who are poor, merely in the sense that there are those in the same society who are richer, *are entitled to a share in the wealth of the latter*...." (p. 101; emphasis added).
3. Wilson (1997) in his excellent comparative study of Islam, Christianity and Judaism, points out that while Christianity urges the rich to help the poor, it does *not* go as far as saying that the poor have a right on the wealth of the rich (pp. 70-74). It may also be noted that the Islamic assertion that the poor have a right in the wealth of the rich directly contradicts the libertarians' claim that the poor do *not* have a moral right in the wealth of the rich.
4. Rawls (1999) defines a *society beyond justice* as one "in which all can achieve their complete good, or in which there are no conflicting demands, and the wants of all fit together without coercion into a harmonious plan of activity" (p. 249).
5. Thus, for instance, it has been argued that since the profit-and-loss sharing (PLS) principle is the only one *most* recommended by the *Sharī'ah*, it alone must be the most efficient and equitable. But this is circular reasoning: it makes the desired efficiency and equity outcomes contingent on the adoption of the PLS principle, which is prejudged as the only one available which is Islamically just! However, as should not be entirely unexpected, there are both theoretical and empirical reasons why an 'unrestricted' PLS-only system is likely to be both inefficient and inequitable [Naqvi (2000)].
6. The problem noted in the text is a historical one. Rahman, F. (1980) notes: "... Islamic ethics proper, systematically based upon a genuine

understanding of the purposes of the *Qur'ān*, did not develop until later in Muslim history...The leaders of the *Sharī'a made practically no distinction between ethics and law...*" (emphasis added; p. 239).

7. Chapra (2000) wisely remarks: "The increasing volume of literature on *maqāṣid al-Sharī'ah* is also a reflection of the realization that the taking of these into account is at least as important as the letter of the text" (p. 107). Also timely is his warning that "if the 'ulamā'....react aggressively and harshly to even moderate forms of rational thinking, which are necessary for enabling *fiqh* to meet the challenges faced by the Muslim ummah, then adverse reaction might occur" (p. 105).
8. The power of reasoning in creating new Islamic knowledge has been duly recognised by modern Muslim religious scholars. Thus, Mustafa Zarqa has laid down: "whatever is against reason has no place in Islam" [cited in Chapra (2000); p. 102]. Kuran (1992) is right in complaining that some Muslim economists ignore the fact that, "like the doctrines they indict so harshly, Islamic economics rests on human reasoning and interpretation" (p. 70).

CHAPTER 2

Morality in Economics

I. Introduction

Economic behaviour since Adam Smith has been *assumed* to be characterised by the ubiquity of self-interest, selfishness and greed. The "butcher", the "baker" and the "brewer" are seen as motivated only by their self-interest ("self-love") in the mutually beneficial *exchange* that follows the production of the goods which consumers demand. Any benevolence they may entertain towards their consumer is not a relevant element in consummating such exchanges to the benefit of both parties.[1] An influential modern (mis)interpretation of the Smithian creed is to go a step further and proclaim self-interest to be an *empirical* reality: "self-interest dominates the majority of men" [Stigler (1975); p. 237].[2] A direct implication of this dominance of self-interest or self-love is a cheerless economics that refuses to include ethical values and moral concerns in the list of explanatory variables of human motivation and behaviour. Yet another is to equate self-interest with rationality: it is entirely rational to be self-interested even in the sense of being self-denying – i.e., "I will never do what I believe will be worse for me" [Parfit (1984)]. Indeed, so overwhelming has been this dominance of the self-interest creed that rationality and rational behaviour have come to be regarded as synonyms for self-interest maximisation; and, any motivation other than profit-maximisation is condemned as irrational!

II. Competing Moral Perspectives

An exaggerated trust in universal cupidity as *the* 'invisible' deliverer has been strengthened both on 'positivist' *and* normative grounds. In the former category, the economic universe is kept efficient by profit-seekers with ambition, vanity and hubris; and any concern for the social good contemptuously shunned as redundant, inefficient and counterproductive. These beliefs have been formalised with tantalising elegance by the (two) fundamental theorems of welfare economics; which show that a state of the economy in competitive market equilibrium (i.e., that which is Pareto optimal) is "unimprovable" by public-policy, or through moral manoeuvring. In the latter category, which is the domain of *non*-market decision-making and where 'market failures' are explicitly admitted, considerable theoretical effort has been expended on matters relating to allocative efficiency (to points on the Pareto-efficiency frontier and those off it). In this area of public enquiry, christened as *positive* public-choice theory, the central assumptions are that "man is an egoistic, rational, utility maximiser" [Mueller (1979); p. 1]. Not only that; even a significant part of what is known as *normative* public-choice theory, supposed to tackle distributional issues, remains exclusively focused on proving the centrality of the Pareto-optimality principle, guided by self-interest behaviour and amoral rationality (see Chapter 1, note 1).

Fortunately, the progeny of Adam Smith has not been completely lacking in imagination. To make the world an interesting place to live, it is increasingly realised (though not always understood) that the vast desert of self-interestedness needs to be flooded with humanity. Thus, Harsanyi (1991) pointedly remarks: "there was a time when many economists wanted to ensure the objectivity of economic analysis by excluding value judgments, and even the study of value judgments from economics...Luckily, they have not succeeded; and we now know that economics would have been that much poorer if they had" (p. 704).[3] The fact is that, beyond the domain of unalloyed self-interest, "valuation and obligations" intermingle with "ascertainable facts" to produce morally acceptable solutions of the vital problems of economic growth, a just distribution of income and wealth, and human development. This is because "a capacity for a sense of justice and for a conception of social good" is required to be able to ask the type of questions just mentioned and seek probable answers to them [Rawls (1999); p. xii]. Thus, to fix the direction of a social transformation that commands popular support the basic structure of society must be so changed that the rights and duties of the people and the distribution of social and economic advantages among them are fair and just.

The fact is that the role of values in human affairs is too extensive to be ignored; and no science of any kind can be divorced from ethical considerations because doing that would limit the scope of human rationality [Boulding (1966)]. An obsession with self-interest is, therefore, artificial and arbitrary. Adam Smith, who is mistakenly credited with having fathered only the self-interest principle, had the foresight to emphasise the great importance of altruism in economic activity, which comprises a lot more than simple acts of exchange. The production and distribution of goods that enter the exchange arena are not necessarily governed by the same motivations. In his *Theory of Moral Sentiments* (1790), he notes that while "prudence" (read, self-interest) remains "of all virtues that which is most helpful to the individual", yet "humanity, generosity and public spirit, are the qualities most useful to others" (p. 191). Would it not be a gross exaggeration, then, to regard self-interest as solely responsible for the success of capitalism?[4] Many empirical studies, like those for Japan, show that a punctilious observance of values like honesty, fulfilling contracts, avoiding (excessive) corruption has contributed nearly as much, if not more, to Adam Smith's "Natural Progress of Opulence". But even common sense suggests that a significant hold of complementary moral values on the human mind is necessary to shape an efficient society that vibrates with justice and fair play, positively values a sharp reduction in the inequities of human condition, and ensures an abundant provisioning of public goods – all issues at the resolution of which capitalism has been singularly inept.

In what follows both the positivistic and normative aspects of economics are presented. It is shown that a purely positivist view (in which self-interest is the oriflamme of economic forces) must be balanced by an ethics-related view (where considerations of social justice, and a commitment to the welfare of the "voiceless millions" guide human endeavour) to produce a creative synergy of the essential plurality of human motivation and conduct. Only thus can the equality of the human condition be ensured, and those adrift in a sea of powerlessness and poverty brought 'on board'.

To set the stage for a fuller discussion of the moral issues in economic matters, let us first recapitulate the case *for* giving a starring role to the self-interest principle as the defender of the economic universe.

III. The 'Universality' of the Self-Interest Principle

The assumption of universal 'selfishness', regarded as a sure sign of rationality, is the regnant idea in much of modern economics. The point of emphasis of neo-classical economics (of which Benthamite Utilitarianism and Pareto-optimality are the central components) as well as of the positive public-choice theory (which admits 'market failure' but still accepts Pareto-optimality as a standard of reference for public policy) is a unifocal quest for efficiency. The moral-economic issues, like distributive justice and helping the poor, wither on the vine of scientific neglect. Even some 'normative' public-choice theories tell much the same story: they highlight such moral values as *neutrality*, *unanimity* and the *priority* of *liberty* to the exclusion of all other worthwhile social goals of what is generally accepted as good life. Yet another feature of this framework of thought is that, in it, a (minimalist) government is *not* expected to do anything positive to maximise social good; instead, it should be confined to safeguarding "negative freedoms". Its only task is, therefore, to set rules of conduct that let self-interested individuals pursue freely the ends they value most.

The discussion in this section revolves around: (a) Pareto-optimality, (b) Libertarianism, and (c) Benthamite Utilitarianism; and it shows the moral vacuity of each of these theories. Thus, for instance, Pareto-optimality claims to be totally 'value free' and *not* concerned at all with issues of social justice; libertarianism advocates policy *inaction* in defence of a special kind of individualistic morality; and utilitarianism manages to maximise social welfare *without* getting any closer to a just society in which the thought of doing good to others would freely insinuate itself into the minds of men (and women).

i) *The "Unimprovability" of Pareto-optimality*

A situation is regarded as Pareto-optimal if there is *no* alternative situation in which at least one person is better-off while none other is worse-off. In other words, it depicts a situation in which the welfare (utility) of someone cannot be increased without reducing the welfare of others. More simply, Pareto-optimality reigns supreme if there is no other state in which *everyone* can be made better off.[5] When there are no ultimate consumers in the model, Pareto-optimality, in a pure production framework, portrays a situation when there is *no* alternative state of the economy in which there is a greater production of outputs, or a lesser use of inputs [Allen Buchanan (1985)]. A Pareto-optimal state is deemed to be *efficient, distributionally neutral, value free, fair* and *liberal*. The central assumption here is that of a well-ordered society – namely, one in which a just distribution of income and wealth has already been accomplished, and where no outstanding socially gnawing interpersonal conflicts of interest strain the rather delicate structure of the free markets. Given this vital assumption, the two fundamental theorems of welfare economics, referred to above, establish a two-way link between Pareto-optimality and competitive equilibrium: assume that all individuals and firms are selfish price-takers. Then every competitive equilibrium is Pareto optimum. Assume, again, that all individuals and firms are selfish price-takers, *and* that the initial endowments have been suitably redistributed by lump-sum transfers, then Pareto optimum can be achieved by competitive equilibrium [Feldman (1991)]. These theorems, subject to the following restrictive assumptions, prove the above-noted nice properties of Pareto-optimality.[6] (i) Market arrangements are the most *efficient* because all points on the Pareto-efficiency frontier denote an 'unimprovable' arrangement of scarce economic resources. But such efficiency guarantees, for whatever they are worth, hold *only* in the space of utility. (ii) By the same token, these arrangements are the most *liberal* in the narrow sense that there is no room here for government interference. (iii) Since the very best state of the economy must *at least* be Pareto-optimal, and in competitive equilibrium, market arrangements must be mutually advantageous and *fair*. (iv) The Pareto-optimality principle could even be regarded as morally non-controversial, because no one can rationally complain about a move from a Pareto-inferior state (in which *someone* can be made better off without making anyone worse off) to a Pareto-superior state (in which *no one* can be made better off without making someone worse off); and because such a move would be in everyone's self-interest.

On closer examination, however, the story looks too good to be true. The rule will *not* guarantee efficiency if only a little bit of reality is allowed into the watertight set of assumptions that sustain it. Thus, if public goods (characterised by the jointness of supply, non-excludability, and non-rivalrous consumption) of various kinds must be produced and consumed, the 'free-rider' problem (i.e., I do not contribute because others most probably will) and the assurance problem (i.e., when I, though not a free-rider, will contribute only if assured that others will also do the same) will *not* let the market produce these goods. In such situations, appropriate state intervention can almost always improve competitive market (and Pareto optimal) solutions [Stiglitz (1991)]. Similar results will follow if such real-life phenomena as asymmetric information, moral hazard, principal-agency syndrome, multiple equilibria are (as they should be) admitted into the analysis; or if markets are missing or incomplete, or if they are liable to complete breakdown. These problems do not go away even when extended to situations of uncertainty and which involve an inter-temporal resource allocation. This is because such extensions require making some additional heroic assumptions – namely, that (i) all economic agents are identically uncertain; (ii) a complete set of contingent markets exists; (iii) transaction costs are zero. True, with these assumptions the Pareto-optimality rule becomes dynamically valid; but it would amount to little else. In particular, this dynamic version too will still fail to deliver if many key contingent markets (e.g., those for sharing risks) do not exist, the information available to economic agents is not symmetric, etc. To add to the rule's woes, the second theorem does *not* settle the issue of distributional equity because Hicksian lump-sum transfers from winners to losers, which must be made to prove the second theorem, are *not* meant to be actually made. Furthermore, even common sense suggests that "there simply is no way to judge the changes that affect distributions while remaining neutral on distribution questions" [Hausman and McPherson (1993); p. 703].

Indeed, the way Pareto-optimality is defined offers *no* solution to problems of distributive justice. For instance, this rule is perfectly consistent with a famine-like situation in which some have none or very little while others get all or most, so long as the agony of the starving multitude cannot be relieved without cutting into the ecstasy of the few rich rolling in luxury! Thus, "a society can be Pareto-optimal and still be perfectly disgusting" [Sen (1970); p. 22]. In other words, Pareto-optimality and competitive markets are immiscible with mutually advantageous production, consumption, and distribution arrangements – which is a particularly damning criticism since the gap between the rich and the poor is much too large to be socially, politically and morally acceptable. And, as if to rub salt into the neo-classical's wounds, Pareto-optimality may even coexist with inefficiency – especially in the non-utilitarian space [Stiglitz (1988)]. Nor is it a big deal that Pareto-optimality depicts unanimity. This is because if unanimity is for the preservation of an unjust status quo, then it would be a recipe for social disaster. Thus, the moral content of the Pareto-optimality principle is next to nil – especially because observing moral principles need not always be (it seldom is) a pleasurable experience for self-seeking individuals. To be able to move towards a reasonably civilised society, a real-life economy had better be delivered from the fetters of the Pareto rule.

ii) *Libertarian Morality*

The priority of individual *liberty*, *unanimity* and *impartiality* in the specific context of constitution-making are the central moral values espoused by libertarians. Yet here morality *misguides* human endeavours into the 'wrong' channel: it promotes distributive inequity and fails to help the poor.

a) The Priority of Liberty

The central proposition here is that individual liberties must be protected *regardless* of the consequences of exercising them for individual well-being and social welfare. The idea here is that individual liberty is intrinsically valuable, to be pursued for its own sake. Thus, for instance, *unfettered* markets are preferred because these are supposed to be the best protection against the dilution of individual liberty. Indeed, capitalism is the most preferred economic arrangement because it means minimising government interference and coercion; it is not just because it most efficiently adds to national wealth [Hayek (1960); Friedman (1962)]. James Buchanan (1985) further shows that unfettered markets are *morally* superior as well because *only* these voluntary arrangements can preserve individual liberty while the involuntary arrangement reached through the government cannot. The job of the government is, therefore, to produce a *legal* infrastructure within which the liberty-preserving markets can function freely. The distributional issues are best settled at the time of making the constitution. At this stage, the individuals responsible for framing the constitution, being uncertain and disinterested about their chances in life, would most likely make rules and procedures which promote a juster distribution of income and wealth and safeguard the interests of the poor in society [Buchanan and Tullock (1962)]. This objective is best achieved by ensuring the *unanimity* and *impartiality* of the rules and procedures agreed upon by these "impartial spectators". However, once the constitution-making activity, done in silence and obscurity, is passed, self-interested individuals go about their economic pursuits, unperturbed by the inevitable trade-offs between individual liberty and other worthwhile social objectives. It really amounts to laying down the rules of a savage justice whereby the "right to life is the right not to be killed, it is not the right to be given sustenance" [Hausman and McPherson (1993); p. 703].

How good are these arguments? Briefly, they do not add up to much. Firstly, Buchanan's assertions, as well as those of Buchanan and Tullock noted above, in support of the free markets suffer from a fatal logical flaw. They *define* specific economic arrangements as *voluntary* or *involuntary* according to whether these are made by the market or by the government; and then proceed to establish the superiority of market arrangements to those made by the government. But this is not a logical result at all; only a restatement of a definition! Secondly, it is *not* empirically a fact that (political) individual liberties are better taken care of in societies where markets are freer and government intervention minimal than where they are less free and government intervention is large. Thus, in free-market economies (e.g., the United States) the civil and political rights of the blacks have been freely trampled on; while in Scandinavian countries, with 'nanny' governments, political liberties are much better safeguarded together with a stellar economic performance record [Allen Buchanan (1985); pp. 78-79]. While this piece of empirical evidence does not prove that 'nanny' governments and suppressed markets are always better, it does prove that markets need not be altogether *unfettered* to produce better economic results and a superior record of political and civil freedoms. Thirdly, guaranteeing individual economic and political freedoms may produce *efficient* results in the Paretian sense (that, no one's substantive freedom can be enhanced without reducing the freedom of someone else), and yet this fact (of giving absolute priority to liberty) does not say *anything* about the equally important issue of equity in the distribution of freedoms. Indeed, the efficiency outcome positively complicates the distribution problem: "the problem of inequality gets magnified as the attention is shifted from income inequality to the inequality in the *distribution of substantive freedoms and capabilities*" [Sen (1999b); p. 119; italics in the original].

Fourthly, the 'unanimity' and 'impartiality' achieved at the constitution-making stage do not make a society any better from the egalitarian point of view. Also, the constitution-makers cannot always ensure *compliance* with what they prescribe; nor can they foresee *all* the distributional issues in the post-constitution making stage, especially those which *result* from the working of the capitalist system itself. Fifthly, the *unanimity* achieved at the constitution-making stage can be extraordinarily conservative: it need *never* permit any social change which benefits all but one person, who can block it no matter what the rest of society wants. True, unanimity about a change in the status-quo can somehow be achieved through public discussion and debate and by a trading of compromises among themselves (which is equivalent to a log-rolling process), yet vested interests would not *voluntarily* endorse it. Finally, Buchanan and Tullock's theory is essentially positivist: what it aims to show is that the unanimity principle can be achieved *entirely* by self-interested individuals: "the uncertainty that is required in order for [the] individual to be led by his own interest to support constitutional provisions that are generally advantageous to all individuals and to all groups seems likely to be present at any constitutional stage of discussion" (p. 78). It is not meant to resolve *any* ethical or distributional issues. The fact is that all this is no more than a smart sleight of hand. It may deepen the neo-classical's unbounded admiration of the state of self-interestedness; but it will not satisfy the curiosity of those concerned about the larger issues of human existence.

b) Non-Consequentialist "Moral Rights"

Nozick's (1974) theory of 'entitlement' and 'historical justice' goes a step further – beyond the standard libertarian's (e.g., Hayek's (1960)) position that individual liberty is *instrumental* in preventing coercion. He deems liberty to be *intrinsically* valuable. In other words, individuals have some inalienable moral rights, which are regarded as deontological 'side-constraints' on action that *must* be satisfied regardless of any (adverse) social, economic or other consequences of doing this duty.[7] But this is a particularly restrictive (indeed, perverse) view of moral rights because it in effect instructs the potential rights violators: "Do not violate the moral rights of others no matter what – not even to *stop* others from an imperfect compliance of these instructions (that is, when some violate the rights of others)". It is not for individuals to minimise the incidence of moral-rights violations but rather to act within the bounds of given moral rights; which, if voluntarily observed by all individuals, will not be violated in the first place. The reward of this state of studied inaction is some kind of 'political egalitarianism': no one has a greater right to liberty than anyone else. In this framework of thought, selfishness is itself a moral right, to be defended no matter what and markets must remain unfettered even though the outcome of such 'unfetteredness' is mutually disadvantageous. This extremist view of the innate morality of the (moral) right to private property, including that in the means of production, rests on the sufficiency of observing legitimate *procedures* in acquiring it: "The general outlines of the theory of justice in [property] holdings are that the holdings of a person are just if he is entitled to them by the principles of justice in acquisition and transfer, or by the principle of rectification of justice (as specified by the first two principles). If each person's holdings are just then the total set is just" [Nozick (1974); p. 153]. He recognises that "past injustices" may shape "present holdings in various ways", but fails to pursue the all-important question of the "rectification" of past injustices, nor does he suggest *any* principle of redress, even in a mild form. On the contrary, he specifically rules out any "patterning" of the existing structure of property (by the government) because "from the point of view of an entitlement theory, redistribution is a serious matter, indeed; involving, as it does, the violation of people's rights" (p. 168). Nozick recognises that past injustices may directly contribute to significant inter-generational inequities, a socially undesirable inequitable distribution of income and wealth, and great poverty. Yet, while all this is "morally unfortunate" or merely unfair – a state of affairs which rich people should be encouraged to remedy by *voluntary* charity – it is *not* morally unjust because no one (even the starving poor) has a moral right to aid![8] Hence, people cannot be forced to be charitable by any coercive government action.

This seemingly impenetrable defence of moral rights has, however, several holes in it. Firstly, as Hayek (1960) maintains, not all distributive patterns or end-states are disruptive of moral rights – e.g., providing minimum sustenance to the poor and the implementation (for redistributive purposes) of long-standing publicised laws specifying tax obligations. Nor are these end-states incompatible with the existence of a stable pattern of expectations which is the essence of the "rule of law". He explicitly states that "coercion, however, cannot be altogether avoided because the only way to prevent it is by the threat of coercion" (p. 21). Secondly, Nozick neglects the need for a balance between charity and efficiency that is necessary for greater social cohesion. The point is that, as Arrow (1974) notes, the act of giving is an "expression of individual volition" based on "an implicit social contract such that each performs duties for the other in a way calculated to enhance the satisfaction of all" (p. 348). More generally, "ethical behaviour is a socially desirable institution which facilitates the achievement of economic efficiency" (p. 354). In other words, downplaying the ethical aspects of social life – e.g., distributive justice, charitable giving, etc., – would erode the efficiency of Nozick's liberty-preserving free markets. Thirdly, it is idle to expect that extreme poverty or distributive inequity can be remedied by uncoordinated voluntary acts of charity on the part of the rich, *even assuming that they are morally upright people of altruistic disposition*: "the laudable desire [on the part of the rich] to be effectively beneficent may be self-defeating where coercion is absent" [Allen Buchanan (1985); p. 73]. The reason is that the free-rider and assurance problems, noted above, are likely to block the generation of a large enough flow of resources by voluntary and uncoordinated beneficence alone. It may, therefore, be necessary to make acts of non-contribution subject to penal action, even if it is accepted that, as Nozick asserts, the poor have no moral right to aid. In this connection a distinction can be made between people *who may desire to be charitable* and those *who desire that the poor should be provided for.* In the latter case, free-rider and assurance problems will apply with even greater force because knowledge that the poor have been provided for by someone may satisfy their rather shallow concern for the poor. What may not be so obvious is that the outcome will be no different in the former case as well. The need for government action, therefore, remains vital in both cases. The point is that foundational issues such as poverty alleviation cannot be addressed just by appealing to moral intuition and voluntary beneficence, and leaving it at that.

Fourthly, Nozick's defence of the nearly unlimited right to private property, on the ground that inequities in income and wealth mostly flow from the differential abilities of the people and their use of these abilities, is also weak. It neglects the *cumulative adverse effect* of the morally unexceptionable individual cases in which merit is rewarded. But "to assume that the cumulative result of a series of just actions must itself be just is to commit the fallacy of composition" [Allen Buchanan (1985); p.

68].[9] In fact, wealthy individuals, even those who earn their wealth legitimately, come to exercise a disproportionate amount of political, social and economic influence, which is then used to deny (poor) people their legitimate political and economic rights. Finally, Nozick's insistence that the state confine itself only to preventing the violations of "negative freedoms" (i.e., the freedoms *from*...., rather than the freedoms *to*...) is altogether extraordinary because *having* some freedoms does not by itself guarantee that the same will also be *exercised* effectively. Thus, for instance, large inequalities of income and wealth preclude poor people's exercise of *their* political rights (say, to free speech and to free political participation). Sen (1999b) observes: "Economic unfreedom can breed social unfreedom, just as social or political unfreedom can also foster economic unfreedom" (p. 8). Whence follows that some coercion (state intervention) is required even to achieve the libertarian's apparently well-meaning aim that no one should have a greater moral right than any other. This is granted even by Hayek (1960), who recognises that a free society has conferred on the state a "monopoly of coercion" to protect "known private spheres of the individual against interference by others..." (p. 21). It is really common sense to assert that the worth of most rights lies in people's ability to *use* them rather than in the mere knowledge that they *have* them. For these reasons, Nagel (1975) has derided Nozick's entitlement theory as "libertarianism without foundations".

c) The 'Morality' of Utilitarianism

Nineteenth century utilitarian philosophy (due to Jeremy Bentham), which has dominated economic thought, has been regarded as a theory of *distributive justice*. The maximisation rule says: "seek the greatest good for the greatest number". 'Good' here has been synonymously used with (mental state) subjectively experienced individual happiness; and it is measured *exclusively* in terms of the metric of utility. Thus, those aspects of life which cannot be translated into a utility number (e.g., the fulfilment/

violation of rights, duties, etc.) are excluded from the utilitarian calculus of human happiness.[10] Sen (1987; 1999a; 1999b) points out that utilitarianism has three irreducible components: (i) 'welfarism', that which reflects the goodness of the human condition in a given state as a function of *only* the utility information about that state; (ii) 'sum-ranking', that which instructs that the utility information about a given state be measured *only* by the sum-total of utilities in that state, paying *no* regard to the distribution of this total among the individuals; and (iii) 'consequentialism', that which weighs the worth of any action and institution by their consequences, as measured by the utilities they generate. The aim of public policy should, therefore, be to maximise social welfare, which is defined as the sum-total of utilities generated by it. It is not always clear whether the maximisation of utility is secured through the market or brought about by the government; but that should not matter. All that utilitarianism requires is maximising the sum-total, regardless of how it is distributed.[11]

The utilitarian approach to distributive justice has the wisdom to seek information about the consequences entailed by specific policies. The objective is to evaluate the worth of such policies and to redesign them on the basis of such information. Quite properly, it worries about the well-being (welfare) of the people in the design of public policy. But its demerits offset its merits as a basis for public policy. Firstly, its central instruction to the policy-maker: "seek the greatest good of the greatest number" is, at best, an ambiguous formula to maximise human economic well-being. Now, if this instruction is taken to mean that, for any given population, "aim at that distribution of resources that maximizes social welfare (measured by the sum total of utilities), and then choose a population size which maximizes this number", then such a policy will, obviously, give no more than is necessary to keep the largest number of population so chosen at little more than starvation level [Roemer (1996)]! More specific instructions are required. To this end, if it is assumed, as some economists do, that utility functions are the same for all people, then the maximisation of total utility, for a given population size, will give equal distribution. However, if utility functions are not the same across individuals (which is a more sensible assumption to make), then the instruction to maximise total utility will result in extremely unequal distribution levels for individuals. This situation is not significantly changed if the maximisation of utility through the market is backed by decent government-backed safety nets. This is because it does *not* follow from it that "maximizing total utility would justify a decent minimum for *everyone*" [Allen Buchanan (1985); p. 59; italics in the original]. Furthermore, utility as a subjective mental state measure does not adequately register the pleasure/pain experiences of different individuals. Thus, a disabled person, or one who is resigned to his/her fallen state (e.g., a slave), may not register the same pleasure/pain as a person enjoying good health and the blessings of freedom. But, on the utilitarian scale, the latter will get more than the former; and some of the former may be altogether excluded from the benefits flowing from public policy. Thus, far from suggesting any progressive egalitarianism, utilitarianism will actually recommend a highly regressive social policy!

Secondly, utilitarianism suffers from a deep dilemma. It works *only* if interpersonal comparisons of the utilities of different people affected by a change is allowed; but in this case all the unsavoury distributional consequences noted above will follow. But, if interpersonal comparisons of individuals are *not* allowed, which is what neo-classical economists have invariably come to believe since the 1930s, then utilitarianism will lose all operational significance.[12] It is for this reason that it has been replaced by the Pareto-optimality criterion, which does not make this assumption. In this sense, Pareto-optimality can be regarded as a second-best indicator of human well-being (the first-best indicator being the inoperational utilitarianism). But, as noted above, Pareto-optimality and utilitarianism, are entirely focused on efficiency and not at all on distributive justice; nor do they represent a mutually advantageous arrangement – the former, because it places restrictions on how the sum-total of utility is distributed as long as the net amount of benefits are as high as possible; and the latter, because it does not recognise any conflict of interest between parties to the exchange. Little wonder, then, that utilitarianism has all but been discarded in modern scientific discourse. The irony is that the inter-personal comparisons of utilities are again back in intellectual fashion; and yet utilitarianism remains discredited. The reason is that utilities are not the proper metric to register adequately and correctly any increase/decrease in human happiness, or well-being.

IV. Towards Altruism

The (positive) collective-choice theories reviewed so far assume no trade-offs between rival interests; public choices, therefore, help *everyone*. We now turn to those (normative) collective-choice theories which postulate a more realistic social setting where ideas and interests and passions clash, sometimes violently. Since the social choices made inevitably generate changes which benefit some and hurt others, there must be a mechanism to redress at least some, if not all, the consequent inequities of the human condition. The problem of social justice is, then, to create a just (democratic) society which puts "all citizens in a position to manage their own affairs and to take part in social cooperation on a footing of mutual respect under appropriately equal conditions" [Rawls (1999); p. xv].[13] This conception of a just society, which distinguishes itself by procedural impartiality as well, differs radically from that presented by a much narrowly defined utilitarian consequentialism – and is light years away from Nozickian non-consequentialism. Rather than compress all aspects of human well-being into just one object of value, i.e., the metric of utility, it is more realistic to recognise it to be *pluralistic* in character. This is because the criteria used to evaluate social states are essentially diverse. To this end, normative collective-choice theories (with some notable exceptions) move away from the subjective mental-state experiences to more objectively 'seen' *evaluators* of human happiness – e.g., primary goods, resources, functionings – all of which assign centrality to human freedom and admit the 'possibility' of improving social conditions by egalitarian public policy.

i) *The Many Faces of Social Justice / Welfare*

The analysis presented in the preceding section highlights the importance of the 'right' moral values – ones that guide individuals to undertake socially desirable activities, and those which enhance social justice.

a) Social Welfare

Social justice, or distributive equity, is generally understood to mean maximising *social welfare* in an individualistic economy. But this usage is not free from ambiguity because social welfare does *not* always imply distributive equity. Positive public-choice theories regard Pareto-optimality as an index of social good or welfare; which, however, is a misnomer. Even some normative public-choice theories toy with the idea of maximising social welfare along the Pareto-optimality *frontier* (i.e., choosing an optimal point on the frontier) with the help of a distortion-free optimal lump-sum taxes and transfer mechanism. This intellectual feat was achieved by Bergson (1938) and Samuelson (1947) who proved that maximising social welfare is equivalent to maximising a Bergson–Samuelson social welfare function.[14] But these efforts have been much ado about nothing! The reason is that the basic components of the Bergson–Samuelson social welfare function do *not* allow it to address the problem of distributive justice. These are: (a) the distributionally-neutral Pareto-optimality criterion, with its unifocal concentration on efficiency-related issues; (b) a neutral lump-sum transfer of resources, which is no more than a hypocritical neo-classical trick of looking egalitarian *without* actually having to distribute *anything*; and (c) the impossibility of making interpersonal comparisons of individual utilities, which are no more than mental-state comparisons of pleasures or desires.[15] The way to cure the neo-classicals' trained incapacity to handle distributional issues is either to discard utilitarianism, or reject the impossibility of making interpersonal comparisons of individual utilities, or both. Harsanyi (1955) rejects the neo-classical's consensus about the *impossibility* of interpersonal comparisons of utility, but retains the utilitarian calculus; while Rawls (1971; 1999) and Sen (1999a) reject both.[16] And, chameleon-like, 'social welfare' changes its 'colour' and meaning in each of these formulations.

b) Harsanyi's Just Social Welfare Function

Take interpersonal comparisons of utilities to be a factual proposition, and assume that if *x* is preferred to *y* by the individuals in a society, it is also preferred by the society as a whole. Then a remarkable result follows – namely, that social welfare (W) is a sum of the individual utilities.[17] Harsanyi's originality is to combine self-interested individualism (i.e., *no* role is assigned to the state even by implication) with the moral quality of caring for others. The *deus ex machina* is to assume that: (a) individual preferences can be divided into one's self-interested *personal* preferences and his/her *moral* preferences which are an indicator of his/her concern for other persons in society; (b) that every individual has an equal probability of being any other individual; and (c) that each individual has the capacity of being in someone else's shoes (determined by mental comparisons alone). Here (b) and (c) provide the ethical foundations of Harsanyi's (1955) formulation.[18] Once these assumptions are made, the *impartiality* of social decisions is ensured. Here, social decisions are made, *not* by the state, but by Adam Smith's "impartial spectator", who possesses the entirely agreeable qualities (a) to (c), and whose preferences are representable by a social welfare function.

The basic contributions here are the following: (a) light is shed on the *processes* of making just collective decisions – namely, by ensuring that these are made by the "impartial spectator", who does *not* have prior information about his/her chances in life. Such *impartial* decisions have a high probability of gaining *unanimity* in a democratic society where individual preferences matter. (b) The additive form of Harsanyi's social welfare function (i.e., that individual preferences should be *added* together to arrive at a *social* welfare function) ensures that *each* individual's preferences count in the making of collective decisions and that no one person (or group of people) is given the right to veto the preferences of any individual, or all other individuals, in society.[19]

This is a plausible enough way of ensuring the quality of social justice in real-life societies. But it suffers from a fatal flaw, which is that if a person is to *become* any other individual in the society, then (in the mental experiment) he/she must also take all his/her individual qualities. However, this is not what happens in the Harsanyi personality-splitting model, in which different individuals in society retain their initial identities and yet *become* any other individual. The point is that, given the assumption of self-interested individual behaviour which is central to the Harsanyi formulation, the whole exercise of an individual becoming someone else is really an artificial one, if not entirely meaningless. Even more damaging is that the *impersonality* of the Harsanyi model does not necessarily form the basis of true *impartiality*. This is because, as Rawls (1971; 1999) asserts, we cannot "evaluate another person's total circumstances, his objective situation plus his character and system of ends, without any reference to the details of our conception of the good" (p. 174). The problem here is the implausibility of one person ("the impartial spectator") having enough information about the positions and the manner of thinking of all other individuals in society.

But Harsanyi's basic ideas are valuable: the *impartiality* of social decisions and the fairness of the *procedures* adopted to arrive at such decisions. The latter is ensured by entrusting them to individuals who themselves are uncertain about their own chances in the future institutional set-up that will come about as a result of the decisions they take. It is only such decisions that can possibly command universal support by free individuals in a democratic set-up. This insight becomes a central feature of the Rawlsian theory of Justice-as-Fairness, which is discussed next.

c) The Rawlsian Concept of "Justice-as-Fairness"

The Rawlsian theory of social justice, perhaps the most influential one in modern times, presents a radically different concept of social welfare. Firstly, it frees the latter from the fetters of utilitarianism, which cannot "provide a satisfactory account of the basic rights and liberties of citizens as free and equal persons..." [Rawls (1999); p. XII]. His aim is rather to provide just such a satisfactory account. Secondly, the basic principles of justice (and of social welfare) should be arrived at through fair procedures which ensure their *impartiality* (that is, they do not represent the selfish interests of those involved in their formulation), generate their own support, and are "stable" for that reason (p. 119). The impartiality of the principles of justice must be maintained so that these can be used to restructure the society in a just manner. The assumption here is that, while natural constraints must be recognised, "men are not powerless to shape their social arrangements" (p. 479). Rawls claims that the actors behind the veil of ignorance will choose the basic principles of social justice – namely, the "Justice-as-Fairness" principle and the Difference principle whereby the least-privileged in the society are accorded priority in any scheme of redistribution. Thirdly, the index of social welfare or human well-being is a pluralistic one; and it is objectively observable rather than shrouded in the mysterious mental-state pleasure or happiness. It consists of the social primary goods which are defined as "rights, liberties and opportunities, and income and wealth [and the bases of self-respect]" (p. 54), which all rational people (in the sense that they prefer more primary goods rather than less) want whatever else they want. It is also stipulated that the flow of such goods to the least-privileged members of society – those which possess the least of such goods – should be maximised. The fundamental principle of justice is that all these (social) primary goods "are to be distributed equally unless an unequal distribution of any, or all, of [them] is to everyone's advantage" (p. 54).

Fourthly, however, he does not make any effort to derive an aggregate index (or a social welfare function) to evaluate the net effect of the creation of just institutions on the economic well-being of the people – presumably, on the ground that what is essentially pluralistic *cannot* be reduced to just one number. Fifthly, the priority of liberty, including some basic political liberties, is emphasised in the Rawlsian concept as well; but such liberties are not made so extensive (as is the case with Nozickian non-consequentialism) as to crowd out social justice in any meaningful sense of the term.

Finally, the Rawlsian concept of justice is mainly a *political* one – one in which even those disagreeing on metaphysical or moral grounds can still cooperate on the basis of mutual respect. It "presents itself not as a conception of justice that is true, but one that can serve as a basis of informed and willing political agreement between citizens viewed as free and equal persons" [Rawls (1985); p. 230]. Thus, the Rawlsian principles of justice, as Sugden (1993) notes, "is a system of fair rules within which individuals with different ends can cooperate to their mutual advantage" (p. 1957). The criteria of justice are, therefore, not that these are true, good or right, but that these are politically workable. The main concern here is *not* about how the economic well-being of the people (or public good) will be maximised by public policy; it is rather to ensure that the rules of justice form the basis of fair terms for cooperation between free and equal citizens.

Subject to these clarifications, and especially the last one, the two central elements of his theory are spelled out below – namely, the *procedure* for arriving at the principles of justice and the principles themselves.

1) *The Procedural Fairness of Just Institutions*

In the contractarian tradition of Locke (1952), Rousseau (1964), and Kant (1948), the procedures Rawls adopts to arrive at a moral judgment about the basic principles of justice are no less important than the principles of justice themselves. This is because it is only if the former are 'seen' as fair (in the sense of being 'impartial') that the basic principles of justice will "be such that when they are embodied in the basic structure of the society men tend to acquire the corresponding sense of justice and develop a desire to act in accordance with its principles" [Rawls (1999); p. 119]. The technique used to derive such a concept of justice is to imagine a group of people who are assigned the task of setting up "a fair procedure so that any principles agreed to will be just", and whose judgment about the emerging structure of society would not be seen as guided by self-interest. This group is assumed to work behind a 'veil of ignorance' "to nullify the effects of specific contingencies which put men at odds and tempt them to exploit social and natural circumstances to their advantage". Thus, for instance, no one knows "his place in the society, his class position or social status; nor does he know his fortune in the distribution of assets and abilities, his intelligence and strength; ... more than this ... the parties do not know the particular circumstances of their own societies" (p. 118). Having passed through the veil of ignorance the members of the group arrive in the "original position" of total equality with respect to the kind of information that each possesses about his/her position in the future set-up. The essential impartiality of the decision-making process ensures that the rules of justice it generates are fair. This is the basic idea of Justice-as-Fairness.

2) *The Principles of Justice*

The central aims of the Rawlsian principles of justice are to "govern the assignment of rights and duties and regulate the distribution of social and economic advantages". These principles, *arranged in serial order*, are as follows: "First: each person is to have an equal right to the most extensive scheme of basic equal liberties compatible with a similar scheme of liberties for others.[20] Second: social and economic inequalities are to be arranged so that they are both (a) reasonably expected to be to everyone's advantage, and (b) attached to positions and offices open to all" (p. 53). These principles of justice are, however, special cases of a more general principle of justice – namely that "all social values – liberty and opportunity, income and wealth, and the social bases of self-respect – are to be distributed equally unless an unequal distribution of any, or all of these is to everyone's advantage" [Rawls (1999); p. 54].

Three points should be noted about these principles. (i) The first principle is prior to the second, which is to assert the priority of liberty. (ii) The inequalities that are *not* to everyone's advantage are unjust. And (iii) it is not just to contemplate, as the Pareto principle does, that the losses of some can be compensated for by the gains of others. Even more important, the stipulations "to everyone's advantage" and "equally open to all" have the interpretation that the principle of fair equality be combined with the Difference Principle, which ensures that "the expectations of the least advantaged are indeed maximized..." (p. 68). In other words, the welfare of the least privileged (i.e., those with the least amount of social primary goods) must be maximised (by a greater supply of social primary goods) *before that of all others*. Indeed, inequalities are only to be deemed justified if these lead to an improvement in the lot of the least privileged.

The question that must be addressed at this stage is: would the Rawlsian theory be relevant to the vital problems of distributive justice, economic equality, poverty and human deprivation in poor societies? The answer is: not necessarily so. This is problematic because Rawls (1971) envisages a condition of "moderate scarcity...and that of conflict of interest" (p. 110), so that the (modest) transfer of resources required by the Difference Principle are expected to improve the conditions of the least-privileged without imposing excessive sacrifices on the rich. Furthermore, although the Rawlsian principles of justice were initially (in 1971) taken as providing a firm base for distributive justice; but, as he later clarified, these principles are not so much about maximising social good as about reflecting "the overarching fundamental intuitive idea ... of society as a system of cooperation between free and equal persons" [Rawls (1985); p. 231]. In the contractarian tradition, his emphasis has shifted over time from the attainment of absolute justice to the fairness of the rules and procedures within which individuals with different ends cooperate.

Some economists regard it as a retraction of the original (1971) version of justice. Sen (1992) doubts "whether [the Rawlsian] political conception gives the idea of justice – even political justice – its due" (p. 79). The problem is that many of the economic problems (e.g., economic inequality) would lie outside the realm of such a political concept of justice, in which things like political liberalism and mutual tolerance are given starring roles.[21] The net effect of the emphasis on the political nature of the Rawlsian concept of justice is to devalue somewhat the value of pressing economic needs (poverty, economic deprivation) should a choice be made between them. True, Rawls recognises that liberty is a luxury commodity, whose importance increases "once the required social conditions and the level of satisfaction of needs and material wants are attained" (p. 476); but this does not mean that the priority of liberty is in any way compromised (though its intensity may be less) at a lower level of development. The fact is that the priority of political and civil rights is quite *absolute* in Rawlsian theory, as he clarifies later on: "the basic rights and liberties and their priority...guarantee equally for all citizens the social conditions essential for the adequate development and the full and informed exercise of their two moral powers – their capacity for a sense of justice and their capacity for a conception of the good..." [Rawls (1999); p. XII].[22] It, therefore, follows that "infringement of basic equal liberties ... cannot be justified by, or compensated for, by greater social and economic advantages" (p. 54).

Yet another limitation of the political concept of justice is that it does *not* apply to those who are prevented, due to some physical disability, from participating as equal contributing members in any scheme of social cooperation – a point which Rawls (1985; p. 234) himself admits. But, as Arrow (1973) shows, such exclusions greatly limit the range and effectiveness of the Difference Principle because these disabled persons are also the poorest of the poor and *the* least-privileged people in society – the "voiceless millions" whom no meaningful ethical theory can possibly ignore.[23]

However, notwithstanding these limitations, the Rawlsian theory does make a valuable contribution. It highlights the difficulties of finding a political solution to the problems of distributive justice. Because such solutions inevitably involve hurting some while helping others, the resulting social tensions must be resolved politically. It is in this context that deriving *fair* rules of justice *impartially* is such an important criterion for resolving the difficult economic trade-offs, and for providing a 'stable' framework of rules which generate support to a 'shared' view of peaceful co-existence. Also, one can hardly think of a functioning society without a consensual agreement about the importance of individual freedom and an equitable distribution of income and wealth.

d) Sen's Capability Calculus

The central point of Sen's analysis is to redefine social welfare by focusing on the circumstances internal to a person which affect the *conversion* of income, the Rawlsian primary goods, Dworkin's resources, etc., into human *well-being*: "If the object is to concentrate on the individual's real opportunity to pursue her objectives (as Rawls explicitly recommends), then account would have to be taken not only of the primary goods that persons respectively hold, but also of the relevant personal characteristics that govern the *conversion* of primary goods into the person's ability to promote her ends", [Sen (1999b); p. 74; italics in the original]. Thus, a disabled (or older) person may acquire larger income, primary goods, and resources and yet be able to convert these into a lesser level of well-being than an able-bodied (or a younger) person can. If maximising well-being be the objective of human activity, then analytical focus must shift to objects ('ends') which determine it *directly* and not to those which do it merely *indirectly* (the 'means'). These objects or 'ends' of human activity are referred to as "functionings" (being healthy, being well-educated, being able to take part in community activity, and enjoy self-esteem) "which are *constitutive* of a person's being" [Sen (1992); p. 39]. A closely related idea is that of the 'capability' to function to achieve alternative feasible combinations of functionings. Capability is thus indicative of a person's *freedom* to achieve valuable functionings. In this context, to be free to choose is a matter of central importance. Thus, for instance, two people who do not eat (the one who fasts and the other who starves) may achieve the same kind of functionings, and yet their capabilities will be different in the two cases, because voluntary fasting is not the same thing as (involuntary) starving!

The significance of the capability calculus from theoretical and practical points of view can be made clear by the following considerations.[24] Firstly, the capability analysis greatly enlarges the informational basis of the evaluative criteria of human happiness and well-being. In this case it makes a definite advance on: (a) the *utilitarian's* unifocal concentration on mental-state experience of satisfaction expressed exclusively in terms of the metric of utility; (b) the *neo-classicals'* non-recognition of trade-offs between parties to exchange and their ruling out the possibility of interpersonal comparisons of individual utilities; (c) the *libertarian's* (such as Nozick's) focus on only the procedures of achieving individual liberty and on preventing negative freedoms in a totally non-consequential setting; and (d) the *contractarian's* emphasis on the processes of arriving at just principles of justice (e.g., Rawls). Secondly, though welfarist in temperament, the capability analysis goes beyond the utilitarian's single-minded concentration on (total) utilities alone, and highlights – like Rawls, whose primary goods include many dimensions of individual welfare – the essential *plurality* of our concerns and objectives in the discharge of social obligations. It focuses on the individual's inner sense of deprivation – which utility (welfarist) analysis does no better than muffle and hide – by recognising the many interpersonal diversities of circumstances which separate the *means* from the *ends* of human endeavours.[25] Furthermore, the capability analysis succeeds in analysing cases of "entrenched deprivation", where a mental-state inter-personal comparison of utilities breaks down completely. Thus, "the extent of a person's deprivation ... may not at all show up in the metric of desire-fulfilment, even though he or she may be quite unable to be adequately nourished, decently clothed, minimally educated, and properly sheltered" [Sen (1992); p. 55].

Thirdly, explicitly allowing inter-personal comparisons of individual welfare, the capability calculus can 'see' the differences between the rich and poor, which recognition is central to an adequate analysis of the poverty problem. Furthermore, Sen's analysis is *not* restricted to the traditional income-based analysis because poverty cannot be disassociated from the misery caused by it, and because poverty ultimately denotes the lack of an opportunity to lead a minimally acceptable life. It is, therefore, a matter of importance "to see poverty as a capability deprivation" [Sen (1999a); p. 361]. This more inclusive view of the poverty problem helps answer the all-important question: why should poverty be regarded as a social evil *irrespective* of the prevailing inter-country and within-country disparities between income and expenditure patterns, especially those between the poor (say, Bangladesh) nations and the rich nations (say, the United States)? Capability analysis offers the insight that "relative deprivation in the space of *incomes* can yield absolute deprivation in the space of capabilities" [Sen (1992); p. 115]. For instance, in a rich country, where the incomes of the poor are much higher than those of the poor in the poor countries, the sense of deprivation may be even greater in the former than in the latter, because in richer countries a much larger income is required to achieve the same level of functionings than in poor countries. This explains "why men in [the] Harlem region of the prosperous city of New York have less chance of reaching the age of 40 or more than Bangladeshi men have" [McCord and Freeman (1990), cited in Sen (1992)]. Fourthly, inspired by Sen's analysis, the UNDP's Annual *Human Development Reports* have made a significant contribution to the empirical information about the many observed features of human well-being – e.g., educational accomplishments, the chances of a longer and healthier life span, the many faces and forms of poverty and human deprivation in addition to the advances achieved in the income and wealth of peoples and nations.

For all its merits, Sen's contribution has some besetting faults. Firstly, drawing too sharp a distinction between the income-related variables and those indicating a person's capability to convert income into the achievement of specific functionings (e.g., to be healthy and literate) tends to overshadow somewhat the significance of the formers' *direct* contribution to enhancing a sense of human well-being. The fact is that income-related improvements in well-being stand apart from those caused by 'hard-core' indicators of capability like improvements in education and health. Also, as Sen (1999a) notes, "in situations of extreme starvation and famine, income deprivation has more immediacy ... than the more subtle – and, ultimately, more informed – distinctions based on capability comparisons" (p. 362). Secondly, there is the difficult problem of 'operationalising' the capability metric of human welfare, to evaluate the authenticity of individual reports about their personal *incapabilities,* which prevent them from efficiently converting income into human happiness. The informational limitation here is significant and so is the cost of collecting the requisite information. Needless to point out, at least some of these *incapability* reports may form an unsuitable basis for public policy [Naqvi (2002)].[26] Thirdly, it has been objected that, at least so far, there is no operational metric for the capability approach like the one that exists for the real-income framework (the metric of exchange value), or like the one "for the Marshallian consumer theory, combined with the Kaldor-Hicks compensation test" (i.e., the metric of cost-benefit analysis) [Sugden (1993); p. 1954]. To these objections Sen (1999b) replies, in my view rather convincingly, that the essential plurality of the capability analysis is an advantage rather than an embarrassment:

"to insist that there should be only one homogenous magnitude that we value is to reduce drastically the range of our evaluative reasoning"... that "heterogeneity of factors that influence individual advantage is a pervasive feature of evaluation", (p. 77); and that "judgmental exercises can be resolved only through reasoned evaluation...rather than any interpersonal agreement (or consensus)" (p. 78).

Yet, notwithstanding these objections, Sen's is perhaps the most comprehensive evaluative exercise which combines ethical and economic considerations into a unified analytical framework. It deals directly with many objectively observed, rather than merely mentally experienced and emotionally felt, causative factors of human well-being.

V. The Possibilities of Public Policy

A central issue in connecting economics with ethics – i.e., determining the influence of moral values held by individuals on their economic behaviour – is about the possibility of a proactive public policy in different public-choice theories. However, as should be evident by now, even theories which are about *non-market decision-making*, take Pareto-optimality as a standard of reference, according to which competitive market solutions produced by the unrestricted sway of the self-interest principle are held to be unimprovable with respect to efficiency. Also, it is assumed that, in 'well-ordered' (Western) societies, the problems of distributive justice have already been solved at some prior date; and that they do not constrain the day-to-day working of these societies. The need for an egalitarian public policy is, therefore, felt only in those normative public-choice theories which focus on problems of social justice, poverty, human deprivation. Even here, the scope of public policy is more restricted in the Rawlsian perspective (concerned primarily with implementing a framework of rules within which individuals pursue activities they value most) than in Sen's (with its focus on maximising social good). It may be instructive to highlight the perspectives on public policy that competing public-choice theories offer by reference to the central normative problem of economic equality.

i) *Perspectives on Egalitarianism*

Sen (1992) notes that a common characteristic of all the *normative* approaches is to seek *equality* with respect to *some* aspects of social arrangement, and tolerate *inequalities* in other respects. Thus, public policy can demand equality in one *space* while neglecting it in another space (spaces). Indeed, equality in one space may even be used to *justify* inequality in some other space. Thus, formally, all theories may claim to be egalitarian in some space, and yet be inegalitarian in some other space.

A useful distinction may, therefore, be made to distinguish between *apparent* egalitarianism and *substantive* egalitarianism: the former goes with universal *selfishness* and an emphasis on efficiency and unfettered markets. The latter, on the other hand, gives a starring role to altruism, with an emphasis on distributive justice. Thus, Nozick, Buchanan and Tullock, etc., seek equality in the moral and political 'spaces' but are unconcerned about *economic* equality, which is not seen as having an intrinsic value, but only an instrumental value, if at all. Political equalities may, therefore, coexist with extreme inequalities of income and wealth. On the other hand, Rawls, Dworkin, Sen, and many others seek economic equality, while also emphasising the importance of political equality for human well-being. Let us begin with utilitarian egalitarianism.

a) Utilitarianism

As noted above, utilitarianism has for long been advertised as consciously focusing on distributive justice; while, in fact, it does not do any such thing. Assume that utility functions are *not* identical for all individuals, then the utilitarian recommendation to equalise marginal utilities across different individuals will result in extremely unequal utility levels for different individuals!

The problem is that an exclusive insistence on using subjective utility information (derived from mental-state experiences alone) as an index of individual and social welfare will most likely lead to a perverse transfer of resources: i.e., *more* income given to the hard-to-please (rich) people and *less* to the poor who manage to build some cheer in their lives even with small mercies. It is for this reason that modern ethical theory has all but discarded utilitarianism as a basis for egalitarian public policy.

b) Rawlsian Egalitarianism

Rawlsian egalitarianism regards economic equality as a baseline standard from which departures must be justified by reference to some other egalitarian principle, i.e., inequalities are allowed only if these are equally beneficial to all. However, equality for all requires, by the Difference Principle, giving more *social* primary goods to those who have the least of it. The point of this principle is that the arbitrariness of the 'natural' distribution of talents and advantages should *not* be allowed to be built into the *basic structure of a just society*. This is because "the natural distribution is neither just nor unjust...what is just and unjust is the way institutions deal with these facts" [Rawls (1999); p. 87]. *Thus, public policy should redress the inequalities of birth and natural endowments by a restructuring of the basic institutions, which represent an essentially unjust meritocratic society*. The need for such redress is the most compelling with respect to the underclass. Hence, following the Difference Principle, social institutions must be reordered "so that no one gains or loses from his arbitrary place in the distribution of natural assets or his initial position in society without giving or receiving compensating advantages in return" (p. 87). The basic idea is to organise societies as a *fraternity* in a cohesive family in which no one wishes to gain unless those left behind are also brought forward: "Those better circumstanced are willing to have their greater advantages only under a scheme in which this works out for the benefit of the less fortunate ... and not wanting to have greater advantages unless this is to the benefit of others who are less well off" (p. 90). However, as noted above, the reach of the Difference Principle is *not* as extensive as one would expect from the above-mentioned general principles. The reason is that: (a) it is meant to work in a society of moderate scarcity so that the well-off are not required to part with much of their wealth; and (b) it altogether *excludes* those who are really poor and physically disabled because they cannot participate in the Rawlsian scheme of social cooperation. Whence follows that the extent of restructuring of the existing social and economic institutions required to generate the necessary resources to equalise the poor with the rich will also be minimal. Yet the basic idea here is a valuable one, and can serve as the basic organising principle of a meaningful social and economic reform in "ill-ordered', societies as well.

c) Dworkin's 'Resourcism'

Closely related to the Rawlsian egalitarianism is Dworkin's (1981a,b) recommendation to bring about equality of "resources", which is mostly of a subjective nature. These resources are not only 'external' to an individual but also those which are 'internal' to him/her (e.g., natural talents, handicaps). But the question is: how can public policy equalise with respect to physically inalienable resources the extant distribution of which Dworkin, like Rawls, regards as "morally arbitrary"? His answer is that equality should be achieved only with respect to those resources for which a person is "responsible", but *not* with respect to those for which he is not responsible. The essence of Dworkin's thesis – which is broadly similar to Scanlon's (1986; 1999) position – is that, while no one is responsible for one's inborn talents and early nurture, a person *is* responsible for the preferences he holds and the risks he takes in life. The latter should, therefore, be rewarded.[27] It may be noted that, like Rawls, Dworkin does *not* recommend (utilitarian) welfare. Thus, for instance, in any scheme of redistribution, one should *not* receive compensation for having cultivated very expensive tastes (which he/she cannot always satisfy) from those whose tastes are more affordable.

d) Sen's Capability Equality

The primary focus of Sen's (1992) analysis is *not* on the "primary goods" or the "resources", which are only *means* to achieving certain valuable functionings, which are "constitutive" of human well-being. His capability calculus rather denotes the individual's free choice to achieve feasible combinations of the functionings an individual values most. Public policy should, therefore, aim to equalise with respect to the capabilities that resources and/or primary goods engender in differing degrees – depending on the inter-personal variations in different people's capability to convert resources/primary goods into personal well-being and happiness. The implication is that for a redistributive scheme to contribute *equally* to human well-being, these inter-personal capability deficits, which will be larger for the poor and/or sick than for the rich and/or healthy, must be redressed. Thus, a person with a serious physical disability must receive *more* than an able-bodied person. It may be noted that functionings and capabilities – unlike utilities and Dworkin's resources, but like Rawls's primary social goods – are observable entities and possess a much wider informational base than any of the competing perspectives reviewed in this chapter. By the same token, the former allow a much larger role for an egalitarian public policy than the latter.

The theories reviewed in this chapter have their weak points; but their main contribution is to emphasise that a greater dose of altruism makes the economic system work better. Yet, private altruistic motives alone are not enough to maximise human beings. To this end, the system of incentives and rewards built into a meritocratic society, or one raised on a feudal system, must be *changed* by public policy. The aim should be to *nullify* the advantages that people come to enjoy due to circumstances of birth, their inborn talents, or a better physical capacity to enjoy life. It should then proceed to create a just society in which the least privileged are given first priority in any scheme of resource transfer, people are rewarded for what they are 'responsible' for, and more is given to the physically handicapped to maximise human well-being. In other words, the *principle of redress*, without which social life would be nasty, brutish, and poverty-stricken, must be the basis of a fruitful public policy, which should not be diverted from its main objective (that is, economic equality) by the irrelevant liberalist *absolutism* about political rights. True, political rights have a due place in any civilised well-ordered society; but economic and political rights are interdependent, so that neglecting economic inequality directly compromises political rights as well. Indeed, "economic unfreedom in the form of extreme poverty can make a person a helpless prey in the violation of other kinds of freedom" [Sen (1999b); p. 8]. For public policy to succeed in achieving a balance between non-economic and economic freedoms and that between political liberty and an egalitarian distribution of income and wealth, it must be *seen* as just and fair and impartial, and not serving vested interests. It is only then that an overarching political consensus can be built and public support gained for a truly egalitarian public policy.

Notes

1. Adam Smith (1776) famously (rather notoriously) remarked: "It is not from the benevolence of butcher, the brewer, or the baker that we expect our dinner, but from their regard to their own interest. We address ourselves, not to their humanity but to their self-love, and never talk to them of our necessities but of their advantages" (pp. 26-27). However, as noted in the text, this quote applies only to the exchange aspect of the economic transactions but not necessarily to its *production* and *distribution* aspects; and also that it does *not* prescribe that the motivational structure (involving *only* self-interest) also applies to the production and distributional aspects as well.

2. A few years later, George Stigler (1981) restated the same position as an empirically testable (indeed, tested) proposition: "Let me predict the outcome of the systematic testing of behaviour in situations where self-interest and ethical values with wide verbal allegiance are in conflict. Much of the time, most of the time in fact, the self-interest theory (as I interpreted on Smithian lines) will win" (p. 176).
3. The leader of these economists, referred to in Harsanyi's quote, is no less a person than Lionel Robbins (1935) who pronounced the formal divorce between ethics and economics: "it does not seem logically possible to associate the two studies [ethics and economics] in any form but mere juxtaposition. Economics deals with ascertainable facts, ethics with valuation and obligations" (p. 132).
4. Sen (1999b) pungently remarks: "We must see the system of ethics underlying capitalism as involving a good deal more than sanctifying greed and admiring cupidity" (p. 266)
5. Formally, if there are alternatives x and y such that if everyone in society is indifferent between x and y, then society need not do any better than be also indifferent between x and y. And, if at least one person in society prefers x to y while the rest consider x as at least as good as y, then society should prefer x to y. In the former case, the society is Pareto-wise *indifferent* between x and y, while in the latter situation x is Pareto-wise superior to y. Pareto-optimality is then defined as a situation when there is no alternative situation which is Pareto-wise superior to x [see, Allen Buchanan (1985); Naqvi (1993; 2002)].
6. The first theorem noted in the text assumes that there are no public goods and externalities of various kinds; and that information between economic agents is symmetric. In addition to these assumptions, the second theorem assumes quasi-concavity of utility functions and convexity of production possibility sets. An explanation of these assumptions is given in Sen (1970); and Feldman (1991).
7. A moral view which insists on moral rights regardless of the consequences (that is, a non-consequentialist view) of their exercise is referred to as deontological.
8. In extreme cases, such defence of property rights may even *cause* famines. Sen (1984) cites such a case: "in guarding ownership rights against the demands of the hungry, the legal procedures uphold entitlements, e.g., in the Bengal famine of 1943, the people who died in front of well-stocked food shops protected by the state were denied food because of lack of legal entitlement and not because of their entitlements being violated" (p. 458).

9. An example of the fallacy of composition is to assert that since the grains of sand in a mountain are light, the mountain is also light!
10. Modern formulations of the classical utilitarian version replace utility by 'desire-fulfillment', measured by some observable choices: if $x > y$, then $xu > yu$. A detailed examination of classical utilitarianism, its criticisms, and possible alternatives to it is given in Sen and Williams (1999).
11. It is, therefore, not surprising that utilitarianism has been used both as an anti-market argument as well as a pro-market one. In the former case, it is contended that *market*-induced inequities do not necessarily maximise *social* utility even when the market outcomes are Pareto-optimal because any redistribution of the total sum of utility will benefit the rich more than the poor. In the latter case, it is argued that, even if a government-backed egalitarian programme is beneficial for overall production, it would compromise the individual's liberty to pursue his/her own happiness and reduce social utility. For details of both type of arguments, see Allen Buchanan (1985); pp. 54-62.
12. Arrow (1951) stated the universal consensus against the possibility of such comparisons: "interpersonal comparisons of utilities has no meaning" (p. 9). This universal consensus, evolved around Robbins (1935), led to a shift from a 'cardinal' to an 'ordinal' measure of utility; and it survives to this day in one form or the other in economic textbooks, even though it has been increasingly challenged. For instance, see Sen (1999b).
13. The quotation is from the Preface to the revised edition (1999) of Rawls's classic work, *A Theory of Justice*, originally published in 1971.
14. Formally, the Bergson-Samuelson social welfare function takes the form: $W = w(x_1, x_2, \ldots, x_n)$ where W is a real-valued function of the economic variables xi. The normative issue is then solved by optimal taxes and transfer to sustain the society at an optimal point along the Pareto-optimal production-possibility frontier with the help of a variant of the Bergson-Samuelson Social Welfare function $W = W(U_1, U_2, \ldots, U_n)$, where U_i are the indices of individual utility.
15. Yet another reason why the neo-classical welfare function is not fit to tackle distributive issues is as follows: since a person preferring x to y is *not* accepted as enough evidence of the person x possessing certain qualities (being poor or rich) in relation to y, it is also not permissible for the society to attribute greater value to x rather than y.
16. There are many other contributors in both categories: e.g., Vickery (1960), Buchanan and Tullock (1962), Harsanyi (1955), Dworkin (1981), Roemer (1996), etc.

17. Formally, Harsanyi's theorem can be written as: $W = \Sigma a_i U_i$, where a_i stand for the values that W takes when, alternatively, $U_i = 1$ and $U_j = 0$ for all *j ' i* [Harsanyi (1955); p. 52]. Furthermore, as discussed in the text, *if an individual has the equal probability of being any other individual,* which is how Harsanyi brings both self-interest and altruism into a single unified framework, then $W = \Sigma U_i$.
18. In Harsanyi's formulation the *unanimity* property is not ethically neutral like it is in the Pareto-optimality formulation (see Part II for a discussion of the unanimity property in the context of the Pareto-optimal principle).
19. It should be obvious that if the social welfare function takes a multiplicative form, then just one individual's zero evaluation of any specific social outcome will reduce the social welfare function (W) to zero. In a dictatorial set-up, as also in a meritocratic society, this can, and does, happen at least to some extent.
20. Rawls clarifies that "primary goods are now characterized as what persons need in their status as free and equal citizens and as normal and fully cooperating members of society over a complete life. Interpersonal comparisons for purposes of political justice are to be made in terms of the citizen's index of primary goods and these goods are seen as answering to their needs as citizens as opposed to their preferences and desires" [Rawls (1999); p. xiii].
21. Important among these liberties are the following: "political liberty (the right to vote and to hold office) and freedom of speech and assembly; liberty of conscience and freedom of thought; freedom of the person; ... the right to hold personal property and freedom from arbitrary arrest and seizure as defined by the concept of the rule of law. These liberties are to be equal by the first principle" [Rawls (1999); p. 53].
22. Thus, for instance, in the Ethiopian famine of 1973, in which Emperor Selassie, who did not provide relief to the famine-stricken people on the grounds that "those who do not work will starve", may not have violated the Rawlsian requirement of political justice; but it was manifestly unjust. Indeed, the Emperor and his opponents were not even interested in "looking for a political solution based on toleration with the desire of living together" [Sen (1992); p. 78].
23. Questions have also been raised both about the Rawlsian procedures for arriving at the principles of justice and these principles themselves. Thus, for instance, liberty is accorded priority behind the veil of ignorance as well, where "free and equal persons" voluntarily agree on the basic principles that are going to affect their lives. "It is perhaps no surprise, therefore, that liberty is 'chosen' as the top priority principle from the original position"

[Mueller (1979); p. 242]. Furthermore, it has been pointed out that the principles required to frame the rules of justice do not serve as an effective compliance mechanism to sort out the many trade-offs in real life because such information does not prefigure in the original position.

24. This analysis draws selectively on Naqvi (2002).
25. The interpersonal variations in individual capabilities, noted in the text, flow from at least four sources: "(1) personal heterogeneties (proneness to illness), (2) environmental diversities (for example, living in storm-prone or flood-prone areas), (3) variations in social climate (for example, the prevalence of crime, or epidemiological vectors), and (4) differences in relative deprivation connected with customary patterns of consumption in particular societies (for example, being relatively impoverished in rich societies, which can lead to deprivation of the absolute capability to take part in the life of the community)" [Sen (1999a); p. 360].
26. There are also somewhat technical objections to Sen's analysis with respect to the 'weighting' of different capabilities and functionings, which are vectors with many elements. This raises the familiar index-number problem, which requires settling, of weights to be attached to each of the diverse elements of these vectors [Hausman and McPherson (1993)].
27. It should, however, be obvious that the preferences that people come to hold and the risks they take later in life are not altogether unrelated to the circumstances of one's birth or early nurture [Roemer (1996)].

CHAPTER 3

Religious Morality in Western Thought

I. Introduction

The central ethical problem in a modern individualist society is to find the right set of moral values, including religious values, that exert the greatest influence on human behaviour. It will be recalled from the previous chapter that the dominant neo-classical paradigm denies the need for *any* exogenous moral or religious stimulus to enthuse individuals to act for society. A spontaneous, doctrineless individualism, powered only by self-interest, is assumed sufficient to produce an (efficient and distributionally neutral) "unimprovable" state of bliss, which is also held up as a moral ideal, one synonymous with the common good. Given the possibility of making non-distortionary transfers from the winners to the losers competitive *equilibrium* can achieve *any* desired distributional outcome. In this wonderland of universal harmony there is not even a pretence for creating socially advantageous arrangements, nor is there any need to make *any* additional distributional corrections, and certainly not on moral or religious grounds. The reason for this aversion to morality is the divorce between economics and ethics, which the neo-classical paradigm has accepted as final. True, it has been acknowledged [Arrow (1974)] that, in so far as the price system is not universal (as it is not), ethical behaviour (reflected in "an explicit or implicit social contract") can contribute to the *efficiency* of the price system; but, such admissions go with the warning that "we do not wish to use up recklessly the scarce resources of altruistic motivation" and that "ethically motivated behaviour may even have a negative value" (p. 355). The divorce between ethics and economics, therefore, remains unchallenged in mainstream (neo-classical) economics. This insensitivity to distributional issues is reinforced by those modern moral-right theories which worry about (negative) individual (political) freedoms, but *deny* that the poor have a moral right to aid! Yet, fortunately, unleashing greed in the economic sphere is not the only activity in the realm of economics. Most normative theories find this insensitivity revolting and emphasise the need for mobilising moral values to nudge self-interested individuals to work for the social good and there are some who are no longer shy of bringing in religious values to do the job of moral manoeuvring.

II. Self-Interested Behaviour and Religious Morality

The question to be addressed now is: how to determine the social role of religion in strengthening the force of moral motivation to induce individuals to contribute to the collective good? The present chapter answers this question in the context of Christianity and Judaism, while the next chapter addresses it in the Islamic context. The expectation in all these cases is that religious morality would, by its confident simplicity, reinforce altruism. However, the problem is complicated by many a slip between the cup and the lip, so to speak. The main slip is that there can simply be *no* role for religion in economic affairs as long as individualist (market) *behaviour* is assumed to reflect individual's selfish *preferences*, because in that case an individual would (rationally) not strive to achieve the public good for *any* reason whatsoever – social, moral or religious. Altruistic behaviour, besides being redundant, would be 'irrational', since *only* self-interested behaviour is rational. But, as Chapter 2 shows, this is not the case; and that morality does make a significant contribution to achieving social goals. Once this much is conceded, religious morality streams in irresistibly. But there are many reasons why the neo-classical's objections to religious (or secular) morality must be brushed aside.

Firstly, the neo-classical solution to the distributional problem, noted above, is nothing more than transparent trickery. Graff (1991) points out that, "the *possibility* of compensation means very little unless the compensation is actually carried out" (p. 254).[1] In other words, the optimal state *is* improvable with respect to distributive equity.[2] This is because there is no way to judge the adequacy of any meaningful distributional scheme while remaining strictly neutral with respect to distributional issues [Little (1957); Streeten (1953)]; and because the postulated size of such 'non-distortionary' transfers – non-distortionary, because any distortionary transfer will make an unimprovable optimal state worse with respect to efficiency and equity – will be too small, even if actually carried out, to bridge the wide gap between the rich and the poor observed in the not so well-ordered real-life societies.[3] That being the case, more genuine and effective transfer mechanisms must be found. Part of the answer to the problem lies in mobilising (even manipulating) individual moral beliefs to effect such resource transfers to the poor. Religious beliefs are presumably more efficient in doing this job if only because the incidence of free-riding can be minimised.

Secondly, in large groups (e.g., big corporations, the nation state, etc.), "unless there *is* some coercion or some other device to make individuals act in their common interest, *rational, self-interested individuals will not act to achieve their common or group interests*" [Olson (1971); p. 2; italics in original]. Not only that. With no binding moral-religious norms to self-regulate, *voluntary* selfish behaviour of the members of a (large) group or society is inconsistent with achieving the common good, *even if* the members know that they would gain by acting in such a manner.[4] This is because an individual member can reasonably free-ride on the assumption that his action (of not giving) will not be noticed by other members of the group. Voluntary self-interest behaviour is ineffectual in achieving social good, even if such non-economic motives as national ideology, the bond of common culture, patriotism are assumed to be strong enough. The fact is that, notwithstanding these sentiments, "no major state in modern history has been able to support itself through voluntary dues or contributions" (p. 13). Thus, the voluntary pursuit of any collective enterprise requires that some coercion, or effective moral norms of a secular or religious kind, be used to link the individual with collectivity.

Thirdly, contrary to the position of positive public-choice theories, individualist competitive behaviour is by no means *the* social norm by which the desirability and feasibility of collective action can be measured. Rather, in many real-life situations, cooperative behaviour comes out as superior to competitive outcomes. This has been aptly illustrated by the Prisoner's Dilemma case, in which each of the prisoners will be better off by cooperating rather than competing. In other words, a strategy which may look rational from the self-interested individual's point of view is likely to be defective from a collective point of view. Individual rationality will, in this case, diverge from collective rationality [Rapoport (1991)]. However, as noted above, any voluntary cooperative effort in a large group, or at a national level, will be defeated by the free-riders. Thus, once again, some sort of coercive action and/or religious sanction is required to organise significant cooperative effort to achieve the collective good.

Finally, it is extremely limiting to define economic rationality as synonymous with self-interest behaviour; for, if this were so, the exigencies of efficiency will crowd out all requirements of a civilised society, involving such vital matters as social justice, helping the poor, or a concept of social good. If only to remain relevant to reality, economic rationality must be capacious enough to accommodate morally motivated behaviour. In particular, *universally accepted religious values like honesty, sympathy, commitment, etc., are collective goods needed to maximise social output.*

Thus, for instance, Reder's (1979) analysis of the economics of honesty shows that net economic output can be secured at significantly lower 'policing' and contracting cost; and Sen (1977) demonstrates that rationality can (and should) account for such considerations as 'sympathy' (which is enlightened self-interest because the welfare of others affects my welfare as well) and 'commitment' (I am willing to accept a cut in my own welfare if it enhances the welfare of others). Rawls (1999) defines rationality as each party trying to ensure the highest index of "social primary goods", without being envious of each other, because "this enables them to promote their conception of the [social] good most effectively..." (p. 125). Thus, it should not be beyond human rationality to be at least as much concerned about the achievements of higher goals and values in life as to be moved by one's own selfish interest. That being the case, it should not at all be an unscientific activity to try to enhance the moral content of economic activity by creating awareness of moral-religious principles that govern human economic behaviour.

III. The Importance of Being Religious

The (utilitarian) belief that if something is good for the individual it is also good for society is misplaced because an individual is not likely to adopt moral standards helpful to the system if the system and what it produces cannot be evaluated (as is the case with the Pareto optimal set-up) on moral criteria.[5] Joan Robinson (1973) remarked: "it is not possible to describe a system without moral judgments creeping in" (p. 19). Rawls (1999) has observed that individuals are motivated by the "conception of a social good" if the system they work for is "just" and if "fair" procedures are adopted. The latter requirement would ensure that the basic principles underlying the system are such that "when they are embodied in the basic structure of society men tend to acquire the corresponding sense of justice and develop a desire to act in accordance with its principles" (p. 119). Historically as well, the capitalist system does not rest on the solid rock of selfishness and greed. Sen (1999) notes: "Within its domain capitalism works effectively through a system of ethics that provides vision and the trust needed for a successful use of market mechanism..." (p. 263).[6] And yet, for all its redoubtable accomplishments, capitalism has remained innately insensitive to distributive equity, poverty and human deprivation. To do better on this count, an open acceptance of a helpful system of moral values by individuals should be important.

The question we ask here is: how far does religion help solve these problems by freeing individuals from the gravitational pull of their own self-interest and work for a 'just' society? It stands to reason that, since the seemingly (secular) moral values that are assumed to make an individualist economy more efficient eventually derive from religious values, the latter too must feature explicitly to explain its operational success. Thus, universal religious moral values like honesty, justice and helping the least-privileged should be strengthened, rather than weakened, to make the individualist economy efficient and equitable. Stephen (1873) argues that religion helps in the secular sphere as well because "duty is so very often inconvenient that it requires a present justification as well as an historical explanation". The only such "historical justification", according to him, is to accept God as a legislator and "virtue a law in the proper sense of the word" (p. 252).

i) *Are Religious Values Irrelevant?*

Before we consider the demand for religion, let us note that the overwhelming consensus in the West has been to *deny* the connection between ethics and religion on the ground that the former antedates the latter. Indeed, according to this view, no theological system which contradicts the 'natural' laws of ethics can be accepted by the people.[7] Even when such a connection is reluctantly acknowledged secular ethical values are held to dominate religious values. Hence, by the Occam's Razor, the latter become redundant as determinants of human economic motivation. J.S. Mill (1874; 1969) did recognise explicitly the religious connection of capitalism, but insisted on the superiority of "the Religion of Humanity" to "Supernatural Religion" as a cultivator of altruistic human feelings. Karl Marx thought religion would wither away as the capitalistic structure of society underwent transformation. This because religion does *not* relate to the intellect; it rather fulfils the needs of the bourgeois society" [MacIntyre (1971); pp. 84-85]. Tawney (1937) reported: "...the doctrine that religion and economic interests form two separate and coordinate kingdoms, of which neither, without presumption, can encroach on the other was commonly accepted by the England of the nineteenth century..." (p. viii). Bertrand Russell (1954), recognised the powerful force of "ethical sanctions" in creating "a happy human society" (p. 150), but firmly rejected religion to be the source of such ethics: "In the Ages of Faith, when men really believed that moral sin, not followed by absolution, would lead to Hell, murder and rape were much commoner than they are in the Western World at the present day..." (p. 147). More recently, John Rawls (1985) denies the connection between his theory of Justice-as-Fairness and religion. He maintains that his concept of justice is based on the notion that free and equal citizens of a society "do not view the social order as a fixed natural order, or as an institutional hierarchy justified by religious or aristocratic values" (p. 231). Joan Robinson (1973) has succinctly summarised the Western position on the relative *unimportance* of religious values: "morality is desired and respected for its own sake; religion is being recommended to us for it supports morality, not morality because it derives from religion", (p. 15); and that: "it does not seem that religion has much to do with our economic ideology" (p. 19). This separation of ethics from religion and the latter being dominated by the former, even if the connection between the two is reluctantly recognised, is thus firmly established in Western thought. Of the latter tendency, Viner (1978) asserts that the trend to secularisation in the West had extended to Catholic religious ethics from the Renaissance period which "brought into existence secular minded philosophers, both lay and clerical...who offered instead a blend of theology, philosophy, and human 'wisdom' which was more secular than Scholastic doctrine..." (p. 116).[8] This moving back and forth between religious and secular values, with a distinct bias in favour of the latter, has created a deep-rooted tension in Western thought, and a kind of dualism in the public domain where "solutions that work have traditionally dominated solutions that have ethical appeal" [Hirsch (1977; 1995)].

There are two main problems with this view of the relation between religious and secular ethical philosophy and its relevance to economics. Firstly, it views religion as another name for arbitrariness and despotism which characterised a bygone, uncivilised age. Thus, for instance, Bertrand Russell (1954) dismisses ethics based on religion as "superstitious ethics", which "come down to us from less civilized times and embody a harshness from which we should try to escape. Affection towards intimates and kindly feeling towards the world at large are the sentiments most likely to lead to the right conduct" (pp. 142-143). Joan Robinson (1973) expressed a similar view: "...religion is a useful way both of strengthening the desire of the individual to do whatever he thinks right, and of imposing a particular view of what is right" (p. 14). A common fallacy of these views is to confound the basic principles of religion with the practice (indeed, malpractice) of religion. True, the Christian Church did in fact do quite a few abominable things to intellectuals and scientists and that it regarded, to quote Gibbon (1984), "reason as the instrument of dispute; [and] interpreted laws according to the dictates of private interest..." (p. 354); and this has been acknowledged by the (Catholic) Church itself and for which it has duly tendered apologies.[9] And yet these historical facts should not be mistaken for the sublime Christian ethical principles which have inspired Christians to do good for society – a clear manifestation of which are the large financial private contributions made to charities, many of which are for all peoples and not just for Christians. Secondly, much secular criticism of religious ethics was based on nineteenth century (secular) Utilitarianism, which has ruled the intellectual climate in the West.[10] It was claimed that it represented an adequate egalitarian ethic which could do better than anything offered by Christianity. But, as shown in Chapter 2, Utilitarianism is by no means egalitarian; indeed it does not pay *any* attention whatsoever to such real-life problems as distributive inequity and poverty – all issues where both morality and religion can (and do) make a contribution. As a result, no one takes utilitarianism as a reference point for an egalitarian public policy. A logical outcome of the decline of utilitarianism should be to strengthen the case for religious ethics, if only because the criticism of religious ethics it inspired is no longer valid.[11]

ii) *The Relevance of Religious Ethics*

An insistence on the autonomous and fundamental character of ethics, and its separation from the ethical *principles* of religion, has not been entirely beneficial for either; nor is it a sound logical proposition. It is clearly valid to argue that if the moral disposition of individuals in the form of ethical beliefs influences economic behaviour, then their religious beliefs (at the level of broad principles) would affect both – especially when these beliefs coincide, as they quite often do. For instance, like most secular ethical philosophies, all the religions in the Abrahamic tradition, i.e., Islam, Christianity and Judaism, feature, to varying degrees, the basic values which sustain efficient economic organisations. It would, therefore, be a case of a major inter-systemic informational breakdown if the former were not influenced by the latter. The fact is that a significant connection between religion and ethics, though hidden from the naked eye, has always been there. Indeed, it has been argued that historically religion and ethics have grown together: "Religion and morality have been advancing and retarding together" [Jafri (2001); p. 93]. There is, therefore, a strong case to link up with this historical trend and make the connection between the two explicit. This will do at least three desirable things. Firstly, the implementation of moral principles will be more effective if secular ethical philosophy and religious principles point in the same direction. Thus, for instance, the aim of helping the poor, which both recommend, will be more easily achieved if religious beliefs, invoked in its support, are stated emphatically and unambiguously. Secondly, an explicit link between ethical philosophy and religion will focus attention *on* those ethical views which encourage economically beneficial economic activities and *away* from those which do not. Thus, for instance, the liberalist philosophy (e.g., that of Nozick (1974)) will be crowded out of intellectual discourse and the realm of public policy because its contention that the poor do not have a *right* to aid runs counter to both logic and religious precepts – indeed, to common sense as well. Thirdly, religious obligations help focus the mind sharply, as secular ethics does not, on real-life issues like unemployment and poverty even when the ruling economic and ethical paradigms may be indifferent to them.

An outstanding illustration of the points just mentioned is the *Pastoral Letter of Catholic Social Teaching and the US Economy* (1985) which recommended, on the basis of "a long tradition of Catholic Social thought", that "the decisions reached [in the US] must be judged in the light of what they do *for* the poor, what they do *to* the poor, and what they enable the poor to do *for themselves*. The fundamental moral criterion for all economic decisions, policies, and institutions is this: They must be at the service of *all people, especially the poor*" (p. 8; italics in original). The *Letter* helped focus the attention of economists and policy-makers on such issues as unemployment, poverty reduction at a time when the individualist liberalist ideas of Friedman (1962), Hayek (1960), Nozick (1974) emphasised the virtues of liberty and the unlimited right to private property and blamed unemployment and poverty on poor people's indolence and lack of interest in work. Thus, Nobel Laureate economists James Tobin (1985) and Lawrence Klein (1985) supported the *Letter*: "The Catholic Bishops have put the present economic debate on a new plane" (p. 364). The point is that egalitarianism can strike stronger roots in public consciousness if leavened by the warmth and clarity of religion; and that drawing upon religious values will help realise fully the former's objectives. The converse statement is also true: religious ethics will lose its populist appeal if its inherent egalitarianism is eroded to placate the powerful, or for any other reason – something that has happened in all religious traditions.

IV. A Religious Vision of Economic Well-being

The claim that economics stands apart from religious beliefs is as unsustainable as the assertion of the autonomy of economics from ethics. Tawney (1937) has ruled that the separation of economics from religious values is a relatively recent phenomenon, and that the criticism which dismisses the concern of the churches with economic relations and social organisations as a modern innovation finds little support in past history. In the Age of Reformation, economics was seen as a branch of ethics, and ethics of theology, and "all human activities [were] treated as falling within a single scheme, whose character [was] determined by the spiritual destiny of mankind" (p. 272). He explicitly repudiates the claim that the estrangement between economics and religion was already complete in nineteenth century England. On the contrary, the economic theories of the Schoolmen and the Reformer's strictures against usury, land grabbing, extortionist prices and the Calvinist's attempts to establish rigorous economic discipline rested "on the assumption that the institution of property, the transactions of the market-place, the whole fabric of the society, and the whole range of activities, stand by no absolute title, but must justify themselves at the bar of religion" (p. VIII). The fact is that to this day, though dominated by the 'secularisation' of economics, intellectual opinion in the West has not been able to free itself entirely from its religious roots. Indeed, there is a growing body of intellectuals who, though still a miniscule minority, prefer to refer their ethical and economic conundrums to the "bar" of religious opinion.

i) *The Weber-Tawney Thesis*

It may be interesting to note at this stage the Weber-Tawney thesis about the causes of the progress of capitalism in the West. They both try to establish the influence of certain [Christian] religious ideas on enlivening the spirit and the *ethos* of capitalism. In this context, their main thesis is that Calvinism was more favourable to its rise than other religious traditions. Non-conformist in attitude, Calvin could give (unprecedented) special religious sanctions to gainful economic activity – something that a tradition-bound Catholic Church could not do at the time. The Calvinist ethic glorified, *on religious grounds*, the unlimited accumulation of wealth through a rigid restriction on personal consumption, a systematic and pitiless exploitation of labour and the strict observance of honesty as a matter of legal formality. It was, as Viner (1978) remarks, "an explicitly 'bourgeois' doctrine, linking non-conformist Protestant religion with bourgeois standards in a harmonious partnership; it is a discipline of sobriety, self-discipline and unashamed pursuit of wealth" (p. 180). This doctrine, though distasteful to the humanistic thinking of the age, was justified as one of the principal means of salvation in the hereafter.[12] The Calvinist creed, in sharp contrast to the Lutherian creed before it, regarded income from business and industry to be at least as honourable (and religiously permissible) as the rental income of landlords which Luther approved of.[13] Whatever may be said of Weber's thesis (and it has attracted a lot of criticism) it goes to the credit of Calvinism that it succeeded in designing religious ethics to suit the realities of a life in which commercialisation held the centre stage, *without abandoning its claim to religion*. Tawney (1937) remarks: "it [Calvinism] no longer suspects the whole world of economic motives as alien to the life of the spirit, or distrusts the capitalist as one who has necessarily grown rich on the misfortunes of his neighbour, or regards poverty as in itself meritorious..." (p. 114). The general point to note here, which is relevant to the main theme of this book, is that the key to the success of growth-promoting reformism – in particular, the one based on religious ethics – is to recognise the contrast between the existing social organisation and the moral standards generally accepted by the people, and then to respond creatively to this contrast by reinterpreting, even modifying, the religious doctrine, rather than accepting it as a *fixed order*, true for all times.

ii) *The Functional Role of Religion*

The Weber-Tawney thesis also illustrates the utility of religious ethical values for the smooth running of an individualist economy. The classical economists, especially Adam Smith and John Stuart Mill, recognised that an economy run on the individualist self-interest principle needed an internalised sense of ethic and built-in religious restraints to maximise social good. Hirsch (1977; 1995) asserts that the modern tendency to keep religion firmly outside the economic sphere has generally "obscured the role it has [historically] played in the economic system" (p. 138). This tendency was strengthened by the general acceptance of nineteenth century utilitarian philosophy, which has consistently insisted on the sufficiency of rational self-interest to achieve private welfare as well as social welfare. However, this has been a costly mistake. The fact is that, as noted at the beginning of this chapter, traditional moral values based on religion perform a useful function to minimise the tendency to free-ride, and induce individuals to work for the collective good. The importance of this functional role of religion has increased manifold as markets become connected within nations and between nations – or to use Olson's phraseology, as "economic groups" get bigger and more complex – in this Age of Globalisation. Correspondingly, the 'policing' and contracting costs of the modern economy have increased the demand for greater cooperative rather than competitive behaviour. But such demands on social organisation can be adequately met only by a matching sense of social morality. The reason being that the more urgent the need to regulate individualist behaviour to meet social goals –

e.g., those of distributional equality, social justice, etc. – the heavier will become the reliance of the economy on such moral values as truth, honesty, respect for law, all of which flow unmistakably from religious beliefs.

However, the assertion about the importance of moral and religious values is not to demand a perfectly, or even a predominantly, altruistic economy. It would be unreasonable to expect individuals to *always* put social interest ahead of personal interest without coercion; because *that* would be demanding a change in human nature. Fortunately, going that far is not necessary. All that is required to produce socially oriented behaviour is a regime of "as-if-altruism" – namely, one in which self-interested *preferences* are accepted but self-interested *behaviour* is not [Sen (1973)]. The strategy is to aim at a socially-influenced behaviour that best serves everyone's interest.[14] Yet, as Olson (1971) shows, individuals may feel 'cornered' by social norms to work for society in small groups; but this is not likely to happen in large groups. Hirsch (1977; 1995) suggests that, to meet these conflicting considerations, "privately directed objectives for choices between alternative spending patterns [should be] combined with socially directed objectives in following codes and rules of behaviour" (p. 148). Religious sanctions and morality mainly work in the latter case. However, altruism, *even when strengthened by religious sanctions*, cannot, all by itself, induce individuals to work for the social good. This is because, as Rawls (1999) points out, there are "definite limits on the strength of social and altruistic motivation .... [and that the theory of justice] supposes that individuals and groups put forward competing claims, and while they are willing to act justly, they are not prepared to abandon their interests" (p. 248). Thus, in order to reconcile the conflicting demands of private and social behaviour, a well-informed public policy must supplement altruism by minimising free-riding and assurance problems (see Chapters 1 and 2).

iii) *Religion For Its Own Sake*

While recognising its secular role – namely, that it contributes to economic progress – the fact is that religion is normally desired for its own sake because it is constitutive of human well-being. The demand for religion is a rational one in the sense that it helps achieve the elusive goal of human happiness by bringing into the open the spiritual problem hidden behind the economic mechanism, and attains an optimal combination of material and spiritual assets. It is in this context that the interaction between religion, morality and economic pursuits becomes really meaningful – and forceful. Such interaction also helps religious moral values evolve over time to meet new social, economic and political challenges, without forsaking their religious credentials. A dynamic relationship between religious imperatives and economic and social exigencies is essential. In its absence, religious ethics will either be replaced by some secularised ethics, which would not have the same operational force as the former does; or else it would turn into an ossified structure of thought unrelated to reality. In this context, the differing responses of the Catholic Church and the Protestant (Calvinist) Church to the rapidly changing composition of human demands as European society became increasingly urbanised make an interesting reading. According to Viner (1978), the Scholastics, unlike the Christian Fathers, showed a generally "tolerant attitude towards economic inequality and the pursuit of profit and did not regard engaging in commerce without recourse to sinful practices" (p. 111). A relevant consideration in this context may have been a grudging move to meet the challenges of the Renaissance, the Protestant Reformation, and those posed by a rising middle class from the sixteenth century onwards. The general attitude was one of condoning human weakness rather than eulogising such activities as contributing to salvation as well. And there was obviously great reluctance on the part of the Scholastics to depart very significantly from the traditional Catholic position, which remained very much the same in the sixteenth century as it was in the thirteenth century. At least to some extent this reluctance of Catholicism flowed from it being "more tightly bound to tradition, less responsive to changing external forces, intellectual and social, than was Protestantism"; and, unlike the latter, "the Scholastic moral theology was increasingly becoming a frozen and lifeless relic of an earlier age, still studied reverently in theological seminaries but steadily losing its influence on social behaviour in the outer world" (pp. 111-112). In sharp contrast, the Calvinist response was to give a "whole-hearted *imprimatur* to the life of business enterprise, which most earlier moralists regarded with suspicion, and had laid upon it the restraining hand of an inquisitorial discipline" [Tawney (1937); p. 232].

In modern times too there has been a revival of interest in looking at religion in terms of its broader scope rather than merely as the means to greater material prosperity. Tinbergen (1985) has advocated (and proved mathematically) the need for an "Optimum Social Order", in which religion appears as a powerful force for reversing the decline in "elementary human values" especially in the West, giving it a "more profound basis" on which to rest a social order, and enriching these human values by drawing upon diverse religious experiences of Christianity, Islam, Buddhism and others. He generally approved of the fact that "an increasing number of Muslims have started thinking about which economic order they have to choose on the basis of the Qur'ān [Naqvi (1981)]. (Western) socialist thinkers should not ignore this process: they may even be able to contribute to it. Neither should they be absent in the neo-Christian manifestations such as – to mention only one example – the Evangelische Kirchentage [Protestant Christian German Church Days]" (pp. 178-179).[15] Fogel (2000) elaborates a similar theme in the American context. While recognising the unprecedented material advance in the United States, he warns against the facile assumption that "improvement in material conditions naturally leads to spiritual advancement". Indeed, the "economist's traditional measure of income inequality" is clearly inadequate to "shed light on the most intractable forms of poverty (those related to the unequal distribution of spiritual resources)" (p. 3). He, therefore, argues for a "greater equity in the distribution of the spiritual assets that have such large effects on both the quest of self-realization and economic success in the market place" (p. 13). Fogel traces the interaction between American egalitarianism and the Christian social reform movements led by the Social Gospellers from 1730 to 1960 and onwards, which he christens as the Four Great Awakenings.[16] The Third and the Fourth Awakenings have had a decisive effect on economic thought. It led to deeper emphasis on the need for transferring more resources from the rich to the poor by greater state intervention as an instrument of redistribution. Also, during this period there has been a progressive tendency to equate "holiness and virtue with disinterested benevolence", regard "individuals the innocent victims of poverty and social corruption" (p. 85), and value the truth of religion in terms of its success in "the elimination of poverty and inequality" (p. 121). The upshot of this interaction between religion and society has been to enrich both in terms of their salience and reach, and achieve a more comprehensive concept of human happiness: "Equal opportunity turns less on the command of physical capital" and more on "spiritual capital" in the "quest of self-realization" (p. 236).

V. Religion as a Mainspring of Economic Virtues

The preceding analysis should highlight the importance of tighter links between religion, ethics and economics for initiating and sustaining a virtuous circle of human development in which economic activities and secular ethics are informed with a sense of the sacred, i.e., with a deep sense of commitment to enhancing human well-being. But, to this end, the edifice of traditional religious values must not dam the fast-expanding intellectual energies; it should rather let fresh ideas stream in. One does not have to be a Marxian to believe that concepts of good are in part absolute and in part relative to the changing needs of society, which create new congenial intellectual and ethical environments. In other words, new economic verities generate their own ethics. Religious ethics cannot remain completely outside of this historical 'ethic formation' process. And yet making radical changes in the scale of religious values is a non-trivial intellectual exercise. Above all, it must be an integral part of a comprehensive plan of moral regeneration. The point is that the new set of religious values should carry the stamp of religious authenticity to be able to influence human behaviour. An important element of such intellectual endeavour is to ask whether the moral qualities required to sustain and accelerate economic advancement – diligence, sobriety, thrift, a sense of justice, a concept of social good, and an intense desire to help others – are also the values on which the edifice of religious thought rests? To answer this question in the context of a Western ethical scale of values, we look at the fundamentals of the dominant Christian ethic, and to some extent the Judaic ethic as well. In the next three chapters, the same question will be answered in the context of Islamic thought. The narrative that follows will maintain a tight focus on religious thinking on such vital issues as rationality, distributive equality, and poverty – the issues on which, as Chapter 2 shows, secular ethics also has much to say. The highlight of this exercise is to allow for a mutually beneficial interaction between religious and secular ethics along the evolutionary path of economic advancement.

i) *Economic Rationality*

To define economic rationality as *only* self-interested behaviour puts artificial constraints on human reasoning and crowds out of circulation any notion of social good. Accordingly, to be able to tackle real-life issues, rationality needs to be defined broadly enough to accommodate such moral values as honesty, sympathy, commitment, etc., all of which relate an individual to collectivity and help resolve perennial problems like social justice, equity and poverty. Such a broader value perspective has always been emphasised by all world religions. Thus, for instance, Wilson (1997) points out; "honesty, justice in economic transactions and a concern for the dignity of the poor are hallmarks of all three religions" [Islam, Christianity and Judaism] (p. 213). The central idea in the ethical value systems of Christianity and Judaism is to relate humankind's this-worldly actions to the corresponding reward (punishment) of these actions in the hereafter. Neusner (1990) shows that Judaism (according to the *Mishnah* or the oral *Torah*) regards altruistic behaviour as perfectly rational. It is recognised that man's actions are governed by avarice as well; but ultimately it is the voluntary sense of responsibility to fellow human beings, rather than coercion, which induces individuals to work for the social good. Similarly the Christian Church believed that the Kingdom of God and the Kingdom of Man on earth are interconnected; and that it is man's behaviour in the latter that determines his reward in the former. St. Augustine in his *City of God* (1878) (cited in Wilson (1997); p. 76) explicitly lays down: "And, in active life, it is not the honours or power of this life we should covet ... but should aim at using our position and influence, if these have been honourably attained, for the welfare of those who are under us" (p. 329). The desire for personal gain from the exercise of power in this world should be subordinated to the collective good with a view to receiving much larger rewards in the hereafter.

ii) *Equality and Distributive Justice*

Achieving greater equality between humankind, and of income and wealth in particular, has been the single-most powerful idea that has driven religious divines and social reformers alike; and yet no other idea has been so much resisted by the privileged class, many a time *on religious grounds*. Indeed, examples of an unholy alliance between religious leaders and the powerful elite to the detriment of the poor and the weak can be found aplenty in all religious traditions. Partly reflecting these conflicting religious perceptions of the dimensions of equality coloured by worldly profit, the (secular) ethical position on distributive justice is also by no means unambiguous – which, incidentally illustrates the (implicit) links between religious and secular ethics. As discussed at length in Chapter 2, the dominant liberalist creed in the West has *opposed* an equitable redistribution of income and wealth. Hayek (1960), the leading light of liberalist thought, explicitly rules out the principle of distributive justice on the ground that it is *inconsistent* with the notion of a free society (p. 100). On the other hand, philosophers and economists like Rawls (1971) and Sen (1992) emphasise the equality of the social primary goods (including income and wealth) and that of the individuals' capabilities respectively. Needless to point out, an unambiguous statement of an egalitarian world order is essential in view of the rising trend to greater within-nation and between-nations inequalities of income and wealth that threaten world peace.

Unfortunately, religious ethics is not free from ambiguity either. Judaism and Christianity have traditionally opposed the *unlimited* right to property *because* all wealth belongs to God, and humankind is only its trustee. However, the notion of trusteeship is not regarded as a negation of the institution of private property; but it restricts its profligate use for personal purposes. And yet, in Judaism, and to some extent in Christianity, religious teachings are *not* always unambiguously egalitarian. God's ownership of wealth has sometimes been (mis)used as an argument *against* changing the existing structure of property rights. Thus, the large differences in income and wealth in ancient Israel were "not viewed as an unjust state of affairs" [Wilson (1997), p. 28]. Indeed, the Divine origin of wealth has been interpreted in Judaism as sanctifying the existing structure of private property rights; and also that the resolution of the inequality problem should be seen"not so much as a matter of redistribution, but rather one of creating a level playing field for each generation so that material advantages acquired through one generation's acquisition of wealth are not handed down" (p. 29). Early Christian thinking, though essentially egalitarian in temperament, was also not very forthcoming on the question of distributive justice. Viner (1978) points out that St. Thomas's views were similar to those of Aristotle's. Both distinguished between "commutative justice" (equality in transactions between two people) and "distributive justice" (which concerns the relation of the community to its members). The latter was taken to mean proportionality according to the status of a person in society. Also, redistribution is confined to "common goods", which cannot be interpreted to extend to income and wealth. In general, the scope for human effort in this regard is not allowed to transgress "natural justice", which in many cases has meant reformative *inaction*. In general, his views do not reveal "preferences as between different possible systems of distribution of wealth" (p. 68).[17] This position is consistent with that held by the Scholastics, who "were hostile towards striving for enrichment, and especially towards striving to rise above one's social status by birth" (p. 66). The early Christian theological position became openly inegalitarian if slaves are included, as they indeed were in those days, as part of private property. Viner has noted that "the early Church itself acquired slaves as soon as it acquired property"; and that, "in order to protect its assets, it imposed restrictions on the right of subordinate Church officials to free Church-owned slaves". Furthermore, it never engaged in, nor advocated, a mass enfranchisement of slaves; and some Fathers themselves owned slaves. But the freeing of slaves on merit was encouraged "especially when the owners were pagans" (p. 26). Much worse, the Church regarded slavery as "a punishment for sin and to some extent a remedy for it" (p. 27). Later on, the rise of Puritan individualism contributed to a substantial weakening of the sense of social obligation, which was earlier emphasised by the Levellers in the seventeenth century. The religious people then would equate distress with demerit; and pointed out the "dangers of pampering poverty" [Tawney (1937); pp. 264-265].

However, of late, greater clarity has been achieved on this score. Modern Catholic theologians take distributive justice as including government intervention to reduce existing inequalities of income and wealth [O'Rahilly (1948)]. The *Pastoral Letter* (1985), referred to above, makes the distinction between "commutative justice" and "distributive justice" that St. Thomas (and Aristotle) made; but it enlarges the scope of both. Now, the former is defined as that "which calls for fundamental fairness in all agreements and exchanges between individuals or private social groups" (p. 22); and the latter as one which requires "that the allocation of income, wealth, and power in society be evaluated in light of its effects on persons whose basic needs are unmet". Yet another category of social justice, called "contributive justice" has been added. It implies that "persons have an obligation to be active and productive participants in the life of society and that a society has a duty to enable them to participate in this way" (p. 23). However, this category, and the other two categories as well, seem to *exclude* from a socially just dispensation those who, because of a physical disability, cannot discharge their "obligation to be active and productive", and whom the society can also not help to "participate in such activities". Fogel (2000) recounts that Social Gospellers in the United States have tended to reinterpret Christian views along egalitarian lines. All these amendments to the original Church position, though incomplete, are illustrations of updating religious ethics on matters of grave social and economic concerns. This has helped, to some extent, Christian religious ethics become relevant as a genuine force for economic change along egalitarian lines. But there is yet another dimension to egalitarianism; where religion makes a contribution: it is with respect to a better redistribution of *spiritual* resources in which *no one* loses. "Not only does this process of redistribution of spiritual resources [through counselling by those who are rich in spiritual resources to those who are poor] leave those who have been deprived better off; it also increases the spiritual resources of those who have them in abundance" (p. 214).

iii) *Poverty*

As on the question of distributive justice, the (secular) ethical position in the West is divided, to the point of being indecisive, on the question of poverty alleviation. This is surprising because, by common consent, poverty is now the world's primary economic problem. Liberalists consider poverty as morally *unfortunate* or even unfair but not *unjust*, because there is no moral-rights violations involved even if a lot of people die of hunger! The 'reason' given is that people only have a right to non-interference with whatever property rights they come to possess through acquisition and/or transfer. Thus, people can help the poor *voluntarily* (and such voluntary giving is encouraged); but the poor have no *right* to aid. Hayek (1960) bluntly states: "There are good reasons why we should...make provision for the weak or infirm...it is an entirely different matter, however, to suggest that those who are poor...are entitled to a share in the wealth of [the rich]...", (p. 101). On the other hand, the Rawlsian Difference Principle accords priority to the needs of the least-privileged in society. But, even in this case, those who are really worst-off (i.e., those who cannot actively participate in economic exchange in the markets because of physical disabilities or whatever) may be excluded from the Rawlsian principles of justice – which he defines as "a scheme of cooperation for reciprocal advantage" – because what is to be distributed justly (or 'fairly') are the benefits and costs of social cooperation. (Incidentally, in this respect, the Rawlsian position is akin to the principle of "contributive justice" laid down in the *Pastoral Letter* (1985).)

The question is: can an appeal to religious morality help dispel the fogginess of secular ethics about the poverty problem? Now there is no question about the emphasis that Christianity, and to a lesser extent Judaism, place on the alleviation of poverty. But, as on the question of distributive equity, the traditional religious position lacks in clarity on how best to resolve this problem. In classical Jewish literature, the guiding principle is the restoration of the Natural (Divine) Order, which is fixed and unchanging;

which, as Wilson (1997) points out, was taken then as a justification for preserving the existing pattern of property holding by the Jews in the (ancient) land of Israel. While man bore a social responsibility to help the less fortunate, "there are no systemic mechanisms [in the *Talmud*] for redistribution, apart from that via the temple through tithes..." (p. 52). Christianity is a little more forthcoming on this issue. Viner (1978) points out that voluntary (*not* coercive) giving was much stressed in the Scholastic doctrine as a matter of charity, *not* of justice. St. Thomas carefully laid down both the maximum and the minimum limits on how much could legitimately be given by way of charity; but "he does not discuss remedial aid as contrasted with mere relief of immediate need" (p. 74). Later on, however, it was stated (by St. Augustine or St. Cesarius) that: "The part of your income as an official or landowner which God bestows on you in excess of what is needed for a simple and reasonable mode of life is not given to you as a true property, *but as a deposit for which you are accountable to the poor*" [cited in Viner (1978); p. 74; italics added]. Also, Latimer stated "the poor man *hath title to the rich man's goods*" [cited in Tawney (1937); p. 260; italics added]. The italicised provisos come close to the idea of almsgiving as a matter of justice. But this does not seem to be the dominant religious position. Wilson (1997) summarises the Christian idea of charity as that "the poor did not have rights or claims upon the rich, but the rich had a religious duty to make charitable donations", and that [according to St. Augustine] while almsgiving is highly desirable, "its function was not to eliminate poverty, but rather to relieve extreme distress" (p. 77).[18] Thus, the general classical religious position is to encourage voluntary giving, without coercion – a position which the (secular) liberalist opinion (e.g., of Hayek) would heartily approve of.

However, modern restatements of both the Christian and the Jewish positions are more openly egalitarian. Thus, Sherwin (1989) thinks that Jewish philosophy is strong on both social justice and poverty alleviation; that it is *obligatory* on the Jews to help the poor; and that poverty is a social calamity rather than as a punishment for past sins. However, the poverty alleviation that he has in mind seems to be class-oriented and not very effective in transferring substantial amounts from the rich to the poor. Thus, he approvingly cites the Jerusalem *Talmud* to elucidate his idea of helping the poor: "If a person (who was rich) has become poor and requires public assistance, if he had been used to vessels of gold (to eat and drink from), then give him vessels of gold; if of silver, then give him vessels of silver" [translated by Issac Klein (1979); p. 65]. However, such a structured programme is not likely to leave much for those who were used to earthen vessels, for example! It may be noted that Sherwin's position is no different from St. Thomas's position, stated above. Once again, the Christian Church has done much better in this respect. Thus, the *Episcopal Letter* (1985) in spelling out the "moral priorities of nation" (the US) explicitly states "*the obligation to provide justice for all means that the poor have the single most urgent claim on the conscience of the nation"; that "investment of wealth, talent and human energy should be especially directed to the benefit of those who are poor or economically insecure"; that "fulfilment of the basic needs of the poor is of the highest priority*" (pp. 26-28; italics in the original). The *Letter* further recommends that the nation make a truly fundamental "option for the poor" to actively help those "who are marginalized and *whose rights are denied have privileged claims* if the society is to provide justice *for all*" (p. 27; italics added). This, in essence, is a radical departure from the traditional position of the Catholic Church, as stated above: Far from being a matter of charity, the *Letter's* exhortation amounts to doing justice to the poor by recognising their prior right on the wealth of the rich. It insists that these teachings – which, incidentally, are clearly echoed in the Rawlsian thinking on the subject – "are rooted in the Christian belief" (p. 27).[19] This claim is probably excessive in the light of the analysis presented above; but there is no denying the efforts of the Church to adapt its traditional teaching to the needs of the time.

VI. Whither Religious Morality?

It should be clear by now that moral values motivate individuals to do social good; and that, contrary to the secularist protestations, religious morality does it even better. At the very least, it is *instrumental* in making an individualist economy work more efficiently at lower policing and contracting costs. But to demand religion only for its instrumental role is to vastly underestimate its potential for human well-being. The fact is that it becomes a truly potent force for good *only* if it is desired *for its own sake*. Through its agency, an economy can become more equitable by instilling in individuals an internalised sense of responsibility to society. This should curb the individual tendency to free ride, encourage cooperative rather than competitive behaviour, and entail lesser coercion than would be the case if the individual's sense of religious obligation to society were absent or weak. A spiritually strengthened person is expected to contribute more to accelerating human development by supporting an equitable distribution of the fruits of economic progress, especially in favour of the least-privileged in society. Conversely, egalitarian reform will be greatly strengthened if it is implemented as part of a vigorous process of moral regeneration – as was done by Calvin in the fifteenth century.

i) *Religious Morality and Social Change*

The central message of this chapter is that, to establish the case for religious morality as a force for social and economic change, there should be a mechanism for reinterpreting, even amending, religious thinking on social and economic issues in the light of the new *knowledge* on ethics and in response to the new economic challenges. In other words, there should be an active interaction between religion, ethics and economics. Also, it emphasises that the following counter-claims are *false*: (a) that individual self-interest can run a modern economy efficiently, without the interposition of moral values; (b) that 'secular' moral values are sufficient to motivate individuals to social action; (c) that religious moral values constitute a fixed, unalterable system; and (d) that, being Divinely ordained, these values need not be improved or amended to meet new economic challenges. The falsity of (a) has been established in Chapter 2 and also in the present chapter and needs no further elaboration; but it may be instructive to elaborate further on what has already been said on (b), (c) and (d).

Firstly, the assertion that religious beliefs play, at best, a second fiddle to secular ethics and are, therefore, redundant as an independent influence on economic behaviour is not well-founded in logic. To see this let us look briefly at how secular ethical belief is defined. Robinson (1973), asserts that the "[secular] ethical system is quite straightforward, as yet untainted by Christian [read, religious] feeling"; and yet concedes that the "ethical system is not derivable from reason either"; nor is it a matter of acting according to the dictates of one's conscience, which can be conditioned by one's experience. Rather, she maintains, this system gets "implanted in each of us by our upbringing": and that "there are certain basic ethical feelings that we share" which were "handed down to us" as they were taught to our predecessors (pp. 17-18).[20] Now it is hard to sustain the argument that what was not derived from reason but learned from people who just believed in these principles and practiced them was never "tainted" by religion, even though when they may have been religious themselves. At any rate, apart from the origins of the ethical system, it has been conceded even by Russell (1954) that religious "tabu has certain great advantages as a source of moral behaviour. It is psychologically far more compelling than any merely rational rules..." (p. 30).

Secondly, an argument for implementing a traditional religious ethical system does *not* imply doing it regardless of its consequences on human development; which really is what Russell revolted against. Indeed, when the unbending absolutism of an ethical system is insisted upon, it becomes a lifeless entity with no relevance to reality; and sometimes it acts as an instrument of oppression. Thus, some traditional religious values may have to be amended, even discarded, to help achieve a higher moral-humanistic objective. An example of this intellectual iconoclasm is the abolition of slavery in the United States *on religious grounds*; and the fact that "American abolitionism began as a theological rather than political movement" [Fogel (2000); p. 105]. The point to note here is that the abolitionists, who were all religious people, explicitly discarded the practice of the early Church, which condoned, even justified, slavery, on religious grounds (that it was a punishment for sin). Not only that; the movement overcame constitutional barriers (because the American Constitution approved of Slavery) and great political resistance. Only ethical beliefs, imbued with religious conviction, could achieve such remarkable results.

Thirdly, it is a historical fact that only those ethical systems survive which respond creatively to a fast-changing reality. In Western Europe, the Protestant reaction to the rising tide of capitalism, which is the subject-matter of Weber-Tawney thesis, is a classic example of how religious beliefs should be reinterpreted as social environment changes.[21] More recently, Fogel (2000) has shown that the Four Great Awakenings, reflected the triumph in the economic sphere of a new "egalitarian ethic that emphasized the equality of condition rather than [the] equality of opportunity. [But] such a shift required discarding a fundamental theological doctrine of the innate depravity of Man, which, in turn, rested on the doctrine of original sin" (p. 117). The New Gospellers instead tended to emphasise "the natural goodness of man"... and "were optimistic about the human capacity for doing good and about the potential for creating a Kingdom of heaven on earth" (p. 119). Also, in the New Theology, "social reform increasingly replaced personal reform ... and the essence of religion became the elimination of poverty and inequality" (p. 121).

ii) *Some General Principles*

To summarise, four general principles flow from the Weber-Tawney-Fogel thesis about the European and American experiences. Firstly, religious values are complementary to, and sometimes far more efficient, than secular ethical values as determinants of economic change – indeed, of social, political and economic revolutions. Secondly, to be able to exert a decisive influence on the course of economic events, religious values must be changed and regenerated by new knowledge and an awareness of the imperatives of changing times, by a sense of purpose, and a vision of the future, because it is only by a shattering of traditional ethical beliefs that all things look new. Thirdly, such changes in religious values must, however, come from 'within', i.e., they should reflect a major reinterpretation of the basic religious principles. This last point is of fundamental importance: the changes in religious values that become necessary to *explain* economic reality more accurately and to *change* it for the better can also (and should) borrow from secular ethical value systems. But this can be done only to the extent that these are consistent with broad religious parameters. Furthermore, such response should be part of a broader programme for religious transformation that changes the way that people believe in religion and about its relationship to the economic aspects of their lives – so that material plenitude *and* spiritual ascension flow from a 'unified' programme of egalitarian reform. Fourthly, as opposed to the wholesome influence of religious ethical values on economic well-being that has been emphasised so far, its detrimental effects must also be recognised. In the European context, as has been noted in Section V of this chapter, the intense Puritanical individualism which helped the Industrial Revolution also had the side-effect of *misguiding* individual inclinations and weaning public policy *away* from a commitment to alleviate poverty. Thus, as Tawney (1937) asserts, the accent on individualism in religion "led insensibly, if not quite logically, to an individualist morality, and an individualist morality to a disparagement of the significance of the social fabric as compared with personal character" (p. 253). This accent on individualism (which has been magnified by the liberalist philosophy) had to be moderated, in religious discourse, to make way for egalitarianism in our own times.

These generalisations will be evaluated in relation to the Islamic approach to the relationship between ethical precepts and economic reality in the next three chapters of this book.

Notes

1. Graff (1991) further remarks: "What does it help to say that, although several men will starve, the cost to the society is low, because they *could* be given sufficient food to prevent their starving?" (p. 254).
2. As noted in Chapter 2, the (Pareto) optimal state is *improvable* with respect to efficiency as well, if such real-world phenomena as externalities and public goods are admitted and if the markets are 'missing' (e.g., the market for risk-taking) or are liable to complete breakdown (e.g., because of moral-hazard, the principal-agency syndrome, etc.).
3. Neo-classical economics postulates well-ordered societies in which there is not much room for a significant redistribution of income and wealth, partly because such distributional issues are *assumed* to have been sorted out at some unspecified prior date.
4. Olson (1971) notes that (self-interested) members of a 'small group' are more likely to act voluntarily to attain the common good because they (at least its larger members) can 'see' their personal gain from having the collective good exceeding the total cost of providing it. However, even in small groups the collective good will not be supplied optimally because of its non-excludability property. Whence follows that *"the larger a group gets, the farther it will fall short of supplying [the] optimal amount of a collective good"* (p. 35; italics in original).
5. The utilitarian belief noted in the text is referred to as the "standard liberal fallacy" by Barry (1973); p. 108.
6. As noted in Chapter 2, Adam Smith, who is (mistakenly) credited with a monocentric focus on self-interest, emphasised in his *Theory of Moral Sentiments* (1790) that such values as "sympathy" and "generosity" which restrain a person's self-interest and "make the

impartial speculator enter in the principles of his conduct" may call for "greater exertions of public spirit" (p. 191). Sen (1999) emphasises that "successful operation of an exchange economy depends on mutual trust and the use of norms – explicit or implicit" (p. 263).

7. Illustrative of the view cited in the text is Collier's (1947) remark: "a good man is the noblest work of God, and a good God is the noblest of man" (p. 51; cited in Jafri (2001); p. 92).
8. Viner (1978) defines these secularisation tendencies as "first the elimination from theoretical discussion, or from the formulation of moral codes of behaviour of reliance on dogmatic theology...; second, the shifting of emphasis from transcendental values to temporal values held on temporal grounds" (p. 114).
9. To some extent, this has been the case with the Muslims as well, especially during the thirteenth and fourteenth centuries in which the rationalists and the traditionalists persecuted each other; and which struggle contributing a good deal to the decline of scientific thought in Muslim societies [Chapra (2000); Ch. 3].
10. John Rawls (1971; 1999), who *rejected* the utilitarian philosophy, noted in 1971: "During much of modern philosophy the predominant systematic theory has been some form of Utilitarianism". Hume, Adam Smith, Bentham and Mill were all Utilitarians. As noted in Chapter 2 of this book, the modern neo-classical paradigm also accepts Utilitarianism, of which the Pareto-optimality is a second-best approximation: "the two Pareto Principles (that is, Pareto Optimality and Pareto Superiority) are usually seen as second-best alternatives to utilitarianism, the assumption being that assessing social states according to the overall utility they produce would be preferable, were it not for the unfortunate fact that interpersonal utility comparisons cannot be made" [Allen Buchanan (1985); p. 8].
11. Thus, Mill, Russell and Robinson, referred to in the text, based their criticism on Bentham's (himself a non-believer) utilitarian philosophy.
12. Vaughan (1843) commenting on Protestant urban communities, writes: "Men are thus taught, that in relation to the affairs of the world, no less than to the affairs of religion, the man who would be successful 'must take up his cross and deny himself'...industry in place of being merely a social virtue, inculcated on the principles of human wisdom or expediency, is made to be indispensable, in the great majority of mankind, to religious consistency, and is enforced, accordingly, by the highest possible sanctions" (pp. 359-360; cited in Viner (1978); pp. 178-179).

13. Calvin wrote to a correspondent: "what reason is there, why the income from business should not be larger than that from landowning? Whence do the merchant's profits come, except from his own diligence and industry?" [cited in Tawney (1937); p. 113].
14. Sen's (1973) argument essentially is that if, say, *not* littering is in everyone's interest and also that some self-discipline is exercised so that no one litters, then it is perfectly rational *behaviour* for everyone to behave as if he/she cares about not littering.
15. Jan Tinbergen in a private correspondence informed me, on reading my 1981 book (*Ethics and Economics: An Islamic Synthesis*), that he himself was working on the Christian contribution to economics. It appears that he could not complete this work.
16. The Four Great Awakenings are chronologically labelled as: First Great Awakening from 1730 to 1830, which coincided with the weakening of the predestination doctrine and the rise of the ethics of benevolence. The Second Great Awakening lasted from 1800 to 1920 and coincided with the rise of the belief that anyone can achieve salvation by a conscious struggle against sin and the deepening of the ethic of benevolence. The Third Great Awakening spanned the period from 1890 to 1930 in which a secular interpretation of the Bible came into vogue. The Fourth Great Awakening, which began in 1960 and still continues, has reasserted the more orthodox religious aspects of Christianity like the concept of personal sin [Fogel (2000); p. 28].
17. St. Thomas in *Summa Theologica* has this to say on "distributive justice": "Consequently in distributive justice a person receives all the more of the common goods, according as he holds a more prominent position in the community. This prominence in an aristocratic community is gauged according to virtue, in an oligarchy according to wealth, in a democracy according to liberty, and in various ways according to various forms of community" (cited in Viner (1978); p. 68). In general, there is room for distributive justice by the exercise of human will "provided it be not, of itself, contrary to natural justice..."
18. Viner (1978) neatly summarises the Christian position on charity, which varied over time, as follows: (i) poverty is a Divine punishment for sin, so it would be an interference in God's Design and wasted effort to try to eliminate poverty on a large scale; (ii) the expediency of helping the poor to forestall social unrest; (iii) the ascetic realisation that poverty, voluntary and involuntary, is really a "blessed" state; (iv) the acceptance of a humanitarian obligation to relieve the misery and pain of the poor; etc. (p. 76).

19. The *Letter* cites Paul VI's position on charity thus: "In teaching us charity, the gospel instructs us in the preferential [treatment] due the poor and the special situation they have in society: the more fortunate should renounce some of their rights so as to place their goods more generously at the service of others" (p. 27).
20. Russell (1954) traces the origins of "ethical feeling and ethical precept", to a kind of "social compromise". He asserts that "this is not dependent, like the kinds of morality that we have been considering hitherto, either upon superstition or upon religion; it arises, broadly speaking, from the desire for a quiet life" (p. 34). That may be so; but it is not clear why an ethic based on religion will be inconsistent with "the desire for a quiet life". Indeed, the Marxian criticism of religion as an "opium of the people" is exactly this: that religion is inconsistent with the antithesis of a quiet life, i.e., a social revolution!
21. Tawney (1937) recounts the Calvinist response to changes in social environment (from a rural economy to a rapidly urbanising economy) as follows: "Early Calvinism, as we shall see, has its rule, and rigorous rule, for the conduct of economic affairs. But it no longer suspects the whole world of economic motives as alien to the life of the spirit ... and it is perhaps the first body of religious teaching which can be said to recognize and applaud the economic virtues" (p. 114).

PART II

Islam, Ethics, and Economics

CHAPTER 4

Religious Morality in Islam: General Principles

I. Introduction

Moral values spark individuals to be in tune with their true self and to be concerned for the hopes and expectations of others. They also highlight such vital issues as distributional inequities, poverty, and economic deprivation which darken the face of human societies.[1] This is because the grasping, disinterested pursuit of personal profit is not, as a general rule, consistent with achieving collective objectives.[2] Indeed, elitist self-interestedness leads to sub-optimal social outcomes [Gauthier (1986)]. What can, then, be done? One way out is to modify individual preferences by binding them to customs and social conventions, so that individualist behaviour produces socially-oriented behaviour.[3] The point is that even self-interested objectives are better served if the flint-hearted individual assumed by the Walrasian neo-classical model shows a decent regard for the welfare of others in the society. In this case, the "policing cost" of running a free-enterprise system would be significantly less than if nobody cared for the social good.[4] Chapter 3 shows that an individualistic economy works better with a respectable degree of altruism. This is especially so when the act of giving is regarded by individuals as its own reward, and if material plenitude is accompanied by moral regeneration, self-realisation and a sense of belonging to the society. In this respect religious ethics is the glue of human relationships; and it has a distinct edge over secular ethics because the former is universally accepted by those who believe in them. Holding a lantern across the divide between right and wrong, it illumines social consciousness and undermines moral passivism with an intensity that secular ethics cannot do. And yet, as an ossified system of beliefs religious ethics cannot play such a salutary social role. The Western experience bears out that religious ethics helps only if it flickers rethinking to lighten up the intellectual horizon when economic reality so demands; and that it becomes an obstruction to social progress when it ordains reality to fit into an antediluvian ethical mould.

The present chapter analyses these matters with reference to Islamic ethical values and its vision of how economic activity contributes to human happiness – that which flows even as a deeply-held sense of justice and a concept of the social good become the mainsprings of human action.

II. What an Islamic Economy is *Not*

The hypothesis presented in this chapter is that Islamic morality can regulate human behaviour by adding a halo of ethical sanctification to the appeal of social good. Without applying *excessive* coercion or trying to change human nature, it aims to purify the heart, sharpen the mind, and lead to transcendence by recapturing the sense of primal identification with the beliefs that Muslims religiously hold. However, this claim must be properly qualified. Firstly, there is *no* presumption that an economy sufficiently suffused with Islamic ethical values will be, wholly or mostly, populated by born-again altruists who *always* put the interests of others above their own; and that in it free-riding will cease to be a problem. Quite the contrary; individuals imbued with a sense of justice are not expected to abandon their individual interests altogether. In other words, altruism will not push an Islamic economy 'beyond justice,' i.e., one in which no appeal can ever be made to the principles of what is right and just. However, it is reasonable to expect that, for all their human imperfections, Muslims entertain some ideas of a *fraternity*, of acting like members of a family in which those who are better placed in life (because of their superior merit or better early upbringing) prefer an arrangement which works to the benefit of its less fortunate ones. Thus, what Muslim societies must aim at is *not* a prototype of a meritocratic or a feudal society in which *equality of opportunity* implies a social order of extreme inequities of economic conditions, a protection of the rights and privileges of the technocratic elites, and a neglect of the underclass who may possess less merit for no fault of theirs.[5] Instead, they should seek to redress social injustice and guarantee *equality of economic condition* for all their members.

Secondly, it is *not* the case that internalising Islamic religious values in individual behaviour will make public policy redundant; instead, the one complements the other. True, the policing and contracting costs will be significantly lower in an altruism-driven (Islamic) economy than in one organised on the self-interest principle alone; but this does not mean that these costs will altogether vanish. There will, thus, be a fairly large room for government intervention in Muslim societies; which, however, will not be so extensive as to extinguish the flame of human freedom, without which social responsibility loses its meaning.

Finally, it is assumed that Muslim societies would normally support a *market* (though not *laissez faire*) economy, which provides ample opportunities for free mutually beneficial exchange. However, in it, to paraphrase Adam Smith (1790), a "greater exertion of public spirit" is expected to dominate "prudence" to tackle the larger issues of human existence; which, again, implies a significant role for the government to regulate production and distribution. Yet another implication is to redefine economic rationality so that "self love" (i.e., the self-interest motive) merges into a complex (and richer) motivational structure which features sympathy and commitment to society as well. This happens, to some extent, even in a secular capitalist society; but it becomes even more prominent when religious morality is mobilised to create a just society that individuals would voluntarily support.

III. The Fundamentals of Islamic Morality

The force of Islamic values, properly spelled out, is expected to be considerable in bringing human behaviour in line with the pursuit of the collective good. The worth of this proposition is best evaluated by reference to what it does to free-riding and assurance problems which, if allowed unchecked, greatly narrow down the scope for voluntary cooperative action and reduce the size of the voluntary transfer of resources from the rich to the poor. However, a distinction must be made here between a situation in which the rich wish that the poor enjoy a higher consumption level and one in which they like to do something about it. In the former case, a higher consumption level for the poor is a public good to the rich, and the free-riding and assurance problems will be very much there. However, if one does something positive to help the poor, then the public-good and the free-riding phenomena become very much manageable [Hochman and Rogers (1969)]. In the former case, the laudable beneficent motive to help the poor by itself will be self-defeating, *even if it is assumed* that a typical Muslim society comprises, mostly or wholly, morally upright people. The main point to investigate is, therefore, the extent to which Islamic ethical values induce people to do something about raising the consumption level of the poor. This point is worth having a serious argument about because, in the Islamic perspective, the act of giving adds to material advancement *and* spiritual edification. It will be shown that at least five elements of Islam's ethical system, universally believed by Muslims, significantly influence their economic behaviour. These are: (i) Islam's is a complete way of life; (ii) Allah Sees our actions; (iii) Allah Owns all wealth; (iv) individuals prefer committed behaviour to unadulterated cupidity, though not denying the existence of the latter; (v) the poor have a *right* in the wealth of the rich.

i) ***Islam's is a Complete Way of Life***

An important aspect of the Islamic economy (and also of a real-life Muslim society) is the absence of conflict between secular ethics and religious ethics – for the simple reason that it is only a sub-set "of the religion of Islam which covers the various branches of life" [Sadr (1982); p. 571]. It regards the distinction between the secular and religious both pointless and counterproductive – pointless, because it fails to recognise that people are ordinarily moved by religious and moral concerns; and counterproductive, because it creates avoidable schizophrenic confusion about the origins of moral values. Muslims are unequivocally enjoined to accept Islam as a complete way of life in which the mundane and the spiritual motives coalesce to strengthen a 'natural' voluntaristic human urge to do good for society [Ahmad (1976); p. 37].[6] As well as being economically beneficial, the act of giving out of love for Allah bridles the corroding appetite for economic gain. Indeed, the travails of the pursuit of salvation are eased not just by the regular performance of the obligatory religious rituals, but even more by reducing human suffering.[7]

ii) ***Belief in Allah's Presence***

A Muslim believes without question in Allah's presence; and this belief motivates his day-to-day economic and social behaviour. Even though it does not exactly conform to ideal Islamic behaviour; yet the departures from it are not expected to be so large and systematic as to negate its importance. Held universally in a Muslim society, this belief takes the form of social norms that effectively check deviant behaviour. Thus, (both voluntarily and for fear of overstepping a social tabu) a Muslim generally avoids (or feigns to avoid) indulging in glaring social malpractices – e.g., gambling, hoarding food items in times of extreme scarcity, charging interest on personal loans, etc. What is distinguishable here is that the influence of religious beliefs is more pervasive in Muslim societies than in any other society, in the sense that such beliefs determine the Muslim's "individual actions and, consequently, the social life of the community" [Boisard (1987); p. 31].[8] Muslim men/women, in the knowledge that Allah watches their actions in broad day-light as well as in the darkness of the night, attempt to behave, however, imperfectly and sometimes only apparently, in accordance with the Divine code of conduct. They seek Allah's help in every significant move they contemplate – by saying *Inshā' Allāh* (Allah Willing) each time they embark on a new enterprise the outcome of which is not known with certainty. Then, as is shown later in this chapter, a substantial amount of charitable giving is done, not to show off, but to please Allah. On the other hand, charitable acts, where explicit religious sanction is absent or ambiguous, do not always get done. This latter attitude, though not justifiable, does nevertheless illustrate the force of religious values in Muslim societies. The susceptibility of Muslims to whatever carries religious sanction also explains the tremendous appeal of the *Sharī'ah* (Islamic Law) in giving a distinctive colour to Muslim societies: "Islamic Law [has been] the most far-reaching and effective agent in moulding the social order and the community life of the Muslim peoples" [Gibb (1975); p. 7]. And, religious symbolism has historically moulded "the world of everyday reality...and has shaped the formation of a number of different but inter-related Muslim societies" [Lapidus (1997); p. XX]. It is not surprising, therefore, that some fundamental Islamic ethical precepts especially those spelled out explicitly in the Holy Qur'ān – e.g., about the equality of all men/women before Allah, etc. – are believed and, to some extent, practiced by Muslims, notwithstanding the fallen state of their societies.[9] Needless to point out, the desire to be governed by Islamic Law has not always been germane to a socially desirable state of affairs; and, in some cases, it may have even nursed an unhealthy conservatism that inhibits social progress; and that, in such cases, clarity and consensus should be achieved on important social issues to motivate Muslims to adopt an informed view of the intent of Islamic Law.

iii) ***Allah Owns all Wealth***

Then there is the powerful concept of Allah's ownership of all wealth and that human beings are mere 'trustees' of this wealth.[10] What this means is that the individual's right to spend his wealth is limited in several ways: (a) he must spend it according to Divine wishes; (b) he cannot hoard it, especially when there are urgent social needs to be met; (c) he must give it to the poor *not* as charity but as a matter of the latter's acknowledged right in his wealth; and (d) he must spend wealth only in moderation because being spendthrift is both a social waste *and* a cardinal sin.[11] In reflecting historical differences of opinion – i.e., about how to reconcile Islamic egalitarianism with a fairly strong tendency to social stratification in Muslim societies – some *'ulamā'* and scholars have held that there are no limits on individual property holdings while a person lives; but even they emphasise that this right ceases after one's death when wealth must be distributed to one's legal heirs according to the Islamic Law of Inheritance.[12] Feudal land holdings have thus been supported, and land reforms opposed, in Muslim countries by many *'ulamā'* on religious grounds. On the other hand, some other *'ulamā'* and scholars, who are keen on changing the status quo, have equally strongly supported the abolition of feudalism because an unlimited individual ownership right to private property violates basic Islamic principles [e.g., Taleghani (1982); Sadr (1982); Chapra (1992); Haque (1977)]. "The fundamental principle", according to Sayyid Quṭb (2000), "is that property belongs to the community in general; individual possession is a stewardship which carries with it conditions and limitations" (p. 137). Happily, this reformist interpretation of the Islamic concept of private property has, of late, gained ground. The consensus seems to be that the question of the ownership of private property should be decided by reference to the overarching egalitarian goals of the Islamic system "rather than [on the basis of] specific legal rulings given in normal circumstances" [Siddiqi (1976; 1981); p. 10].[13]

It is, thus, hard to find Islamic scholars and *'ulamā'* who regard the existing structure of private property rights to be a reflection of some kind of unchanging Natural Order – as was, for instance, the Jewish opinion about the structure of property holdings in the ancient land of Israel (see Chapter 3). Also, the liberalist opinion [e.g., Hayek (1960); Nozick (1974)] – that there exists an unlimited individual moral right to private property and that any restriction ("patterning") of the existing property structure even to help the poor is a violation of moral rights – would be summarily rejected even by the most conservative of Islamic jurists and scholars. The historical fact is that, notwithstanding the pervasive conservatism of the *'ulamā'*, Islamic egalitarianism has never been altogether tamed by the existence of social privilege. Thus, "the elites who benefited from hierarchical forms of social organizations in the Islamic world found themselves in moral difficulties that their counterparts in other civilizations did not always share, or at least not to the same degree or in the same way" [Marlow (1997); p. 10].

iv) *The Principle of Commitment*

In so far as the three elements of the Islamic ethical system identified so far belong in the 'feeling-good-about-it' category rather than being a matter of 'doing-something-about-it', they still leave considerable scope for free-riding, which greatly reduces the chances of voluntary effort succeeding in generating sizeable resources to help the poor. What should be distinctive about a typical Muslim society is that it be imbued with the spirit of commitment. While self-interest motivation is recognised as a weakness of human nature, it is rejected as the prime mover of the economic universe (see Section IV-(i) below). Islam would not regard selfish behaviour as a sure sign of 'rationality', much less an empirical truth. However, the Islamic rejection of the self-interest principle is not altogether exclusive; the support for this narrow view of human motivation is no longer universal even in mainstream economics. Thus, being 'committed' to the welfare of others is *not* regarded as being totally other-worldly. Indeed, being insensitive about the misery caused by distributive inequity, poverty, and social deprivation would normally be looked at with a sense of shock by a society of sane people. Committed behaviour *is* both normal and rational because it would (or, at least, should) be regarded by the individual and the society to be the morally right thing to do.[14] At any rate, Islam goes out of the way to inculcate commitment in individuals. This is done in at least four related ways: (a) men/women are encouraged to give in the way of Allah what he/she loves most, and that which involves some self-sacrifice; (b) giving to the poor is believed to bring manifold reward in this world and in the hereafter; (c) *not* helping the poor is odious because it is condemned in the Holy Qur'ān as a denial of faith; (d) and helping the poor *means* attaining social good as well as spiritual ascension.[15]

v) *The Poor's Right in the Wealth of the Rich*

The Holy Qur'ān unambiguously states that the poor have "a due share" in the wealth of the rich.[16] In sharp contrast, the liberalist tradition does *not* recognise the poor's moral right to aid, though it encourages the rich to give to the poor voluntarily. Even the Rawlsian Difference Principle, which explicitly stipulates helping the poor on a priority basis, does *not* include in the rich man's wealth the right of those who cannot participate in market exchange. Western theological systems are generally ambiguous about recognising the poor's *right*. Little surprise, therefore, that the dominant refrain of Western moralising, academic thinking, and practical politics is that of self-help by the poor themselves, absolving the rich people and countries alike, from the *responsibility* of helping the poor. In sharp contrast, the originality of the Islamic position stands out; it ordains "returning" to the poor their rightful *share* in the rich man's wealth – the presumption being that a malfunctioning of the economic system has enabled the rich to deprive the poor of what was legitimately theirs. It is for this reason that Islam enjoins taking extreme care in giving to the poor in a manner which does not hurt their self-respect and esteem; and condemns giving just to show off *because* that would amount to a disbelief in Allah.[17] An implication of this position is that the public-good problem, noted at (iv) above, goes away. The reason is that Islam emphasises urging people to give to the poor what is rightly theirs rather than being merely happy in the knowledge that the poor are being helped (presumably by others).

However, it should be recognised that there has been an important theological *(fiqh)* opinion which seems to water down, though unwittingly, the explicit egalitarian intent of Qur'ānic teachings by pointing out that the poor's right in the wealth of the rich is limited to compulsory Islamic taxes *only*. But this view is defective. Firstly, many of the Islamic levies are no longer relevant in a modern Muslim society – e.g., *kharāj, jizyah, ghanīmah, fay'* in particular; while the remaining ones – e.g., *zakāt, 'ushr, Ṣadaqah al-Fiṭr* – do not yield sufficient revenue to meet the needs of the poor, as these are proportional and in some cases even regressive. At best, the yield from such Islamic taxes will not be enough to eliminate poverty, or even reduce it much. Secondly, the opinion that, barring some extra-ordinary events like fighting a war or in famine, the governments in Muslim countries are *not* allowed to impose more taxes than are stated in *fiqh* books, has posed problems for some Muslim states. For instance, there is opposition among *'ulamā'* to modern taxes, like income or corporate taxes or death duty, which are progressive in incidence and a highly effective means of preventing the concentration of wealth in the hands of the rich (which is the Islamic intent as well).[18] Consequently, considerable free-riding, tax evasion and fiscal irresponsibility prevails in Muslim societies. Fortunately, there is a growing convergence of opinion, which should be strengthened, that imposition of taxes, in addition to those listed above, is legitimate to meet the recognised needs of a Muslim society.

IV. Religious Ethics and Economic Reality

Religious morality performs a functional (instrumental) role, in which moral values are public goods in material output. However, unlike in the West, such a truncated vision of religion would not have much appeal in a Muslim society. The presumption is that Islam is universally demanded by Muslims as inherently valuable and an end in itself. Indeed, generally speaking, the fluorescence of religion, in any society, requires a comprehensive role, i.e., when it comes to defining the individual's entire personality. It, then, helps internalise in the individual a sense of social obligation, lowers the incidence of free-riding, promotes cooperative (rather than competitive) behaviour, and strengthens the flow of voluntary giving from the rich to the poor. Having said that, it must be recognised that overly conservative interpretations (which sometimes border on misinterpretations) of the religious message can greatly undermine its potential to do good to society. Chapter 3 gives examples of this phenomenon from Christianity and Judaism. Islam has not been immune to it either. For instance, especially during the second/eighth to seventh/thirteenth centuries, attempts were made to dilute the egalitarian content of Islamic ethics in large parts of the Muslim world [Marlow (1997); p. 93]. It is, however, a tribute to the clarity of Islamic egalitarianism that such attempts have never succeeded in subduing it.[19] But the problem must be faced, especially in areas where ethical principles are not that clear, or are only implicitly stated. It is, therefore, essential to achieve clarity with respect to Islamic ethical values to be able to address such modern problems as: (a) equality; (b) distributive justice; (c) poverty alleviation and (d) economic growth. We begin this analysis by clarifying the concept of economic rationality in Islam.

i) *Economic Rationality in Islam*

The preceding section mentions the centrality of sympathy and commitment in Islam's ethical system. This contrasts sharply with the unsympathetic isolationism of the dominant neo-classical model in which the economic agent jealously guards only his/her own bundle of commodities.[20] However, four observations may be made in this context: firstly, Islam does not minimise the fundamental importance of "trade by mutual consent"; indeed, being mutually beneficial, such trade is encouraged as morally just.[21] In this limited sphere, self-interest is expected to play a socially beneficial role. But looking at the entire economic universe from the prism of self-interest alone amounts to virtue paying tribute to vice! If personal advantage is all that counts, then, as noted in Chapter 2, the vital problems of human existence (inequity, poverty, etc.,) cannot be addressed. In the Islamic perspective, it is *not* an either-or situation: namely, that *either* you repose complete trust in your self-interest and be like a Homeric Cyclops who lives "in sovereign disregard of all his peers", *or* you be a practitioner of pure altruism and care only for others, disregarding personal advantage in situations riddled with conflict of interest. Instead, there are many intermediate situations of concern between selfishness and altruism, all ennobled in the Eyes of Allah: e.g., the concern for one's parents and relatives, orphans, and the needy in society – presumably, in that order.[22]

Secondly, Islam lays great store by the individual's sense of social responsibility. Indeed, the dimensions of people's inborn freedom are enhanced to the extent that they discharge social responsibility: caring for others is a sign of individual freedom, for one who is unfree cannot take responsibility either. A central feature of caring for others is that it is entirely rational. It has been shown that commitment (and many other moral values other than the pursuit of self-interest) are entirely consistent with a maximising of behaviour, which includes *the process of choice itself.* Thus, it is entirely rational if my commitment to the cause of justice, for instance, is included in what is being maximised (the maximand) because socially it is the right thing to do; or because being moral carries some weight in making me look respectable in society; or because my personal (feeling of) well-being is enhanced by making a choice that may not be optimising in the neo-classical sense but is maximising nevertheless. However, in these (*normal*) cases, the act of choice is itself included in the maximand to arrive at a comprehensive outcome [Sen (1997)].[23] Thirdly, and related to the first point, is that it is motivationally rational for a person to sacrifice his selfish interests because: (a) "success" is measured, as Islam does, in terms of one's distance from greed and avarice; or (b) making a sacrifice in this world enhances the expected reward in this world as well as in the hereafter.[24] Fourthly, as Rawls (1971; 1999) points out, a person can become committed to working for society, beyond one's selfish interest, if it is based on 'fair' and 'just' principles. Whence follows that in a just Islamic society, commitment can reasonably be expected to dominate selfishness and greed, without attracting the odium of being 'unscientific'.[25]

ii) *On Economic Equality*

Nothing has exercised secular and religious (including Islam's) philosophy more than what should be equalised (liberty, opportunity, income and wealth), to what extent the goal of equality should be pursued (complete or partial, structural or incremental), and/or by what means (redistributing private property and/or taking appropriate fiscal policies)? Islam's view on equality derives from an unequivocal emphasis on the equality of humankind before Allah *and* with respect to each other, regardless of affluence, rank and social status [e.g., Hodgson (1974a); Lapidus (1982); Marlow (1997)]. Here we confine the discussion to the equality of income and wealth. In this context, three broad principles seem to govern the Islamic viewpoint: (a) since wealth belongs to Allah, all human beings are equally entitled to it; (b) from an arbitrarily chosen position of inequality of income and wealth between people, society should move towards a position of equality over time; and (c) in addition to whatever is accomplished in this respect in the aggregate, the claims of the least privileged must be addressed *first* by virtue of their prior claim in total wealth.[26] These general principles are strengthened by four specific observations: (i) the superiority of one person over another is recognised *only* on the basis of knowledge and piety; (ii) the concentration of income and wealth in the hands of the rich is undesirable; (iii) hoarding wealth is an evil act; and (iv) the morally illegitimate exercise of wealth and power by the rich is condemned. Indeed, they are held directly responsible for the ruination of human societies.[27]

Following these principles, a just and stable Muslim society can be created that enjoys the voluntary support of the people. It should be clear from these statements that what Islam aims at is not the *equality of opportunity* to acquire income and wealth; it rather insists on the *equality of the economic conditions* of the people with respect to their current and expected holdings of income and wealth. The reason for rejecting the former is that "equality of opportunity means an equal chance to leave the less fortunate behind in the personal quest for influence and position" [Rawls (1999); p. 91]. On this principle, people with different starting points in life, by virtue of the circumstances of their birth as well as early nurture, will end up increasing the existing inequalities of income and wealth if they are given only the equality-of-opportunity option to pursue their plans in life. In particular, this formula will not care to relieve the immense misery of those whose brutal childhood has left them with stunted souls. Whence follows, that the equality-of-opportunity principle can be acceptable if and only if substantial differences in people's *capacities* to make use of the opportunities are *redressed* by a significant redistribution of income and wealth to provide them all with equal starting points in life. But, in this case, the equality of opportunity and equality condition principles coincide. Thus, the former usage should be discarded to avoid confusion at the policy-making level.[28]

It will be interesting to see as to which of the moral theories, discussed at some length in Chapter 2, would find broad support in Islamic philosophy. This should also help crystallise the Islamic point of view in terms of the requirements of a modern Muslim society. The closest (but *not* identical) to the Islamic point of view is the Rawlsian general principle of justice, according to which "all social values – liberty and opportunity, income and wealth, and the social bases of self-respect" – are to be distributed equally unless an unequal distribution of any, or all, of these values is to everyone's advantage" [Rawls (1999); p. 54]. There are three aspects of this principle which are broadly consistent with the Islamic position outlined in the preceding paragraph: (a) equality should be sought with respect to a broader set of variables than just income and wealth, which together are referred to as "social primary goods", and the actual possession of which determines the degree of equality of the human condition in the widest possible sense of the term. In particular, individuals should be able to enjoy equal opportunities and liberties; and, as Adam Smith (1790) puts it, they should be able to appear "in public without shame" and take "part in the life of the community" (pp. 351-352). (b) The general principle with respect to the possession of social primary goods is one of equality, so that any departures from it (i.e., inequality) must be justified by showing that these work to everybody's advantage. (c) The least-privileged in society – i.e., whose possession of social primary goods is the least – must receive the most of these goods, which is the Difference Principle. (d) Also relevant from the Islamic point of view is the Rawlsian emphasis on the impartiality of the procedures to arrive at the basic principles of justice, so that people voluntarily support these principles.

However, the Difference Principle is deficient from the Islamic point of view in that it excludes those who cannot participate in economic activity due to some physical disability or whatever (see Chapter 2). The general Islamic principle is more comprehensive in that all living beings are entitled to a minimum level of sustenance.[29] In this context, relatively nearer to the Islamic position is Sen's (1992) position that equality be achieved *not* with respect to the resources (the Rawlsian primary goods) that people need or possess to carry out their life plans; but with respect to *every* individual's *capability* to function (the capability to be well-fed, well-educated, enjoying a long life, etc.), especially of those who are physically disadvantaged. Thus, the physically disadvantaged need *more* of primary goods and resources than a healthy person does. In other words, *equal* capabilities would normally imply giving an *unequal* possession of primary goods, *more* to the poor and *less* to the rich.

iii) *The Question of Distributive Justice*

If the equality of the human condition is what Islam aims at, then the next logical step is taking concrete measures to bring it about by an egalitarian distribution of income and wealth (including, other elements of the social primary goods noted above). But before we take up this issue, an important clarification is in order: it is that achieving *equality* in the 'space' of income and wealth is perfectly consistent with having *inequality* in some other 'space' [Sen (1992)]. For instance, as noted in Chapter 2, the libertarian moral-right philosophies – especially, Nozick's (1974) – insist on equality in the space of libertarian moral rights (of unlimited property rights) but are content with inequality in income and wealth. Indeed, they oppose any effort to redistribute property rights because *that* would upset the equality of the individual's moral rights. Conversely, an attempt to bring about greater equality in the distribution of income and wealth normally requires constraining at least some of the bizarre libertarian rights. Whence follows that one cannot insist on achieving the same degree of equality in all spaces exactly and simultaneously – e.g., that with respect to income and wealth, as well as rights and freedoms at the same time. And, yet, with differences in emphasis, Islam would require keeping a balance between the efforts to equalise made in different spaces. Thus, egalitarianism must be informed by a recognition of the competing claims of substantive freedoms, i.e., political freedom as well as freedom from hunger. This seems to be the import of Sadr's (1982) contention that social justice in Islam is a matter of "social balance" and "reciprocal responsibility" (pp. 60-62).

Keeping this proviso in mind, three definitive statements can be made about the legitimate claims of distributive justice in Muslim society. Firstly, as a corollary of the concept of Allah's ownership, justice should be maintained in the basic structure of property rights. Indeed, this is the essence of Islamic egalitarianism. The state is *not* allowed to confiscate private property without demonstrating unambiguously its social benefits; and certainly not when the intent of the state is to hurt the people.[30] If the right of private property is to be restricted in the public interest, it must be justified by reference to the terms of a social contract which is voluntarily accepted by the people, promotes social cooperation, and aims at maximising collective good. The point is that Allah's ownership implies that every individual has an equal *right* to own private property; and the *duty* of the state is to promote an egalitarian distribution of property or property rights. Whence follows that a feudal system of private ownership, which excludes the cultivators from the ownership of land, is not allowed in Islam [Sadr (1982); Taleghani (1982)]; and the state *cannot* perpetuate such a system. In addition, the provision of assuring a minimum (but respectable) sustenance to the poor is the collective responsibility of the society.

Secondly, the extent of the redistributive effort, however, is an empirical matter. It will be determined by the size of inequities in the initial structure of ownership, subject to the proviso that the planned redistribution will ensure an equitable access to the flow of benefits to all the people. The general principle is that injustice in the basic structure of property right should be reduced, not enhanced, with the passage of time. This means redressing initial differences in the size of holdings which confer artificial advantages on the initial owners of wealth and widen the differentials of income and wealth in subsequent time periods. Thus, incremental egalitarianism will be ineffective unless associated with *structural* reforms during the initial period [Naqvi (1997)].[31] Large inequalities of income and wealth must be reduced to establish a just economy because these are not only inequitable but inefficient as well in that they lower the growth rate and increase poverty [Tinbergen (1985)]. Birdsall and Londono (1997) find that "initial inequalities in the distribution of...human capital have a clear negative effect on economic growth, and the effects are almost twice as great for the poor as for the population as a whole". In other words, a lower growth rate due to initial inequalities in income and wealth, makes the poor poorer.

Thirdly, it follows from the preceding observations that the extent of redistributive effort must include abolishing the feudal system in Muslim countries, which has obstructed agricultural productivity and impeded human development by restricting access to education, health and other poverty-reducing social services. It has also been parent to many a social evil, including an open violation of the spirit as well as the letter of Islamic Law. A glaring instance of this is the almost universal practice of denying women their legitimate rights in property in almost all rural areas of Pakistan. Yet, there have been considerable differences in religious opinion, duly noted in the literature, about the limits on redistribution based on the competing claims of the individual's freedom to hold property and the needs of society as well as regarding the role of the state in reconciling these claims [e.g., Kuran (1992; 1995a,b); Behdad (1989; 1992)].[32]

This lack of clarity on the issue of distributive justice is surprising because it has also been emphasised by religious thinkers and Muslim economists that private property rights are neither absolute nor unlimited. Part of the reason for this ambiguity is probably historical: the conjunction of Islam's strong egalitarian message and the tendency in the early Middle Ages to social differentiation that inevitably became evident as Muslim societies grew richer and more powerful [Marlow (1997)]. The *'ulamā'*, depending on their individual perceptions of society, cultural backgrounds, interests and political leanings, could not remain entirely immune to such influences. Some *'ulamā'*, therefore, honestly tried *not* to disturb the existing structure of private property rights to minimise social tensions. But there were others, who equally honestly and with some more conviction, regarded such tensions as necessary to bring about changes in this structure to let the pristine translucence of the Islamic ideal illumine the fabric of Muslim society. Yet another important reason for a lack of clarity on the issue may have been that not all *'ulamā'* have supported the role of government in an Islamic economy. Indeed, some have been openly sceptical about the government's intentions in this regard.[33] They, therefore, overemphasised voluntary beneficence as *the* means to achieve distributive justice while at the same time recognising the power of the self-interest motive as well [e.g., Shafī' (1968); pp. 7-9; Mawdūdī (1970); p. 23].[34] But, free-riding and assurance problems will ensure that this 'motivational' mix will be the vehicle of only a limited transfer of resources from the rich to the poor. On the other hand, a large number of *'ulamā'* have emphasised the need for land reforms on the ground that private property rights are *not* absolute in Islam. They also explicitly acknowledge the role of government in an Islamic economy [Sadr (1982); pp. 54-62; Taleghani (1982); pp. 22-28 and pp. 37-38]. Fortunately, a growing consensus has evolved on the need for land reforms and the role of government as a redistributive agent to operationalise Islamic egalitarianism [Siddiqi (1981); esp. pp. 6-10 and 18-21]. The time has come to reflect this consensus in Islamic Law as well so that the Courts of Law, which continue to be guided by the most conservative interpretation on this issue, can implement such reforms.[35]

iv) *Reducing Poverty*

Notwithstanding some tensions among religious scholars on the question of distributive justice, there have been practically none on the question of helping the poor. The result has been equally unambiguous: confined into a narrow channel and driven by a sense of religious obligation, voluntary beneficence has run with great strength in Muslim societies. A recent survey of 1,365 individuals across Pakistan, conducted by the Aga Khan Development Network (AKDN) in 1998/99 to measure the dimensions of individual giving in Pakistan, shows some remarkable aspects of a typical Muslim society: (a) in 1998 alone,

Pakistanis, belonging to various classes and social backgrounds, contributed Rs. 41 billion ($ 820 million) in cash and goods by way of *voluntary* philanthropic giving. This, at a 58 percent participation rate, is almost twice the world average and exceeds even the high rate of voluntary giving in the United States. (b) 98 percent of voluntary philanthropic giving has been motivated by religious (Islamic) teaching. (c) Voluntary giving has been a matter of religious conviction, humanitarian concerns, social responsibility, and civic duty in that order. The primary objective has been to do good (in a religious sense) to the poor; and to be cooperative rather than competitive in achieving it. In particular, this activity is *not* linked to securing tax incentives etc., [AKDN (2000); pp. 43-53]. These findings, for Pakistan, are probably typical of practically all Muslim societies, where a great many financial resources are transferred from the rich to the poor, some even without the latter's knowledge of the person who gives *because* Islam encourages *incognito* giving. These results illustrate the main contentions of this book – namely, that (a) Muslims do care for Islamic values; and that (b) Islamic religious values tend to lower free-riding by inculcating a sense of commitment in individuals to give to the poor. Having said that, the widespread poverty in Muslim countries illustrates that private giving alone is *not* adequate to generate enough resources to finance an effective anti-poverty programme; it should be supported by an egalitarian public policy. These matters are taken up again in Section VI.

It may be useful at this point to pull together the strands of thought which have enhanced the effectiveness of Islamic ethical values on the poverty issue. (a) There is no hint in the Islamic ethical system to suggest that (involuntary) poverty is ennobled in the Eyes of Allah; that the poor themselves are responsible for their misery; that widespread poverty is in any way an unalterable social state; and that the poor should do nothing about their fallen state. On the other hand, it is emphatically stated that: (a) poverty is a curse, caused by the immiserising behaviour of the rich which obstructs (even diminishes) the flow of resources to the poor; (b) men/women have it within their power to improve their lot by following the laws of Allah.[96] Islam suggests that poverty is not only an economic issue; but it has moral, social and political dimensions as well – moral, because it deprives people of their sense of self-esteem; social, because it prevents the poor from taking part in the life of the community; and political, because alienation from life's mainstream foments interclass tensions.

Poverty-reduction programmes in Muslim societies should, thus, be multi-dimensional to implement Islam's moral vision. The following components of this programme follow *directly from the first principles of Islamic ethics*: (a) the poor are *entitled* to their share in the wealth of the rich. This establishes the principle that the transfer of resources from the rich to the poor is not a matter of *charity* but of doing *justice* to the latter. Whence follows that this resource transfer should come about not only through the voluntary actions of the rich but by coercive actions as well.[37] (b) These clear statements imply that the poor need *not* be ashamed of claiming their right in the wealth of the rich. Furthermore, the rich are warned that the act of giving should not be accompanied by hurting the self-esteem of the poor; and that those who do so incur Allah's wrath and their giving will go to waste.[38] (c) Islam prohibits hoarding, especially of food-grains, in the strongest possible terms, and enjoins that the required amount of help be provided by the state to avoid extreme poverty and famine-like conditions. (d) Recognising that poverty is directly associated with inequalities of income and wealth and is created by the socially irresponsible behaviour of the rich, the state must arrange the necessary transfer of resources *in addition* to normal taxes like *zakāt* etc.[39] (e) Islam creates irresistible social compulsion to help the poor by declaring the act of giving to the poor as being materially beneficial as well as spiritually uplifting; which strengthens the individual's sense of *commitment* to the point of making it psychologically compelling and an act of supreme rationality. (f) In the Islamic view, poverty should not be alleviated only temporarily but reduced to the minimum, if not altogether eliminated, on a long-term basis.

To highlight the originality of the Islamic message on poverty, it will be interesting to compare it, at the level of first principles, with secular and (Western) religious ethics. Firstly, Rawlsian thinking should, to some extent, be congenial to Islam. In particular, the concept of primary social goods – "liberty and equality, income and wealth, and the social bases of self-respect" – is broadly consistent with Islam's multi-dimensional characterisation of the poverty problem. However, *not* consistent with the Islamic point of view are the following aspects of it: (a) the assumptions of a well-ordered society with only "moderate scarcity" so that the poor can be made better off without great sacrifice to the rich [Rawls (1971); pp. 127-128]; (b) the exclusion from the Difference Principle of those who cannot participate in market exchange because of physical disability or whatever [Mueller (1979); pp. 240-241]. However, Sen's (1992) capability theory redresses these drawbacks of the Rawlsian principles of justice and, to this extent, is nearer to the Islamic point of view.

Secondly, the following aspects of secular and Western religious ethics are totally *unacceptable* to Islam: (a) the *utilitarian's exclusive emphasis* on maximising total utility and its deafening silence on how to distribute it, especially to the poor. (b) The *Pareto optimality principle*, which is (at best) neutral on issues like distributive equity and poverty and does not envisage anything more substantial than the (unfulfilled) promises of lump-sum non-distortionary resource transfers to the potential losers in market exchange. (c) The *liberalist doctrine*, which is opposed to doing *anything* to lessen poverty on the ground that it would suppress individual liberty and violate the individual's unlimited moral right to private property; and which contends that the poor do *not* have a right to aid, that poverty is *not* morally unjust, though morally unfortunate and that the act of giving be purely voluntary. (d) A *minimalist government*, so that the state can prevent the violation of the individual right to private property but do *nothing* positive if these rights have been violated![40] (e) *Christian thinking* that the poor do not have a *right* in the wealth of the rich. And, finally, (f) the *Jewish* (as well as the Christian) *principle* of "commutative" justice, whereby a person who once was rich but has become poor should receive more assistance than one who has always been poor. [Wilson (1997); p. 77 for the Christian position; and pp. 65-66 for the Jewish point of view].

v) *Economic Growth*

It is well-known that a necessary (though not sufficient) condition to reduce poverty on a durable basis is that a growth rate of per capita income (i.e., the growth rate of the Gross National Product *minus* the population growth rate) of at least 3 percent per annum be sustained for several decades. Furthermore, there is a two-way linkage between high rates of growth and egalitarianism. While a high rate of growth tends to promote equity, an equitable distribution of assets itself increases the growth rate of income. Consequently, the share of incremental incomes due to growth that accrues to the poor people tends to increase [Naqvi (1995); World Bank (2000); pp. 55-59]. And, yet on these dynamic-economic relationships, Islamic morality provides, at best, indirect and tangential guidance. We will discuss in the next chapter the problem of making Islamic ethics capacious enough to handle problems of growth in a modern society. Here, we simply assert that Islamic moral values are *not*, in principle, a hindrance to growth. This assertion can be deduced from the first principles of Islamic ethics. Assume that the problems of equality, distributive justice, and poverty have an *inter-generational* dimension as well; and that the present generation is committed to making a sacrifice of current consumption for the well-being of the next generation. In other words, the present generation must keep a balance between current consumption and future consumption. The problem of growth in an Islamic economy is, then, to maximise a social welfare function, which depends on the commodity basket to be consumed over time *and* on the per capita capital stock to be used for the production of the commodity basket. Making due allowance for the growth of the economy over time and for pricing capital and using it efficiently, it can be shown, that the growth rate will be optimal if and only if: (a) there is a steady transfer of resources from the rich to the poor; (b) adequate provision is made for the production of wage goods consumed by the least-privileged people in society; and (c) a steady flow of income accrues to the poor. Furthermore, maximal *and* equitable growth requires that: (d) an egalitarian redistribution of income and wealth be done to offset the widening inequalities that usually accompany the growth process; (e) the share of wage goods in the commodity basket must rise to satisfy the incremental demand for these goods over time; and (f) the wealth differential in the initial period is held down to a minimum. This proves the assertion that Islamic ethical values are positively helpful in achieving the required growth rate of the economy [Naqvi (1997)].[41]

To achieve the growth objective, Islamic morality can be 'factored' into the following elements: (a) wasteful consumption is condemned as immoral in the strongest possible terms. (b) The concentration of income and wealth in the hands of the rich is discouraged. (c) The consumption needs of the least-privileged in society are assigned priority over those of others. (d) The rich have a social responsibility to society's welfare, which they must discharge in a manner that the self-esteem of the poor is not hurt. (e) Everyone has a right to minimum sustenance.[42] (f) Islam emphasises universal education.[43] Together these considerations help growth by reducing poverty, enhancing human capital, and raising people's aspirational level.

V. Problem Areas in a Traditional Islamic Ethical System

Economic progress is vital to human well-being. The Islamic ethical system must, therefore, facilitate it. However, the fact is that Islamic ethics has not been stated explicitly enough to strengthen the individual's commitment to economic development *as a matter of his/her moral duty* in the same way as it does on matters relating to distributive justice and poverty reduction.[44] A lack of interaction between Islamic ethics and the requirements of economic development hurts both. Inasmuch as religious ethics has not lent *direct* support to economic growth, it has compromised economic and human development in Muslim societies. This incongruence between Islamic ethics and economics must, therefore, be removed, especially because the former, as noted above, is essentially pro-growth.

In this respect, Western (Christian) efforts to adapt an ossified ethical structure to the ethos of the Industrial Revolution are relevant. As related in Chapter 3, the traditional Christian value system, meant to serve the needs of rural societies, could not even comprehend the dynamics of a fast-changing urban society. It was thus confronted with the choice of either being helpful to the cause of economic change, or becoming totally irrelevant to it. Fortunately, however, the Christian theological doctrine was practically rewritten, first in Western Europe and then much later in the United States, to be able to respond positively to the challenge of economic growth and urbanisation, *while retaining its religious credential*. Calvinism took up the challenge in Europe. Tawney (1937) notes that from its "reiterated insistence on secular obligations as imposed by the divine will" flowed the principle that, "not withdrawal from the world, but the conscientious discharge of the duties of business, is among the loftiest of religious and moral virtues" (p. 239). This was a radical departure from the traditional (Roman Catholic) Christian position, which regarded the economic motive as entirely alien to the life of the spirit. It is, therefore, no exaggeration to state that Calvinism's was "the first systematic body of doctrine [in Christianity] which can be said to recognize and applaud the economic values" (p. 114). Much later, the Social Gospellers performed a similar feat in the United States. They discarded, around 1890, the fundamental Christian theological doctrines of "original sin and innate depravity" to make Christian ethics usable for tackling the problems of growth and distributive inequities [Fogel (2000); p. 119].[45]

Fortunately, Islam does not have to go so far as the Christians had to. It is *not* necessary to rewrite Islamic theological doctrine to make its ethical values helpful to economic progress. Islam does explicitly recognise the excellence of human creation and his/her freedom from any original sin or innate depravity. Instead, human beings, freed from the chains of an irrelevant past, are entrusted with the task of rebuilding societies on strong economic *and* moral foundations. What, then, explains the historical ineffectiveness of Islam's ethical system in inculcating a commitment in Muslim men/women to roll back the forces of economic, social and moral decline of their societies in the last one thousand years or so? And why is it that even in the modern age of high growth they remain mired in economic stagnation, notwithstanding their success in achieving political independence against heavy odds. Even at the risk of oversimplification, three reasons seem to account for this paradoxical situation. (a) Rather than respond to the challenges of economic development, an illusion has been created of an immutable Divine ethical system (as represented by Islamic Law), which contains sure-fire solutions to all human economic problems, including economic development. (b) Insofar as attempts have been made to evolve an ethical system (*maqāṣid al-Sharī'ah*) to emphasise the relativity of Islamic Law to its underlying objectives (i.e., to improve the economic, social and moral well-being of the people), nothing concrete has come out of this noble project. Much worse, as if to strengthen the state of intellectual stagnation in Muslim societies, Islamic ethics too has remained static since it was born some fifteen hundred years ago, when the forces supporting the supremacy of human reason were defeated by the combined might of religious conservatism and truculent dogmatism.

It may be useful to elaborate on these critical comments in order to clear the way for future progress.

i) *Economic Statis in Muslim Societies*

Muslim societies have suffered, literally, from an economic and political sclerosis for centuries. Back in the Middle Ages, even though blessed with great geniuses in natural and social sciences, Muslim society seemed set on the road to moral, economic, and political decline [Al-Shakaa (1994)]. Even the greatest period of splendour and fluorescence of the sixteenth and seventeenth centuries was *not* of a type when all traditions are questioned and recast into new ones, and in which everything is rediscovered in a pioneering spirit. The world of Islam, though the most influential and widespread at the time, was weighed down by a "conservative spirit". "The great figures and events invoked as authoritative by the Muslims of the sixteenth and seventeenth centuries were the same as had been invoked for generations before; in the most central aspects of civilizations they went back to the beginning of Islamic times" [Hodgson (1974c); p. 14]. It is this conservative spirit, this irrepressible desire to look back to find answers to new questions, which became the greatest single hindrance to the development potential of Muslim societies through the ages. The story has been one of economic and social statis, especially from the eighteenth century onwards. Starting with the Western domination of the Muslim world in the wake of the Industrial Revolution – which completely transformed production technologies helped by rapid capital accumulation and mass markets and to which no matching response came from any other civilisation including the Muslims – the world of Islam completely lost its poise and bearing in "the long night of colonial hegemony: a period during which the key institutions of the Muslim society were supplanted and substituted, the moral fibre of the society was destroyed...." [Ahmad (1994); p. xiv]. The tragedy is that, even though the Muslim world has gained political independence by making great sacrifices, and has been in possession of much (badly utilised) wealth for several decades now, its response to the modern challenges remains, as before, weak and indecisive, and, in many cases (e.g., human freedom, especially for women), downright perverse. The ideas most suitable for basically agrarian societies still hold sway in the Muslim world. This is especially the case in oil-producing countries where tremendous wealth remains inaccessible to productive use. These countries seem to have followed what is derisively labelled as the Amazon's Law: "the more money it took, the more it lost". In particular, a fast rate of economic growth, which comes about *only* with sustained "structural transformation, i.e., when the share of the manufacturing sector in the Gross Domestic Product steadily rises, has eluded them. Abundant oil wealth has given the people of these countries indolent Welfare States, weighed down by a life of luxury and fed by unearned rents; but little scientific advance and intellectual sophistication has flowered. These countries are located in the growth-killing fields of the Middle East and North Africa (MENA) region where the per capita growth rate has been zero or negative for nearly 30 years. A lot of foreign investment has flowed into 'enclaves', with little or no spill-over into the rest of the economy. By contrast, non-oil producing countries have made good economic progress (and Malaysia has done extremely well); but even these countries have had lower growth rates than the non-Muslim countries of the region. On average, the *non*-Muslim world has grown faster, with lower growth rates of population, a lesser gender discrimination against women, and much greater political freedom than the Muslim world, which is much worse in all these respects (see Chapter 6). The net result of this irresponsible use of wealth is that the dream of the Islamic revival, dreamt half a century ago by Muslims, now appears to fall between the adolescent and the deranged. Needless to add, all this must change to turn social, economic and political discontent into a full-blown spring of material and spiritual progress.

ii) *The Immutability of Islamic Law*

As a reflection of the distemper of bad times, the Muslim societies seem to have cultivated a *trained incapacity* to face up to social, political, moral, and economic challenges. This incapacity shows up most strikingly in the case of Islamic Law, where "little effort [has been] made to *rethink* and reformulate the actual body of *fiqh* [Law]...and no thinker, however bold, [has] dared to touch it" [Rahman (1979); p. 115]. As if to completely foreclose all possibilities of reinterpreting Islamic Law to meet its social and ethical objectives "no real and effective boundaries were drawn between the moral and the strictly legal aspects in Islamic Law..." (p. 116). There is an influential view that Islamic Law already incorporates its underlying moral objectives. An assumption of the immutability of each and every element of Islamic Law has produced a non-consequentialist legal structure, which insists that following the letter of the Law itself guarantees good consequences.[46] But this is circular reasoning; because like any system of law, Islamic Law must also be judged by reference to an exogenous set of ethical principles. To achieve social good it should be possible to reinterpret it in the light of the nature of the *consequences* that it produces in different societies and at different times because of radical changes in both the production relations and the factors of production. A moments' reflection should show that a deontological view amounts to asserting the following propositions. (a) Either all possible (good and bad) consequences of the Law were already anticipated in the original formulation of Islamic Law (in the Middle Ages); (b) *or* that the consequences of the implementation of the Law do not matter. Needless to point out, neither of these propositions can be logically sustained.[47] As if to make matters worse, it is further believed that the supposedly Divine origin of Islamic Law guarantees its success at all times. But this argument is also logically invalid: the Divine origin of Islamic Law does *not* carry with it the Divine guarantee of its success in specific situations. Islam does not offer any such guarantees because, being Allah's vicegerents on earth, human beings must themselves decide in specific situations about what would best maximise individual and social welfare – though always praying for Allah's guidance in reaching the right decisions. The immutability of Allah's word *cannot* be extended to its human interpretation (which is what Islamic Law is) in specific contexts to meet the needs of society at a certain point in Muslim history.

There is a historical reason for such conservative attitudes. It is that an Islamic ethical system, based on a genuine understanding of the intent of the Holy Qur'ān, did not evolve for a long time after the full development of Islamic Law so that "the leaders of the *Sharī'ah* [Islamic Law] made practically no distinction between [Islamic] ethics and [Islamic] law" [Rahman (1980); p. 239]. Kamali (1999) has voiced a similar concern: "for almost three centuries, no one took interest in relating Islamic Law to the *maqāṣid* [the objectives of the Law]. It was left to al-Ghazālī (d. 505) and al-Shāṭibī (d. 790) to emphasize the vital importance of this connection to formulate "both a set of rules and a value system" (p. 198). Obviously, the ultra-conservative attitude has been in the wrong because "the underlying theme in virtually all of the broad spectrum of [legal injunctions] *aḥkām* is the realization of benefit (*maṣlaḥah*)" (p. 195). Whence follows that the beneficial potential of the specific provision of Islamic Law must be independently established by their ability to deliver the promised benefits. Thus, beyond its literalist reading, Islamic Law must be re-evaluated from time to time in the light of its (empirically) demonstrated consequences. It is interesting to note that from the nineteenth century onwards, nearly all political opposition movements in the Muslim World have nearly always been "accompanied by appeal to *Sharī'ah* as an ideal of social justice" [Calder (1997); p. 325]. Yet, having achieved the political objectives, this link has generally been forgotten. As a result, Islamic Law has come to acquire a sanctity of its own; and the aim of religious thinkers has become just to preserve the letter of the Law, unrelated to the ethical and economic consequences of such an exercise.[48]

iii) *The Static Nature of Islamic Ethics*

As noted above, it is now being increasingly realised that Islamic Law must be made consequence-sensitive and linked firmly to its *maqāṣid*. Yet, for all such protestations, little progress has been made to implement this commendable agenda. Thus, for instance, even though a constructive consensus has already been achieved among Muslim scholars on some basic elements of economic and human development – e.g., implementing land reforms, ensuring distributive justice (especially an egalitarian redistribution of assets), universalisation of the access of the poor to the basic necessities of life like education and health, putting restrictions on wasteful consumption, etc. – the same has not yet been unambiguously reflected in Islamic Law. But the problem runs deeper: it is that Islamic ethics too has remained placid for centuries. Thus, we have the unfortunate situation that the challenges of the rapid advances in the knowledge and the onset of new ideas and economic interests are met by a generalised appeal to the traditional views on Islamic ethics. Thus, the *maqāṣid*, spelled out by al-Ghazālī (around the year 1000 A.D.), and confirmed by al-Shāṭibī (around the year 1350) as definitive, are still cited approvingly as the repository of ultimate wisdom on Islamic ethics. True, these *maqāṣid*, i.e., (a) faith; (b) life; (c) progeny; (d) intellect; and (e) wealth, must have made an interesting list of objectives, in the time these were formulated, to address legal and metaphysical issues; yet they need to be refocused, expanded and amended to become useful guides for public policy in modern times. Leaping between totally different eras and time zones to cull nuggets of traditional wisdom is, at best, an exercise in futility.

There are many reasons why such an exercise has *not* been undertaken so far. Firstly, these *maqāṣid* are not amenable to a straightforward extension to social and economic matters. In this context, it would not be wise to accept Shāṭibī's claim that both the *maqāṣid* and their *ordering* be regarded as final (*quṭ'ī*), presumably for all times [Nyazee (2000); p. 204]. Indeed, an insistence on the proposed ordering of the ethical value can introduce inconsistencies in the framing of public policy. Thus, for instance, intellect would be required to determine the worth of the remaining four elements; and life does not have much meaning with poverty. Also, an overemphasis on progeny may lead (as it has) to a pro-natalist bias in population policy, which tends to aggravate poverty. And so on. Secondly, in this ordering, intellect is degraded to a rather low position. This is not surprising, because both al-Ghazālī and al-Shāṭibī distrusted human reason in determining what is good (or harmful) for human beings: "The primary purpose of *Sharī'ah* [and of its *maqāṣid*].....is to free Man from the grip of his own whim and fancy..." [Nyazee (1994); p. 235]. This opinion must be put into its time and place.[49] It may have sounded reasonable in the Middle Ages when extinguishing the flame of human reason was all the rage in the Muslim world; but this medieval contempt for intellectual freedom needs to be radically revised in modern times. This is especially true of economic growth ("wealth"), whose acquisition would be dismissed as a mere weasel word in al-Ghazālī's eremitic asceticism. Obviously, a phenomenon which first appeared in human history around 1776 in Europe and gained momentum only in the last 50 years or so, could not be understood when al-Ghazālī (d. 505/1111) wrote, or even when al-Shāṭibī (d. 790/1388) lived. But in modern times, economic progress, without which sustained poverty reduction is impossible, must appear near the top of the *maqāṣid* – if only because poverty, according to a Prophetic tradition, undermines faith. We should, therefore, not hesitate to acknowledge that the traditional scheme of ethical priorities has outlived its utility. The emphasis should now be on the *creation* of knowledge which can help change the Muslim world for the better.

VI. Public Policy in Muslim Societies

The next question to be answered is: to what extent would public policy be required to supplement Islamic moral values to attain common good in Muslim societies, i.e., achieving distributive justice, giving the poor their share in the nation's wealth, and ensuring high rates of economic growth to raise the economic well-being of the people (especially, of the poor) on a durable basis? To answer these questions, the basic relationship between the self-interest motive, moral imperatives, and public policy, discussed several times in the book, may be recalled. Public policy achieves the above-mentioned social objectives *both* when the self-interest motive is regarded as supreme and when altruism is assumed to dominate human motivation. The reason is that, since each individual attempts to 'free-ride' in the hope that his/her own non-contribution will not be noticed by others, *self-interested individuals will not, as a rule, work for the common good even if they expect to gain by doing so*. True, in "small groups" social and moral norms will be enough to make free-riders contribute to the common good; yet in "large groups", (i.e., at the national level), a proactive public policy is required to strengthen the hold of moral norms on human behaviour. The same problem arises if altruism is assumed to motivate the individual: free-riding may be curbed in small groups, but the problem re-emerges in large groups. And even if it does not, public policy is still required to *assure* the altruistic individual (one who is *not* inclined to free-ride) that his contribution will not go to waste and that others in society will not be allowed by the government to withhold their contributions. Essentially, the problem is one of generating the right information about individual behaviour which, being a public good, can only be provided by the government. Altruism lowers the policing and transaction costs in the economy; but it does not eliminate them altogether. Furthermore, public policy economises society's demand on scarce altruistic resources. This is a very important consideration because an excessive insistence on altruism can create a permanent tension between what a Muslim society is required to do and what eventually gets done in practice. Indeed, *there is a real danger that if moral perfection is demanded at all times, then the entire social system will become dysfunctional for want of the required supply of altruism*. Thus, in general, appropriate public policy must keep a balance between self-interest behaviour and moral imperatives because the principles of altruism and exchange are both mutually supportive as well as antithetical [Boulding (1973)].

Keeping these qualifications in mind, the problem is to determine the extent of policy intervention to achieve growth and social justice, which is regarded by Muslims as "the greatest of the four foundations of Islam" [Quṭb (2000); p. 131]. The aim here is to determine the system of rewards and incentives that Muslim societies offer to motivate individuals to work for the good of society; inspire a sense of commitment in them to support the system; ensure its stability at a given point in time as well as over time; and *change* the existing system if it is inconsistent with the principles of justice. In other words, to create a 'well-ordered' society, the government must set the basic rules of a 'social contract' which the members of the Muslim society will assent to voluntarily. These rules would require that the *processes*, whereby the basic principles of social justice are generated are fair and impartial to enhance the credibility of these principles and to facilitate reaching consensual agreement on them. The first requirement is best met, in a democratic framework, at the constitution-making and legislative stages, when a compliance mechanism should be devised to oversee the implementation of the basic principles of justice agreed to at these stages.[50] Once the impartiality of the basic rules of justice is established, the government in a Muslim society should adopt achieving the equality of economic *condition* (not just of *opportunity*) as its moral and social ideal, from which departures should be justified only if they are shown to be to work out to everybody's advantage.

It may be noted at this point that, while the role of public policy in Muslim societies would be fairly extensive, this does *not* imply that their governments can enjoy an inherent *right* over individuals. The correct position is that the government's *rights* are derivative and proportional to its *duty* to ensure a balance between the individual's freedom and social well-being. These derivative rights extend to the ownership and use of natural resources (e.g., mines, forests, rivers, etc.). The reason is that these belong to society and no individual or group is entitled to own these to the exclusion of others.[51] However, the government's right ceases to exist once it abdicates its social duties and starts safeguarding the interests of a group of individuals. Thus, for instance, beyond the rights of the cultivators, the state *cannot* support feudal systems of ownership prevalent in many Muslim countries because such systems find "no support in Islamic ordinances and the laws derived from them" [Taleghani (1982);

p. 37)]. On the other hand, the government can suspend the individual's rights to own and use private property when an irresponsible exercise of these rights enhances poverty – and, in extreme cases, may even cause famines.[52] This is because in such situations the government's failure to act on behalf of the poor will amount to abdicating its duty to provide the latter their "acknowledged right" in the wealth of the rich.

Notes

1. The statement in the text implies a refutation of the meleorist "eighteenth century heresy" – that rational human-beings normally behave in such a manner that the pursuit of self-interest and altruistic behaviour would not conflict. There is not much support now for the simplistic (utilitarian) view that, "if men were actuated by self-interest, which they are not – except in the case of a few saints – the whole human race would cooperate" [Russell (1954); p. 173]. Surprisingly, Russell regards self-interest (which he interprets as "enlightened self-interest") as a moral ideal while idealistic motives are seen as "disguised hatred" or "disguised love of power" (p. 174).
2. An important aspect of the Keynesian Revolution was that it "brought back the moral problem in economics by destroying the neo-classical reconciliation of private egoism and public service" [Robinson (1973); p. 80]. Keynes (1932) stated: "It is *not* a correct deduction from the Principles of Economics that self-interest always operates in public interest. Nor is it true that self-interest generally *is* enlightened;...Experience does *not* show that individuals, when they make up a social unit, are always less clear-sighted than when they act separately," (pp. 312-313; italics in original).
3. The point here is that market behaviour does not necessarily reflect an individual's true *preferences* that are formed, in no small measure, by social conventions. Once preferences are modified, individual *behaviour* may become *as if* every individual is altruistic [Hirsch (1977); pp. 146-147]. The perfect-altruism alternative is here ruled out because that would amount to changing human nature.
4. Except in small groups, socialised norms – which require that individuals in fact do what they are expected to do by the group or society – are inefficient means to achieving the collective good. But, even in small groups, these may be extremely oppressive. A system

which expects people to think *only of others* may be rejected as much as a system which expects people to *think only of themselves.*

5. A meritocratic society is defined as one that "follows the principles of careers open to talents and uses equality of opportunity as a way of releasing men's energies in the pursuit of economic prosperity and political dominion. There exists a marked disparity between the upper and lower classes in both means of life and rights and privileges of organisational authority. The culture of the poorer strata is impoverished while that of the governing is securely based on the service of the national ends of power and wealth [Rawls (1999); p. 91]. See also Young (1958) for a discussion of the dangers of a meritocratic society.
6. The Holy Qur'ān enjoins upon all Muslims: "O Believers, come to full submission to God" (2:208).
7. The Holy Qur'ān unequivocally declares: "Piety does not lie in turning your face to the East or West; Piety lies in believing in God, the Last Day,...and disbursing your wealth out of love for God among your kin and orphans, the wayfarers and mendicants, freeing the slaves..." (2:177).
8. In the same vein, Bell (1953) remarks that: "No book has exercised a deeper influence upon the spirit of man than [the] Qur'ān ... it is the basis of Muslim's religious beliefs, their rituals and their law; *the guide of their conduct, both public and private.* It moulds their thought and its phrases enter into their literature and their daily speech" (p. 1).
9. The statement in the text is consistent with the fact that many Muslims do frequently violate the Divinely approved code of conduct. What is asserted is that, on average, Muslims consciously try to act correctly and feel bad when they fail to do so. Indeed, there is the widespread practice of trying to justify actual behaviour (even that which is *not* Islamic) on religious grounds; which, though borders on hypocrisy, does nevertheless explain the strength of religious beliefs in a typical Muslim society.
10. The Qur'ān lays down: "Allah's is the heritage of the heavens and the earth" (3:180). See also verse (57:10) at note 11 (a). However, Allah's ownership does not dilute individuals' ownership in the eyes of Islamic Law.
11. The Qur'ānic verses supporting the statements in the text are, in that order: (a) "And what has come on you that you do not spend in the way of God, when the heritage of the heavens and the earth belongs to God?" (57:10); (b) "That which they hoard will be their collar on the Day of Resurrection" (3:180); (c) "And in whose wealth a due share is included for the needy beggar and those

dispossessed" (70: 24-25); (d) "So give to your relatives what is their due, and to those who are needy and the wayfarers and do not dissipate your wealth extravagantly. Those who dissipate (their wealth) are brethren of the devils..." (17: 26-27).

12. There is, however, a provision for earmarking one third of the private property of the (dying) individual "for the sake of settling claims of the family members, for charitable undertakings, or to meet the claims of the society" [Taleghani (1982); p. 39]. Note that this is also the nearly unanimous opinion of Muslim jurists.
13. Taleghani (1982) states a widely held opinion among the *'ulamā'* that, "the problems of life cannot be solved, nor public justice secured through [legalistic] formulations...that by and large fail to accord with the realities of life..." (p. 42).
14. These matters are discussed in the Islamic context in Naqvi (1981). Incidentally, Adam Smith (1790) was the first to recognise these concepts. He explicitly notes that "sympathy" entails "no self denial, no self-command, no great exertion of the sense of propriety, since such acts (which involve sympathy) are prompted by what sympathy would of its own accord prompt us to do" (p. 191); but "humanity, generosity, and public spirit are the qualities most useful to others" (p. 189). Sen (1982) explains these distinctions in detail.
15. The Qur'ānic verses corresponding to the observations in the text are the following in that order: (a) "You will never come to piety unless you spend of the things you love" (3:92); (b) "The semblance of those who expend their wealth in the way of God is that of a grain of corn from which grow seven ears, each ear containing a hundred grains" (2:261); (c) "Have you seen him who denies the Day of Judgement? It is he who pushes the orphan away, and does not induce others to feed the needy" (107:1-3); (d) "How will you comprehend what the steep ascent is? – To free a neck (from the burden of debt and slavery) or to feed in times of famine, the orphan near in relationship, or the poor in distress" (90: 12-16).
16. The corresponding Qur'ānic verse is stated in note 11 (c) above. It may be noted that this right is *not* restricted to only the Muslim poor but to the non-Muslim poor as well [Mawdūdī (1976); p. 19].
17. The Qur'ān explicitly states: (a) "God has favoured some of you over others in the means of sustenance. Yet those of you who have more do not give [return] of their means to their dependants so that they (may not) become their equals. Will they then deny Allah's beneficence?" (16:71). Jauhri (1984) holds that here the emphasis on "returning" the poor's share shows that it is their right in the rich man's wealth, which mistakenly was put (by the economic system) in the rich man's hands (pp. 28-29). (b) "O believers, do

not nullify your charity by giving to oblige and flaunting (your favours) like a man who spends of his wealth only to show off, but does not believe in God and the Last Day" (2:264).

18. See, for instance, the Report of the Council of Islamic Ideology, Pakistan (1992), especially pp. 55-84. It explicitly rules out the imposition of income tax (p. 80) and does not even mention death duties. However, at other places this position is modified. See note 39.
19. Marlow (1997) notes: "The realities of power and status meant that in time the social significance of [the Islamic egalitarian spirit] was diluted. It was not, however, eliminated" (p. 41).
20. Indeed, this narrow view of the economic universe, and a restatement of the 'eighteenth century heresy', is regarded as a supreme achievement of economics in Arrow and Hahn (1971) definitive text: "There is by now a long and fairly imposing line of economists from Adam Smith to the present who have sought to show that a decentralized economy motivated by self-interest and guided by price signals would be compatible with a coherent disposition of economic resources that could be regarded, in a well-defined sense, as superior to a large class of possible alternative dispositions" (p. VI).
21. The Qur'ānic verse corresponding to the statement in the text is: "O believers, you should not usurp unjustly the wealth of each other, but trade by mutual consent; and do not destroy yourselves. God is merciful to you" (4:29). Three points may be noted here: (a) the alternative to "trade by mutual consent" is to "usurp unjustly the wealth of others"; (b) the former is just while the latter is unjust; (c) the former saves men/women from the destruction caused by indulging in the latter.
22. The Qur'ānic verse in support of the statement in the text is: "They ask you of what they should give in charity. Tell them: 'What you can spare of your wealth as should benefit the parents, the relatives, the orphans, the needy, the wayfarers, for God is not unaware of the good deeds you do'" (2:215).
23. A person's preferences are seen over *comprehensive* outcomes if the act of choice is *included* in the maximand; but not if these are only *culmination* outcomes, *not* counting the act of choice. The latter is the standard *optimisation* exercise done to determine the rationality of individual behaviour in neo-classical economics. However, this is not correct because (volitional) maximisation in economics is not like the non-volitional maximisation in physics and related disciplines [Sen (1999); p. 745].

24. The Qur'ānic verses corresponding to the statement in the text are: (a) "Whoever preserves himself from his own greed will be prosperous" (59:9); (b) "The semblance of those who expend their wealth in the way of God is that of a grain of corn from which grow seven ears, each ear containing a hundred grains" (2:261).
25. Kuran (1995) has criticised Islamic economics for "countering a key element of modern social thought [that selfish actions can, and often do, end up serving the social good] by reviving a very old belief pattern – one that is traceable to Aristotle's teachings on the household" (p. 398). However, the analysis presented in the text shows that, at least, in this respect – namely, in pointing out the untenability of the amorality of neo-classical (even classical) economics – Islamic economists have anticipated much of modern debate on the issue. The reason is that the connection between religion and economics focuses the mind, as nothing else does, on the inevitability of introducing moral considerations in the economic calculus as well.
26. The relevant Qur'ānic verses are those given in notes 11 (a); 17 (a); 11 (c).
27. The Qur'ānic verses supporting the statements in the text are: (a) "He who has more integrity has indeed greater honour with God" (49:13); (b) "so that it [i.e., wealth] does not concentrate in the hands of those who are rich among you" (59:7); (c) "To those who accumulate gold and silver, and do not spend in the way of God, announce the news of painful punishment" (9:34); (d) "And leave those to Me – the lovers of ease and comfort – and bear them for a while" (73:11); and (e) "when We destroy a human habitation, We send Our command to warn its people living a life of ease; and when they disobey, the sentence against them is justified, and We destroy them utterly" (17:16).
28. It should be obvious that in this respect the position taken by some Muslim scholars is not correct. Thus, for instance, Sayyid Quṭb (1976): "Islam does of course, recognize the principle of equality in opportunity, and the principle of justice among all" (p. 129). But these are obviously contradictory statements. Indeed, the former principle would *not* normally imply the latter outcome. On the other hand, it would require that if, initially, there are substantial inequalities of income and wealth, these must be redressed by *unequal* opportunities, *more* for the poor and *less* for the rich.
29. The Qur'ānic verse is: "There is not a creature that moves on the earth whose nourishment is not provided by God..." (11:6).
30. Abū Dharr, a distinguished Muslim egalitarian and a Companion of the Prophet, was opposed to the confiscation of private property

by the state. According to him, Islam insists on *collective* ownership and not *state* ownership of private property (especially in land). The Holy Qur'ān prohibits arbitrary confiscation of one's private property: "And do not consume each other's wealth in vain, nor offer it to men in authority with the intent of usurping unlawfully and knowingly a part of the wealth of others" (2:188). This verse makes it clear that (powerful) individuals cannot usurp other individual's wealth with the explicit intent of hurting them. The same observation applies to the powers of the state with respect to the property of its citizens. However, it does not prohibit regulating private property rights with a view to enhancing social weal.

31. The reason for the statement in the text is that even if the income of the poor is rising faster than the income of the rich, the absolute gap between them will *not* begin to narrow until the ratio of their wealth holdings is equal to the inverse ratio of the growth rates of their relative incomes. For a detailed proof, see Naqvi and Qadir (1985) and Naqvi (1997).
32. Nomani and Rahnema (1994) give an illuminating account of the *post*-Revolution differences of opinion on the question of land reforms. Of special interest in this context is the role of the *'ulamā'*, who have taken sides in this debate. Thus, for instance, "the landlords managed to obtain some *fatwās* (formal religious proclamations)...*against* land distribution" (p. 166; emphasis added). The issue still remains undecided, having become an on-going "debate between members of parliament and the Guardianship Council" (p. 166).
33. This scepticism about the government's role in promoting social good goes back at least to the 'Abbāsid period when a fundamental conflict of the worldviews led to "a struggle between the Caliphate and the urban *'ulamā'* communities over the contents of the Islamic belief, religious authority and the role of the Caliphate in the governance of the Muslim community" [Lapidus (1997); p. 123].
34. Chapra (1993) – who himself advocates land reforms to supplement the Islamic Law of Inheritance (p. 76) – cites a large number of Muslim scholars, including Mawdūdī, who had earlier opposed the imposition of limits on land holding (p. 144; footnote 5) but have since revised their opinion in this regard. See also [Siddiqi (1981); p. 9] on this.
35. Kuran (1995) cites some examples of an overly conservative interpretation of the Islamic Law by the *'ulamā'*. There are some among them according to whom "the Islamic injunction against excessive consumption puts no limits on wealth accumulation" (p. 166). The anti-egalitarian conservative religious opinion often draws

strength from a misinterpretation of some of the Qur'ānic verses: (a) "It is He who made you trustees on the earth, and exalted some of you in rank over others in order to try you by what He has given you" (6:165); (b) "Are they the ones who dispense the favour of your Lord? It is He who apportions the means of livelihood among them in this world, and raises some in position over the others to make some others submissive. The favours of your Lord are better than what they amass" (43:32). However, even a cursory reading of these verses should show that the Holy Qur'ān, while recognising a social reality (that some are rich while others are poor, with the latter serving the former), gives a strong warning to those who make this a pretext for perpetuating an unjust social order in which the rich "amass" wealth at the expense of the poor. Such social differences are Allah's way to "try" those who use their positions unjustly; with the explicit warning that those who fail the test would be punished *both* in this world and in the hereafter. At any rate, none of these verses bespeak an unalterable Natural Order based on social injustice; nor do they prohibit redistributive changes to redress such injustices.

36. The Qur'ānic verses in support of the claims made in the text are: (a) "But when He tries him by restraining his means [i.e., making him poor] he says: 'My Lord despises me'; No. In fact, you are not generous to the orphans, nor do you urge one another to feed the poor, and devour inheritance greedily, and love wealth with all your heart" (89:16-20); (b) "But if the people of these regions had believed and feared God, We would surely have showered on them blessings of heavens and the earth, but they only denied, and We punished them for their deeds" (7:96).

37. Mawdūdī (1976) citing from the Holy Qur'ān and *Ḥadīth* clearly states that: "if a Muslim comes to know that a person is without the basic necessities of life; then, irrespective of whether he asks for assistance or not, it is the duty of the rich to give all help that he needs; and that "the Islamic State should support those who have nobody to support them" (p. 31).

38. The Qur'ānic verses corresponding to the text are: (a) "O believers! do not nullify your charity by giving to oblige and flaunting (your favours) like a man who spends his wealth only to show off..." (2:264); and (b) "Saying a word that is kind and forgiving is better than charity that hurts" (2:263).

39. On this there seems to be widespread agreement. The Islamic Ideology Council, Pakistan (1992) clearly states that the state is responsible for arranging the necessary assistance to the poor if the *zakāt* funds are not enough to do the job. In this context, it cites the

unanimous opinion of the Companions of the Holy Prophet that *Allah has earmarked in the wealth of the rich the amount required to meet the needs of the poor*. The reason is that if the poor go hungry and naked it is because the rich are not discharging their social responsibility (p. 82). Sayyid Quṭb (2000) states that *zakāt* is "the lowest limit of the statutory duties on property...it gives the ruler wide powers to assign levies on capital..." (p. 167).

40. To take only two representative specimens of the liberalist's (unacceptable) thinking: Hayek (1960) maintains that it is incorrect "to suggest that those who are poor, merely in the sense that there are those in the same community who are richer, are *entitled to a share in the wealth of the latter*..."; and that the "principle of distributive justice...would produce a kind of society which in all essential respects would be the opposite of a free society" (pp. 100-101; italics added].
41. The point has been made by Rodinson (1978) that the Holy Qur'ān neither prescribes nor prohibits (capitalist) development. Thus "as for the ideological resistance to the constant driving for profit, the driving force of capitalism ... there was certainly less of it in the Islamic World than in the Christian West..." Indeed, since the emphasis in Islam is on the good use to be made of one's possession and not, as in Christianity, on the lack of it, Islamic values are "more favourable to economic expansion than that of the Christian theologians" (p. 108).
42. Ahmad (1976) emphasises that to ensure economic growth, among other factors, "production would be concerned with things which are useful for man in the light of the value pattern of Islam..." (p. 181).
43. Every Muslim is enjoined to pray: "O Lord, give me greater knowledge" (20: 114). Also knowledge (*'ilm*) is the second most cited word after Allah in the Holy Qur'ān.
44. In al-Ghazālī's essentially static scheme of the objectives of Islamic Law (*maqāṣid al-Sharī'ah*) the "preservation" of wealth cannot be interpreted to mean its growth over time as well.
45. In this context, Weber's thesis about the *uniqueness* of Protestant ethics as more congenial than other religious traditions (including Islam's) is highly suspect. For, as Rodinson (1978) has shown, Islamic values are also not inimical to growth.
46. An outstanding example of this logically invalid reasoning is the near-unanimous recommendation of Muslim jurists and Islamic economists that the profit-and-loss sharing (PLS) principle is the *only* one that guarantees both the efficiency and equity of economic outcomes. Even though the PLS principle has already lost out in

the process of 'natural selection' by financial institutions and consumers, it is still argued that the fault is one of implementing it and not of the principle which being firmly based in Islamic Law could *not* go wrong [Naqvi (2000)].

47. To continue the argument in note 45, if it can be logically and empirically established that a PLS-only system tends to concentrate income and wealth in the hands of the (rich) risk-takers and that it exposes the economic system to instability, it should be possible to amend the principle suitably to avoid these adverse consequences (see Chapter 6 for more details).

48. It was decided by the *'ulamā'* in the second and third centuries (A.H.) that "because the principles on which this logical structure was built up were immutable, so also the system itself, once formulated, was ... immutable, and indeed ... divinely inspired as the sources from which it was drawn. From that day to this, the *Sharī'ah* or *Shar'*, as it is called, the 'Highway' of divine command and guidance, has remained in essentials unchanged" [Gibb (1975); p. 64].

49. The comment in the text is not intended to diminish the greatness of al-Ghazālī, which rests on his success in synthesising such diverse fields of knowledge as philosophy, theology, law and mysticism, achieving an unparalleled degree of unity and harmony in the fundamentals of faith, and presenting a picture of Islam that was acceptable to religious opinion at the time. From his work "emerged the image of a new organism, a complete body with mysticism or Sufism as the heart, theology as the head, philosophy as its rationality binding the different parts together, and law as the working limbs. Islamic civilization had come to maturity," [Glasse' (1989); p. 138]. Also, contrary to popular belief, his denigration of the philosophers (in his masterly *Tahāfut al-falāsifah*) was *not* directed to their contribution to natural sciences which he praised, but to the worthlessness of metaphysics in finding the truth about faith. Also, "the intellectual flowering of the Earlier Middle Ages" took al-Ghazālī's synthesis of *kalām, falsafah,* and Sufism [Hodgson (1974b); p. 192}.

50. It will be recalled from Chapter 2, that the basic idea of the two-stage scheme to devise fair rules of justice is due to Rawls (1971; 1999); but the requirement that the impartiality of the 'process' is met at the constitution-making stage is due to Buchanan and Tullock (1962). However, Buchanan and Tullock hope (vainly, in my view) that once the constitution-making is done the working of the economy can be left to self-interested individuals, who will respect the rules for distributive justice agreed at the constitution-making stage. The argument in the text borrows only the very broad ideas

from these contrasting theories – contrasting, because the former is normative theory while the latter is a positive one.

51. Thus, Taleghani (1982) states: "On the principle that the earth and all resources belong to everyone ... the state, the guardian and the representative of the general welfare, has the rights of supervision and distribution" (p. 29). Similarly, Shafī' (1968) states: "Islam ... has not permitted any individual or group to have a monopoly over the primary source of wealth, but has given every member of the society an equal right to derive benefit from them" (p. 9).
52. Sen (1981) shows that most famines and extreme starvation have occurred when there is no shortage of the supply of food grains. In such situations, safeguarding the rights of the individuals to hoard food will clearly be an illegitimate use of government's authority.

CHAPTER 5

An Islamic Ethical System: Continuity and Change

I. Introduction

The analysis presented in the preceding chapter suggests that it is important to have an Islamic ethical *system* to systematise diverse Islamic ethical teachings, make them implementable, and light up areas where misinterpretations have taken away their clarity and forthrightness. It should also help evaluate the Islamic credentials of new thinking about ethics and economics with a view to broadening the scope of traditional knowledge. In this manner the Islamic ethical system can be sensitised to modern ethical and economic concerns, *without losing its religious credentials.* The italicised proviso is fundamental because it is only with the spiritual strength of religio-moral convictions that people agree to make the sacrifices needed to bring about socio-economic changes that uproot established institutions and familiar modes of thought. The converse of this statement is also true: cataclysmic changes succeed in re-establishing new social equations, propitious for a humane existence *only* when these are helped, not hindered, by universally accepted religious moral values.

Fogel (2000) attributes the emergence of the modern egalitarian ethic in the United States to radical changes in the Christian theological principles rather than to any advances in economic theory (p. 117). This has been true of Muslim societies as well whenever they decided to change the course of Muslim history: in each case religious beliefs have quickened the pace of social, political and economic events.[1] True, in such cases, Islamic moral values did not have to undergo a change of the same order of magnitude as Christian values had to; yet the former too had to be refocused by throwing off the excess baggage of some conservative interpretations. To make such events happen again, the centuries-old belief in predestination and the denial of human freedom and social responsibility, both of which are repugnant to Islam, must be finally put aside to pave the way for political, economic, and moral regeneration and growth.[2] The lesson is that the necessary flexibility in traditional thinking must be introduced, and the commitment to human freedom renewed to satisfy the imperatives of social change. To usher in an Islamic Renaissance we should draw on the traditional wisdom to the extent that it is relevant, borrow from secular knowledge and ethical knowledge, and learn from Western religious traditions. It is important that attachment to the fundamentals of faith is neither allowed to degenerate into a false belief in intellectual and moral self-sufficiency, nor be mistaken as a licence for free-wheeling intellectualism.[3]

II. The Nature of Islamic Morality

A few preliminary remarks are in order to clarify the nature of Islamic morality. Firstly, a confidence in the veracity of Islamic moral beliefs is not to assert its complete exclusivity; nor does it necessarily imply a total rejection of modern (secular) ethical thinking, or even of Western religious morality. As shown in the preceding chapter, the latter can help crystallise Islamic ethical thinking, analyse in greater fullness its moral and economic implications, and help *create new knowledge which is socially relevant, yet religiously authentic.* But, to this end, Islamic moral values should be treated as scientific statements whose worth can be established, theoretically and empirically, in specific institutional contexts. This is especially the case when, in the absence of historical precedence and because of doctrinal ambiguity, the Islamic point of view needs to be re-focused on foundational economic, social and moral issues.

Secondly, religious values must not become fossilised doctrinal structures, with no evolutionary possibilities. Instead, they should be flexible enough to respond creatively to new political, social, moral, and economic challenges. Thus, for instance, traditional ethical principles, formulated a thousand years or so ago when the Age of Reason in the Muslim world was succeeded by doctrinal rigidity and religious superstition, are prime candidates for revision in modern times. A key element in systematic thinking about basic ethical principles is a willingness to evaluate its social and economic worth. To this end, a two-way interdependence between ethics and economics should be established to 'operationalise' the former and 'moralise' the latter – both of which are vital to human well-being.

Thirdly, Islamic moral exhortations must be axiomatised to turn them into an operational ethical system which can generate principles of sufficient generality to be able to deal with even those problems which traditional religious ethics does not explicitly address, or those where the Holy Qur'ān is reasonably explicit but subsequent interpretations of it have obfuscated the original message – e.g., social and political equality between men and women, economic growth, human development, etc.[4] A systematic and internally consistent procedure, rather than a mere cataloguing of moral precepts, is required to stick together diverse Islamic teachings on the central issues of human existence, and extend their reach and salience by using universally accepted rules of logical deduction. There is yet another philosophical point in this context. It is that the efficient working of the systems of governance requires only a *minimum* number of ethical rules. An uncompromising insistence on moral perfectibility would be a counter-productive exercise.

Finally, as emphasised in the preceding chapter, Islamic Law should be reinterpreted to make explicit its underlying moral objectives (*maqāṣid*), i.e., to facilitate economic and social progress and create the necessary motivational momentum to make individuals work for the common good in Muslim societies. This is a vital consideration because Islamic Law *is* taken seriously by Muslims in regulating their economic and social behaviour, and is *the* medium through which Islamic ethical values can play a beneficial social role.[5] But, the problem is that the traditional *maqāṣid* themselves need to be restated, as part of a wider 'endogenous' process of intellectual and moral regeneration, to meet the vastly different needs of modern Muslim societies. The present chapter shows the way to solve this problem.

III. The Axiomatisation of Islamic Ethics

The problem is, essentially, to find a set of ethical principles which faithfully reflect the Islamic ideals, and devise a scientific mechanism to generalise the known Islamic positions on specific situations about an (idealised) Islamic economy. Al-Ghazālī (d. 1111) and later al-Shāṭibī (1388), keeping in view the requirements of their time, attempted to prepare just such a list of Islamic ethical principles *(maqāṣid al-Sharī'ah)* to relate Islamic Law to its presumed benefits or consequences. In modern terminology, the purpose of *maqāṣid* is to make Islamic Law consequence-sensitive. This implies, among other things, that the former is a separate entity in its own right which provides the basis of amending the latter as circumstances, time, and institutional framework change. They identified five basic ethical values: faith, life, progeny, intellect and wealth.[6] It is interesting that al-Shāṭibī derived these principles from a collective understanding of the Qur'ānic injunctions, even though none of these principles are listed as such in the Holy Qur'ān. He further claimed that "such conclusion and positions that are so established are the general premises and overriding objectives of *Sharī'ah* and thus have a higher order of importance than specific rules" [Kamali (1999); p. 203]. This list of principles is obviously of considerable theological interest, but is not much use in deriving any meaningful economic statements in the modern context, especially if the order in which they are stated is an integral part of the scheme.[7] Thus, an uncritical acceptance of these principles and their ordering is likely to introduce contradictions in public policy, both if they are introduced sequentially, or if implemented simultaneously. Furthermore, al-Shāṭibī's insistence that this list is final (*qaṭ'ī*) for all times further reduces its utility. Yet, his method of scientific enquiry – using general principles to derive specific statements of Islamic Law and regarding the former as prior to the latter – is an important insight. This is the broad approach of this section as well.[8]

i) *On Axiomatising An Ethical System*

Following al-Ghazālī's and al-Shāṭibī's bold generalisations, we derive a set of Islamic ethical principles (axioms) of sufficient generality, from which a large number of specific statements about economic issues can be deduced. Before we do this, it is important to recapitulate the relevant aspects of deductive logic. The general principle here is that the axioms themselves are reached, as Einstein put it, through informed intuition about the 'universe' in question; and that these are not derivable from particular statements, the latter being of a lower order of generality. Given this principle, the following procedure must be followed to prepare a list of valid axioms: (a) in most social and economic situations, the set of chosen axioms must be a *plurality*. This is because, contrary to the standard philosophical reductionist procedure, it is not particularly useful in economics, or even in ethics, to 'reduce' the list of axioms to just one 'original' cause when the existence of more than one original cause is normal.[9] (b) Having said that, a number of axioms must be found which can serve as a *basis*.[10] The aim is to use this basis to generate a wide variety of empirically *falsifiable* statements of sufficient generality about economic and ethical matters.[11] (c) The basis should contain only a *minimum* number of axioms to avoid making redundant, even logically inconsistent, statements about the same, or similar, issues. If the number of axioms were not a minimum then for every axiom in the set there will exist another axiom 'outside' the list to serve the same purpose. (d) The list of axioms should be an *adequate* representation of the Islamic viewpoint on ethical and economic issues.[12] This is essential to form a consensus of scholarly opinion on the chosen axioms. (e) The axiom system should be *comprehensive* enough to include both its *process* aspects and the *opportunity* aspects.[13] An example should make clear the importance of this distinction. As between the non-consequentialist moral philosophy (e.g., Nozick's, Hayek's) and the strictly consequentialist moral philosophy (e.g., the Benthamite Utilitarianism), the former aims to satisfy only the process (or the procedural) aspects of the chosen moral principle, unmindful of its social, economic consequences; while the latter insists only on the consequences of the principle, disregarding the procedures. The point here is that the chosen axioms should pay attention to both these aspects. (f) Each element of the axiom system must be *independent* of every other element in the set in the sense that *no* element of the system is derivable from any other of its elements. This is really common sense. If an element of an axiom system is derivable from any other in the set, then it is a candidate for elimination from the *basis*, which comprises only linearly independent vectors (see note 10). (g) Yet another indispensable property of a logically valid axiom system is that each of its elements is *consistent* with every other element in the system. Indeed, this is a requirement of sanity, because the existence of an inconsistent element in the set will reduce it to pure 'noise', i.e., an inconsistent axiom system can be made to yield any number of statements we please, depending on our subjective preferences/tastes. A proof of the consistency property simply checks that the truth and falsity of a statement are not asserted in the same breath, so to speak. In other words, the truth of one element should not be denied by any other axiom in the set. (h) The system should be *sufficient* to generate all the possible statements belonging to the axiom system, and exclude all superfluous assumptions.

The general purpose of these conditions, which make an ethical system truly 'fertile', is that it does the job it is required to do – i.e., of deriving statements of lower order of generality from axioms of higher order of generality – efficiently and reliably, without being contradictory and superfluous. Thus, it is not permissible to *add* to the chosen ethical system any number of axioms to the selected minimum number in an arbitrary fashion. The *only* way to do it is to check whether the conditions mentioned in the preceding paragraph are still met each time an axiom is added to (or subtracted from) the set. If these conditions are not met then this is a proof that the proposed system is not complete in the sense stated above. The procedure to decide on the exact number of axioms in the set is, therefore, not guesswork; it requires doing some systematic thinking about it. Each time such a procedure is repeated its validity must be proved by following the above-noted general principles.

ii) *The Axiomatised Islamic Ethical System*[14]

The preceding analysis makes clear the inadequacy of the simple assertion that Islamic economics reflect its moral values. It is obvious enough once it is stated, as has been done repetitively, that Islam's is a complete way of life of which its economic aspect is a sub-set. Reflecting these moral values in economic decisions is, however, a step further, and a non-trivial undertaking; it takes turning an unwieldy catalogue of ethical values into a countable number of axioms, which then form an ethical *system*. The main attraction of such an exercise is that it makes modern methods of scientific reasoning accessible to Islamic economics.

It is asserted here that a complete and consistent Islamic ethical axiom *system*, in the meaning of the term defined above, comprises exactly four elements: (a) unity (*tawḥīd*); (b) equilibrium (*al-'adl wa al-iḥsān*); (c) free will (*ikhtiyār*); (d) responsibility (*farḍ*). Each of these elements of the system has been selected by reference to "informed intuition" about widely held Islamic beliefs, philosophy of life, and the centrality of human reason – all of which are highlighted in the Holy Qur'ān. However, these axioms are used here *not* as a set of theological beliefs (which these undoubtedly are) but to serve as higher-order generalisations from which specific statements of a lower order generality can be *deduced* about the moral imperatives which motivate individuals to work for social good in an Islamic economy.

a) *Unity* (Tawḥīd)

Unity is the supreme attribute of Allah and denotes both a "metaphysical truth and a living spiritual reality…" [Nasr (1987); p. 313]. It is also the central concept of Islamic ethics, symbolising "a unitary and a purposive will creative of order in the universe" [Rahman (1979); p. 34]. By the same token, all human activity, secular and spiritual, is unified and integrated into a mutually supportive totality. An all-embracing overarching unitary vision of social processes informs human action with a sense of morality on the one hand and invests him/her with a voluntary *commitment* to working for the social good. Within this holistic framework of thought material good 'effortlessly' translates into spiritual bliss – effortlessly, because achieving the former directly contributes to success in the latter. An unconditional surrender to Allah links all human beings to Him on an equal footing and makes them equal to each other.[15] This is the *vertical dimension* of Islam. Its unifying force works not only for the Muslim society but throughout the world, beckoning different peoples, races, nations and tribes, men and women to the common goal of mutual understanding and universal peace, without discrimination.[16] Thanks to it, a society of diverse people is transformed into a *fraternity*, i.e., the more prosperous members of which are inclined to share their wealth and power with the poor and the weak.

There are at least three elements in this unitary framework which play a central role in refocusing human motivation towards common good: (a) Allah's Omniscience; (b) His Omnibenevolence; and (c) His Ownership of all things.[17] The perception is one of the essential *relativity* of humankind's knowledge and worth to Allah's absolute knowledge of all things and His benevolence. Also emphasised is the limited nature of the human ownership of wealth in relation to Allah's absolute ownership. These perceptions instil into the human mind humility, frugality, and altruism in place of arrogance, extravagance, and cupidity. Human consciousness is raised to a higher plane which guarantees the stability of the social fabric because people then become voluntarily committed to achieving the central goals of human happiness. In short, "unity determines not only the doctrine and the organization of society but also the entire life of the individual and in particular his piety...." [Schuon (1987); p. 49].

b) *Equilibrium* (Al-'Adl wa al-Iḥsān)

If unity is the vertical dimension of Islam, then equilibrium (*al-'adl wa al-iḥsān*) constitutes its *horizontal dimension*.[18] On the plane of social existence all things exhibit in relation to each other a kind of (approximate) dynamic equilibrium, a perpetual movement towards human betterment (*aṣlaḥ*). Thus, for instance, the benefits and costs of any scheme of social cooperation must be shared in proportion to the contribution made by each participant. This is *al-'adl*, which indicates balance and reciprocity in human relations. But society must also make provision for those who, because of their physical disability or whatever, cannot reciprocate in equal measure the benefits accruing to them from social cooperation nor bear its costs. This is *iḥsān* – which Murata and Chittick (2000) translate as "to do that which is beautiful, or to make beautiful" (p. 269). The latter requirement is that the poor and the weak should receive *more* than their share in social cooperation in order to achieve an overall social equality of the human condition. It makes human societies caring, considerate and beautiful in the Qur'ānic sense of informing humankind with a sense of commitment to the "oppressed in earth". Together, these principles show what is so distinctive about the Islamic moral vision: this overarching concept of social justice indicates both a *state* of equality as well as a *process* of making people equal in their access to the fruits of economic and social progress. The latter characteristic underscores the importance of ensuring that the chosen principles of social justice are *seen* as just by the individuals in a society to elicit their support for them. An essential feature of social justice in this sense is that the least-privileged in society are rewarded in proportion to their *needs* and not on the basis of a *quid pro quo* from them. It also signifies a just ordering of all legal, political and economic social institutions, determines a fair system of social rewards and incentives, and provides for a corrective mechanism to bring the system back to a just state if it is unjust to begin with. The provision of a corrective mechanism is an integral part of a just society and is important because the antonym of *al-'adl* is *ẓulm,* which denotes a perverse flow of resources *from* the poor *to* the rich. This situation obviously requires correction because it is in clear violation of the Qur'ānic injunction that wealth should not concentrate in the hands of the rich. By the same token, meritocracy and feudalism denote *ẓulm* because these social systems directly contribute to extreme inequalities of social, political and economic conditions.

Whence follows that to provide only for "equality of opportunity" for all would essentially be a *perverse* social arrangement. The supporting argument that 'natural' differential in intellectual endowments and abilities must be unequally rewarded ignores that the circumstances of birth and early nurture of different individuals in society contribute significantly to the existing differentials between them. What appears as innocuously 'natural' – i.e., the reward for greater merit must also be greater – is *not* just. Indeed, the equality-of-opportunity principle is an example of true and deep compassion for humanity surrendering to hypocritical pragmatism. It is really common sense that people should *not* be rewarded for the differentials in their abilities *caused* by initial advantages for which they are not responsible, and that the consequences of initial social injustice must be redressed, not exacerbated. A consistent application of the twin principles of *al-'adl* and *iḥsān* would redress the initial (unearned) advantages to put all people on the same 'line'. There is another important application of these principles: it is that it calls for maintaining equity within a generation and between generations. The full implications of this remark will be worked out later in this chapter.

c) *Free Will* (Ikhtiyār)

Man is born with free will, unburdened by innate human depravity or original sin; and *not* chained to predestination. He is *the* author of all of his actions, the wielder of the God-given power of reason, and the maker of choice – which exalts humankind over all His creation. Armed with such extensive powers, he enjoys the exalted status of Allah's viceroy on earth.[19] "Gifted with intelligence ... he alone of all creatures is capable of knowing the Reality of which he himself is a manifestation..." [Eaton (1987); p. 358]. He is free to use his freedom to do good and achieve the *virtuality* of Allah's vicegerency; or go astray from the "Right Path" and become the lowest of the low – or, as the great Mu'tazilah scholar al-Jubbā'ī' put it, *Qudratun 'alayh wa 'alā ḍiddih* (see note 36). The guidance from Allah comes when it does; but it is conditional on Man "putting his own house in order", so to speak.[20] This is the Islamic concept of *ikhtiyār*, which guarantees human freedom as the individualist's *birthright*. It implies that human beings cannot sit idly and still expect Allah to make choices for them. They should *act* for their own betterment as well as to enhance social welfare. Indeed, "those who sought to escape action, taking refuge in divine omnipotence, were repudiated [by the Holy Qur'ān]" [Rahman (1979); p. 85]. However, *ikhtiyār* must *not* be confused with *tafwīḍ*, which is *not* allowed in Islam: the former denotes "the freedom of human will", while the latter signifies "unqualified discretion in the choice of wrong and right". In other words, while man is free to take the road to vicegerency or to self-destruction, yet he is denied the right to turn "evil into good or sin into virtue" [cited in Ali (1988); p. 339]. The point is that it is within the parameters of right and wrong laid down by Allah that man's free will can be exercised.

Whence follows that Islam would deny the contractarian concept of the absolute autonomy of the individual.[21] The Islamic position contrasts sharply with that taken, for instance, by Kant – namely, that men/women themselves choose the guiding principles of their action as the most adequate expression of being free and rational persons [Murphy (1970)].[22] The relativity of the freedom that human beings enjoy in Islam means that he/she will not voluntarily transgress the social limits on individual freedom. The same is the Islamic stance with respect to the ownership of wealth, which too is relative to Allah's absolute ownership. The purpose of imposing constraints in both cases is not to take away human freedom or his right to ownership on the pretext of Allah's ownership.[23] It is rather to prevent humankind from arbitrary social behaviour. In the first case, the purpose is to restrain him/her from undermining the very foundations of morality and civilised behaviour, and to achieve "success" by not becoming a slave to avarice and greed.[24] In the second case, the aim is to prohibit the squandering of wealth and depriving the poor of their due. These constraints on human freedom are ways of winning the "moral struggle" and successfully resolving innate "moral tensions that are necessary for creative human action" [Rahman (1979); p. 35]. And, yet notwithstanding these constraints, human beings have it within them to go astray from the Right Path and destroy themselves. In both cases, the ultimate choice is theirs.

However, in practice, there is not much difference between the Islamic position on the relativity of individual freedom and the Western concept of absolute autonomy because individual freedom to own wealth and spend it is constrained by the latter as well (quite severely in the Scandinavian Welfare States) through fiscal devices. Yet social tensions have arisen in the West from a belief in absolute human autonomy because religious ethical values (including Christian and Jewish values) are then ignored in the name of individual freedom. This sets the individual's sense of morality at variance with the social sense of morality. To give an example, men/women exercising their autonomy, can take their own lives *even though* Western society also prohibits such practice. Similarly, individuals believing in their absolute ownership of wealth (presumably under the influence of liberalist ideas) may squander it on trivia and yet the government's attempt to constrain this right is resisted (through powerful lobbies). Obviously, such tensions between the individual and society can be greatly decreased if religious morality emphasises the idea of trusteeship and is explicitly understood by the individual and reflected in public policy in that sense. There is yet another dimension to the problem: it is that in a democratic society (which Islam also prescribes) sometimes a belief in absolute individual autonomy gets translated into arbitrary social legislation. Two examples should illustrate this point: the permission recently given in some Western democracies to same-sex marriages, and the recognition to take one's life in some circumstances.

Hirsch (1977; 1995) shows that modern developed economies are operating less efficiently and equitably than they could because the "individualistic, rationalistic base of market [has] undermined the unseen religious support" (p. 143). In other words, *any* society, Muslim or non-Muslim, functions better, more 'naturally', and with a lesser incidence of coercion if religious ethical values are made explicit rather than kept implicit, so that they are observed by the people. As to the observation that the (religiously oriented) Muslim societies are much worse than the secular Western societies in terms of their social behaviour, the answer is that when this is the case it is not the fault of the Islamic principles but that of the Muslim's deviant practices. Indeed, it is one of the tragedies of Muslim societies that they themselves have let down their superior ethical values. The reasons for this perverse behaviour are many; but for this state of affairs, highly conservative interpretations of Islamic ethical values must take a significant part of the blame. In the present context, the substitution of the principle of predestination for the true Islamic principle of free will has greatly undermined the forces of activism and innovation since the Middle Ages.[25] While the influence of these ideas has greatly diminished, yet these are still common currency in ultra-conservative religious circles.

There is yet another important dimension of the Islamic concept of free will and the derivative notion of human freedom. It is that these include the more substantive economic freedoms as well and not just political freedoms. Furthermore, in Islam (as also in Christianity and Judaism), the poverty of the soul is regarded as no less devastating than material poverty. Freedom from want, poverty, and avarice are, therefore, integral parts of the Islamic concept of freedom. This point is reinforced by the explicit Qur'ānic perception that the poor have an acknowledged share in the wealth of the rich and a right to a minimum decent standard of living. In other words, in Muslim societies, they are entitled to freedom from hunger and starvation *both on legal and moral grounds* – legal, because such freedom is their God-given right; and moral, because the state of poverty also denotes the spiritual bankruptcy of rich peoples and nations. Similarly, when the individual's right to health care and education is denied, it bespeaks moral poverty as well, for the observance of the sanctity of life and being knowledgeable are the most distinguishing attributes of a good Muslim (and of all human beings) [Naqvi *et al.* (1980; 1984)].

Two additional clarifications of the Islamic concept of freedom are in order. Firstly, Allah's omniscience does not detract from the freedom to make a choice between alternative courses open to an individual. Secondly, and this is important from the practical point of view, the *fact* that Divine guidance sheds light on what is right and what is wrong in no way diminishes the uncertainty facing the individual in making the 'right' choice; nor, for this reason, would the demands on human ingenuity to 'face the music', so to speak, be any the less. With few exceptions, Divine guidance is broad enough to leave enough room for reasoned choice about the most appropriate course of action in specific situations. And the risk of failure is not lessened just because this possibility is also within the purview of Allah's omniscience.

d) *Responsibility* (Farḍ)

Once it is accepted that man is the creator of *all* his actions, his total responsibility for these actions and his liability to reward and punishment for what he does follow as a logically corollary. This is because "obligation and sanction can only be understood in reference to a responsible being" [Gimaret (1993); p. 790]. Not allowed to hide behind predestination, the Holy Qur'ān unambiguously lays down that human beings are free to choose between good and evil and that their's is the responsibility for the consequences of the choices they make.[26] In general, with free will (and, its corollary, individual freedom) goes the individual *and* social responsibility to preserve and enhance it. The reverse of this proposition is also true: the exercise of responsibility requires that men/women be free, economically, socially, and politically. The one implies the other. However, to avoid confusion, it must be immediately noted that this reciprocal relationship between freedom and responsibility does *not* mean that the two are one and the same thing. The fact of two objects being equal or inter-related does not imply that they are identical. It is, therefore, surprising that for all the clarity of the Islamic position, many a Muslim scholar and religious leader *denied*, for several centuries, both human freedom as well as human responsibility on the ground that men/women simply do (indeed, they are constrained to do) what Allah Wills them to do.[27]

But the view that freedom and responsibility are vital elements of the Islamic message has also been asserted with equal intensity throughout Muslim history. Indeed, in early theological debates among Muslim scholars, these principles were seen as directly flowing from Allah's transcendence and Unity and His being Just [Lapidus (1997); pp. 105-109; Rahman

(1979); pp. 87-94; Gimaret (1993); pp. 789-791]. The inescapable conclusion is that the denial of these Qur'ānic principles, which were widely believed by the Muslim community and the Companions of the Holy Prophet, was politically motivated. Thus, the widely respected Ḥasan al-Baṣrī (21-100/642-728), when questioned about his views in favour of human freedom and responsibility, replied: "There was none among our (Muslim) predecessors who rejected this (viz., that human beings are free to choose); nor did anybody dispute with regard to this since they were (tacitly) agreed and unambiguous about it" [cited in Rahman (1979); pp. 55-56]. At any rate, in the absence of the political compulsions of the Middle Ages which led to the formulation of the principle of predestination and the denial of the twin principles of human freedom and individual responsibility, it must now be accepted that "Man, within the limited sphere of his existence, is absolute master of his conduct. He is responsible for his actions, and for the use or misuse of the powers with which he has been endowed" [Ali (1988); p. 335].

The Islamic concept of responsibility has the following important facets. Firstly, the foundational nature of the responsibility principle flows directly from the need to introduce individual morality, especially that based on religion, as an integral part of human motivation. The assertion that the self-centred, selfish and greedy individual of neo-classical economics inevitably contributes to social good is now regarded as no more than a bad piece of economic fiction. What is special about the Islamic concept of responsibility is the intensity with which the moral motivation of human behaviour is insisted upon. It assigns a starring role to *commitment* on the ground that this is *the* rational thing to do. The point is that, in the Islamic perspective (as also otherwise), discharging one's responsibility to others is not all pain; it becomes a pleasurable act because committed behaviour is its own reward and is normally regarded as respectable in all civilised societies. Secondly, human responsibility runs in three directions simultaneously – in relation to Allah, to one's own self, and to society. And these three aspects of responsibility merge with a single goal, which is to help the poor out of love of Allah so that this act becomes *the* means to achieving spiritual ascension.[28] Thirdly, the responsibility principle is not confined to individuals alone; it extends to society as well. Unlike libertarianism, Islam does *not* make the individual solely responsible for *all* of his problems. This is because it would be unjust to hold a person entirely responsible for his poverty, as a lot of it flows from the malfunctioning of the economy. This is the reason why, in Islam, the state is made responsible, no less than rich people, for expanding people's substantive freedoms by taking steps to minimise poverty and human deprivation. In particular, it is the responsibility of the state to change the pattern of incentives – those which reward people for advantages in the acquisition of which they had no hand (i.e., being born in a rich family) – concentrate wealth in few hands, and increase poverty. The general theological principle is that individual responsibility does not exceed his capacity to bear it (*taklīf mā lā yuṭāq*); and beyond that the state must take over. Thirdly, a theological aspect of the responsibility principle, which is also relevant to the individual's motivation to do good to others, is that he is neither responsible for what others do; nor would he be held accountable for that which his forefathers did; nor is he chained to some original sin. This freedom from an irrelevant past over which individuals have no control, and from any guilt complex, conserves individual responsibility, and is one of the most original aspects of Islamic morality.[29] Fourthly, indifference to human suffering and a failure to act when circumstances do so warrant is incompatible with a free man's sense of responsibility. It is, therefore, condemned.[30] Similarly, even ritual prayers, though obligatory by virtue of human responsibility towards Allah, become unacceptable in the Eyes of God when not associated with the discharge of his/her social obligations.[31] The essence of the Islamic message is that, beyond one's personal well-being, an individual has an 'agency' aspect as well, which values personal accomplishments in terms of the achievement of universally recognised social goals.

iii) *The Historical-Doctrinal Roots of the Proposed Axiomatised Ethical System*

The preceding discussion of the Islamic axiom system should make it clear that each element of it is based on explicit Qur'ānic injunctions. But it also has a long doctrinal history behind it. It will be interesting to note in more detail the philosophical and doctrinal contents of the elements of the proposed Islamic ethical system – elements, because the *system* as given here was not proposed at the time. With the beginning of theological formalisations in the second half of the second century (A.H.), the Jabriah school of thought, reflecting the fierce Arab fatality, stressed Allah's Omnipotence more than His Justice; and took the position that Allah's Will (reflecting His Omnipotence) *directly* acts on affairs of men, being in no need of any human agency. And since His Will emanates from His Omniscience, man is bound by predestination. Whence follows that there is no free agency in men/women who, therefore, are not responsible for what they do. Since this doctrine implied that Allah is party to what humans do, including evil, it evoked a strong reaction from the piestic school of Qadariyyah and the rationalist school of the Mu'tazilah.[32] The latter, though recognising Allah's Omnipotence, put emphasis on Unity as the *only* eternal attribute of Allah, rejected an ascription of injustice to Him, and insisted that Allah does what is for the betterment of humankind. Furthermore, Allah's Omnipotence does not imply that Allah's Will is arbitrary; nor does it preclude man's freedom of will and his responsibility for what he does. The latter assertion contradicted the "coercionist" (*al-mujbirah*) thesis that acts are created by God. This is because "the only one authentically responsible for an act is the one who is the author of it in the full sense of the term; and who 'makes it to be' [Gimaret (1993); p. 790]. He has the power to act or not to act. Whence follows that man is the "creative efficient of his actions, good and bad and gets reward and punishment in the future world by merit of what he does; and that no moral evil, or inequity of action or unbelief or disobedience, can be referred to God..." [Ali (1988); p. 344]. To them "God's Unity [His Justice] and man's responsibility [along with his freedom] seemed to be the very essence of Islam itself" [Lapidus (1997); p. 106].[33] In the context of this book, the Mu'tazilah's most original contribution lay in the use of human reason to find rules of Islamic ethics. Thus, what is morally good or bad is known to us through reason and predates revelation, because man is an intelligent being. Revelation confirms this prior understanding of the good and the bad and makes knowledge more precise. It also eases the thorny path of finding the truth by reason alone. Contrary to popular misunderstanding, Mu'tazilī rationalism worked strictly within theological limits. This is to be expected because the Mu'tazilah were primarily theologians *par excellence*, and they derived their arguments from the Holy Qur'ān. Indeed, "theirs was the first overall orthodox school of theology" [Ess (1987); p. 222]. What made them rationalists was their belief that "certain awarenesses are accessible to man by means of his intelligence alone, in the absence of prior revelation" [Gimaret (1993); p. 791]. However, *they insisted on complementary, rather than competing, roles of revelation and reason*. The latter is the faculty required to grasp the possibility of making a choice between good and evil; but this faculty, or capacity, humankind receives from Allah. Their rationalism drove them to argue, from general principles, to tackle specific (theological) problems. Thus, to prove their central thesis about the absolute justice of God, they proceeded from two general principles: (a) every adjective has a cause (*'illah*); and (b) there is the analogy of the invisible to the visible (*Qiyās al-ghā'ib 'alā 'al-shāhid*). From (b) follows that God *cannot* do injustice *as we know it in this world*. The second part of the proof that Allah does only that which is morally good and is exempt from all that is morally bad also follows from (a). Similarly, the principle of free-choice (*ikhtiyār*) is proved by the general principle that the fact of a person being powerful (i.e., the power to make a choice) is established by his authority not to use this power or to choose the opposite of an act (*Qudratun 'alayh wa 'alā ḍiddih*). Once this principle is accepted, the conclusion follows that the power to act must of necessity exist *prior* to the act. This is because if the power to act comes into being concomitantly with the act itself, as their adversaries believed, then it would lead to the absurd conclusion that the fact of coming of power to man from God would *simultaneously* lead to the creation of an act as well as the fact of it not being created [Gimaret (1993); p. 789]. Even modern logic cannot do any better in terms of the tightness of the Mu'tazilah argument on this score.

However, the rationalisations of the Mu'tazilah about what God can or cannot do drew the ire of the orthodox *'ulamā'*, led by Abu'l Ḥasan al-Ash'arī (d. 330 A.H./942 A.D.).[34] He, instead, believed that revealed law is the *only* foundation of what is good and evil; and that God is necessarily just whatever He does and would be so if He acted in a contrary fashion (as it appears to us). He also pointed out the seeming incompatibility, in ordinary logic, between Allah's Omnipotence and His Omnibenevolence, reaffirmed His Omnipotence (reflected in Divine Will) in relation to the rewards and punishments for human action, and argued that His Will be accepted without further explanation, or justification.[35] But even He could not absolve humankind of its responsibility. To this end, al-Ash'arī formulated the doctrine of 'acquisition' (*kasb*). According to this doctrine, all acts are directly created by Allah Himself, but in some actions there is superadded to them a special quality of voluntary acquisition (*kasb*) which "by God's will makes the individual a voluntary agent and responsible" [Hodgson (1974); p. 442; Vol. 1]. However, if man has the consciousness of owning his acts then what prevents him from producing these acts in the first place? A direct implication of al-Ash'arī's thesis is that "all the power is referred to God while responsibility must remain with man" [Rahman (1979); p. 92]. But to argue that man can at the same time be responsible for an act and yet not be its only creator is neither just nor logical.[36]

And yet, notwithstanding its obvious weaknesses and manifest ubiquity, Ash'arite theological doctrine remained for long the official creed in the Islamic world. The subsequent refinements of the Ash'arite doctrine, e.g., by Māturīdī (d. 333/

945), allowed greater importance to the efficacy of human will, but did not much change in its overall thrust. And, somewhat paradoxically, the towering figure of al-Ghazālī (d. 505 A.H.), who opposed the Ash'arite doctrine, in the end "imparted to Ash'arism an idealism it did not previously possess", [Ali (1988); p. 386]. The paradox disappears once it is remembered that both al-Ash'arī and al-Ghazālī had a common adversary: the use of human reason in exploring the fundamentals of faith, especially about God's actions. However, the entirely *unintended* effect of these sterile theological disputes between the rationalists and the orthodox *'ulamā'* was a reinstatement of the doctrine of predestination, the progressive decline of reason and progressive thought, and the ascendancy of truculent traditionalism in the Muslim world – unintended, because al-Ghazālī did *not* rule out the importance of reason (philosophy) in natural sciences. Indeed, in some extreme conservative theological formulations, reason was succeeded by superstition. Even as Allah's Will in smaller minds overshadowed His *'Adl* (Justice), new arguments were advanced to discredit the principles of human free will and responsibility as well. For instance, Fakhr al-Dīn al-Rāzī advanced the argument that human beings cannot even own their acts – as was allowed by the Ash'arite principle of *kasb* – because they cannot anticipate all the consequences of their actions. But this argument is entirely specious because, as we know now, *complete* information about the consequences of one's actions is neither a necessary nor a sufficient condition for human beings to create specific acts; and much less information would be needed to 'own' them.

Fortunately, since the thirteenth century A.H. (nineteenth century A.D.), there has been some serious challenge to the Ash'arite literalism, anti-rationalism, and its status-quo preserving tendencies. Ahmad Amin (1936), a leading Egyptian scholar, stated: "In my opinion, the demise of Mut'azilism was the greatest misfortune to have afflicted Muslims", and Zahid Hussain (1947) regards the decline of the Mu'tazilah as the "victory of obscurantism" [both cited in Gimaret (1993); p. 786].[37] What they bemoan is the decline of rational thinking in general, and in religious matters in particular. Happily too a more guarded Mu'tazilah rational approach was revived by such scholars as Shaykh Muhammad 'Abduh of Egypt, Zia Gokalp of Turkey and Jamāl al-Dīn al-Afghānī, Sir Syed Ahmad Khan, Allama Muhammad Iqbal, and Syed Ameer Ali of Pakistan. More relevant in the present context is that there is now a broad agreement about each of the elements of the axiom system presented in the preceding section – namely, that Unity is the eternal attribute of Allah, that He is Just (*Al-'Adl*) by His Nature, that man is born free; and that he is responsible for all his acts, good or evil. There is an urgent need to cement this consensus, which conveys the correct vision of socio-economic processes that the Holy Qur'ān offers to humanity, and reflect it in the Islamic Law in order to mobilise public opinion in support of the progressive forces of reason and against doctrinal obscurantism. Perhaps this is the only thing to retain from the doctrinal debates of the Middle Ages – namely, the importance of rational thought in general, and of reasoned dialogue in religious matters in particular. The latter becomes absolutely central because of the *necessity* to use religious ethical principles to derive the solutions to the socio-economic problems of society, like the ones we have discussed in this book.

iv) *The Logical Coherence of the Axiomatised Ethical System*

Having shown that the proposed ethical system possesses solid religious and historical credentials, the next step is to prove, though only heuristically, its logical validity, i.e., to see whether it satisfies the criteria set out in section III-(i) above. That is, beside offering an adequate representation of the Islamic ethical viewpoint, it should be shown that the axiom system is a plurality, and that it is consistent, complete, comprehensive, capable of making the largest number of predictions and able to generate sensible statements about the ethical and economic contents of an Islamic economy. This is important because if it does not meet these criteria, then the statements deduced from it will also be suspect, if not altogether invalid – notwithstanding their religious virtuosity. Firstly, let us see why the axiom system must be a *plurality* (greater than one) rather than just being non-trivial (greater than zero). This is an important point which has both logical and doctrinal dimensions. Logically, the issue is how far can the reductionist process go to produce a *basis*, i.e., that which contains the *minimum* number of independent and logically consistent elements. The philosophical tradition has been to carry this process back to *the* 'first' cause. Thus, some authors, quite properly, regard unity [Sayyid Quṭb (2000)], or unicity [Choudhury (1995)], as the first cause of all that exists or happens in the universe. It is, therefore, argued that unity should suffice as *the* axiom to generate all the relevant information about the economic universe as well.[38] The central question about this argument is: is this one-axiom system an adequate representation of the way Islam visualises the economic universe to operate? Ultimately, the answer depends on whether one believes that Divine Will directly orders all things, and acts *directly* on the springs of human thought and action; or is it that Divine Will manifests itself through human agency? Now, obviously if the former is the case – so that human freedom and responsibility are not relevant (as the Ash'arites believed) – then there is no room for any other axioms. However, if the latter is the case, then there is room for more axioms, *in addition* to the unity axiom, to describe the characteristics and behaviour of the human agency. As noted above, the overwhelming weight of the current consensus is in favour of the latter opinion.[39] But once this position is taken, the rest of the three axioms *must* enter the system. The equilibrium axiom becomes relevant because, unlike in the physical universe, this is a *requirement* for the smooth functioning of a social milieu that humans inhabit; and it must be met for making it work reasonably (thought not always perfectly) smoothly. However, man with free will can go against equilibrium, in which case disorder and anarchy will prevail. Responsibility, therefore, enters the picture to keep a balance in the economic universe. Thus, *all* the four axioms follow from the doctrinal position that Divine Will operates through the human agency. This proves our first assertion unambiguously, that the axiom system must be a *plurality* in the sense indicated above.

Secondly, the assertion, i.e., that the proposed system comprises *exactly* four elements, no more, no less, needs to be proved. Now, it has just been shown that there must be *at least* four axioms in the set; so the remaining assertion to be demonstrated is that it cannot *exceed* four, i.e., that any additional axioms can be expressed in terms of the four basic elements (in other words, from those which form a basis).[40] But, this is a self-evident proposition and requires no further proof.[41] However, let it be noted in this context that since *a* (not *the*) basis is non-unique there can be other axiom systems as well which can live *peacefully* with the one proposed – peacefully, because the proposed axiom system neither denies the existence of other possible axiom systems, *nor* does the existence of other systems constitute a refutation of the proposed system.

Thirdly, it must be shown that the axiom system is an adequate and legitimate representation of an ideal Islamic society. But this has already been proved above; and, at any rate, *no one* has denied it ever since it was first proposed by Naqvi (1978). Indeed, there are some who have endorsed it, e.g., Ahmad (1981); Sirageldin (1995; 2000). Fourthly, there is the important question: is the system *consistent* in the sense of being *not* self-contradictory and uninformative? (To this end, it should be possible to separate statements that are compatible with it and those which are not [Popper (1980; p. 92]. This proposition will be proved in the next section.) The consistency property is established by the fact that from each of the axioms issues forth the same message: that Islam aims at establishing a harmonious and just society (by the *al-'adl* component of the equilibrium axiom); that individuals exercise their freedom (by the free will axiom); that they are committed to looking beyond their own self-interest (by the unity axiom); and that they work for the welfare of others, especially for the least-privileged in society without expecting a *quid pro quo* from them (by the *iḥsān* component of the equilibrium axiom, and the responsibility axiom). In other words, in order to generate a 'complete' statement about an efficient and a just Islamic economy all the four axioms are needed.

Fifthly, the *independence* of the axiom system can also be demonstrated by the statement just made – namely, the property that none of its elements are deducible from any other element in the set. This is because if it were so then not all the four elements would be required to generate a complete statement.[42] Finally, the *comprehensiveness* of the system (that it includes both the process aspect and the opportunity aspects) can also be established by noting that it is concerned not only with the *process* of generating a just system (unity and free will axioms) but also with the opportunities it provides to all people, and especially the least-privileged in society (the equilibrium and responsibility axioms).

IV. The Domain and the Range of the Axiomatised Ethical System

Before we pass on to the task of deducing *empirically verifiable* ethical and economic statements (of lesser order of generality) from the axiomatised ethical system, two clarifications are in order about its domain and range. Firstly, the axiomatised system is *not* most useful in checking the validity of those aspects of the Islamic economy where the Holy Qur'ān is explicit even though it does that duty as well by drawing out the full implications of these instructions. Rather, it is most useful in analysing those aspects of our social and economic life where the Qur'ānic instructions are implicit or indirect but which need to be highlighted to help public policy. Secondly, the axiom system seeks to revive the spirit of the Qur'ānic observations/instructions where it has been diluted by lifeless exegetic commentaries which, in most cases, meant bending the Islamic ethical principles to meet the social, political and cultural reality of Muslim societies in the Middle Ages.

The analysis presented below is only illustrative of the large number of questions that can be asked, and answered satisfactorily, about specific ethical and economic issues that an

Islamic economy – and a real-life Muslim society – is expected to face. It shows that with every shake of the axiom system's kaleidoscope, the overall pattern of the Islamic point of view on ethical and economic questions becomes clearer. The cases we analyse below fall into three categories: (i) those which deal with the manner of recognising those aspects of modern ethical knowledge which would not be usable in an Islamic economy; (ii) those which make the analyses of some vital economic issues presented in the preceding sections logically more coherent; and (iii) those which address some new vital issues that Muslim societies face today.

i) *Axioms as Basis: Unacceptable Ethical Statements*

Let us begin by first getting out of the way those ethical and economic statements which *cannot* be deduced from Islamic ethical axioms. Chapters 2 and 4 give a fairly detailed description of such ethical and moral theories, and their *irrelevance* from the Islamic point of view. Here, even at the risk of some repetition, these theories are re-evaluated with reference to the Islamic ethical axioms. It should have been obvious by now that Pareto-optimality, Benthamite Utilitarianism, and the Liberalist non-consequentialist 'moral-right' theories are contrary to the Islamic point of view. The Pareto-optimality rule is unacceptable because of its total disregard of the equity issues, and of any moral considerations that may warrant an improvement of a Pareto-optimal situation that is manifestly unjust. Benthamite Utilitarianism cannot be accepted because of its insistence on maximising total utility regardless of its distribution, its failure to distinguish between the rich and poor, and because the maximisation rule that it recommends, i.e., an equalisation of people's marginal utilities, inevitably leads to extreme inequalities of income. The liberalist philosophy fails because it disregards distributive equity altogether, considers any steps taken to promote it a violation of individual's moral rights and denies the right of the poor to any aid or assistance. Yet, Pareto-optimality remains the headstone of neo-classical economics, which, notwithstanding its 'other-worldly' agenda, continues to be the dominant economics paradigm, and is in no immediate danger of being thrown out. Also, Benthamite Utilitarianism has been accepted by neo-classical economics. And notwithstanding all its moral blemishes, liberalism has been influential in moulding 'rightist' Western intellectual opinion and public policy since the 1970s, and is one of the main reasons for discrediting Welfare State principles in Europe and for inducing aid fatigue in developed countries.

It is, therefore, important to establish the unacceptability of these theories by reference to the Islamic ethical system. The *Pareto-Optimality* rule violates the unity axiom because of its undiluted positivism (i.e., that morality has no place in economics); it contravenes the equilibrium axiom for being insensitive to distributive issues; and it denies the responsibility axiom because economic agents are expected (indeed, mandated) to be guided *only* by selfishness and greed. The free will axiom is apparently satisfied but Islam does not accept the absolute autonomy of the individual because human freedom when separated from a sense of responsibility leads to social anarchy. *Benthamite Utilitarian* philosophy is consequence-sensitive as Islam requires; but it is unconcerned about distributive justice, in violation of equilibrium and responsibility axioms. It fails to provide substantive economic freedoms and is incapable of distinguishing the rich from the poor on moral or economic grounds. For these reasons it violates both free will and responsibility axioms. And, though it is presented as a moral principle, yet there is hardly anything moral about it. Thus, the unity axiom is also violated. Similarly, *libertarianism* fails the unity axiom for being morally inconsiderate: i.e., it is not obliged, on moral grounds, to help the poor. And, while it accords priority to individual liberty as Islam does, yet it goes to extremes in the defence of individual freedom and leaves no room for egalitarian reform – in violation of equilibrium and responsibility axioms.

ii) *The Axiom System as a Basis of Acceptable Ethical Statements*[43]

Next we look at some *normative* public-choice theories that *are* attractive from an Islamic point of view. They offer something valuable to better understand the full meaning of Islamic ethical values. The most important candidate in this category is the Rawlsian theory of Justice-as Fairness. As explained in Chapter 2, it consists of two parts. The first part is concerned with the *procedure* that ensures the fairness of basic principles of justice agreed to in the "initial situation". The guiding moral value here, which is also highly rated in Islam, is the *impartiality* of the people who are expected to arrive at these principles without any prior knowledge of their position in the emerging social order. This satisfies all the four Islamic ethical axioms – the unity and responsibility axioms, because the people involved here are motivated by the welfare of others in society, beyond their own selfish interest in any future social set up; the equilibrium axiom, as the aim here is to establish a just society; and the free will and responsibility axioms, since the people involved in decision-making act freely and voluntarily, and accept the consequences of their actions. The second part of Rawlsian theory deals with the principles of justice themselves, both of which are of great importance from the Islamic point of view. The first principle – namely, that each person is to have an equal right to basic liberties compatible with similar liberties for others – requires that the basic structure of society be redesigned, if need be, to assure a just assignment of rights and duties to facilitate a just distribution of advantages and costs in society. For these reasons, this principle satisfies all the four axioms. The second principle, i.e., the Difference Principle, is generally consistent with the Islamic insistence on meeting the needs of the least-privileged as a compulsory social obligation. Also, there is the point that the burden of inequalities, to the extent these are necessary for economic development, must be so arranged that they work out for everyone's advantage. Yet another point which an Islamic theory of justice would accept is that these principles are presented as the basis of social cooperation among individuals such that its costs and benefits are equitably divided between the contracting parties. An aspect of Rawlsian theory which, subject to the qualification just noted, is congenial to the Islamic point of view is the concept of 'primary social goods' – namely, rights, liberties, and opportunities, and income and wealth, and the social bases of self-respect – and that the least-privileged in society (who possess the least of such goods) should receive most of these goods. An important point here is that human welfare is not just a function of the possession of wealth. However, *not* acceptable from the Islamic point of view – indeed, from the point of view of *any* moral theory – is that, as Arrow (1973) shows, the Difference Principle *excludes* from the distribution of the benefits of social cooperation those who cannot participate in it by virtue of their physical or mental disabilities. This violates the *iḥsān* part of the equilibrium axiom and also the responsibility axiom.

Also useful in clarifying the Islamic point of view is Sen's Capability Calculus in at least two respects: (a) its contention that it is not the *possession* of primary goods but the capabilities that they engender which needs to be equalised, i.e., the capability to be well-nourished, well sheltered, well-clothed, to be able to move about freely in society without a sense of shame, etc. (b) Its emphasis on the individual's capabilities broadens the concept of social justice – which is that justice demands not simply equalising capabilities across individuals, but giving *more* to those who have the least capability to enjoy the possession of these goods. For instance, a sick person needs more money (to buy more primary goods) to reach the same level of capability that a healthy person with less money would. It can be easily seen that this aspect of Sen's theory satisfies the requirement of *iḥsān*, while Rawlsian theory does *not* meet it. Readers can check for themselves that some other theories (e.g., Harsanyi's equiprobability model, Dworkin's equality of resources conjecture, etc.,) are also congenial, though not entirely acceptable, from the Islamic point of view.

iii) *The Axiom System as a Basis of Economic Statements*

a) Poverty Reduction

It has been noted in Chapter 4 that the clearest Islamic injunction is against *income* poverty, and *capability* poverty.[44] As to the former, transferring resources from the rich to the poor is a highly recommended activity – one that simultaneously brings some cheer in the lives of the poor *and* spiritual happiness to the rich. An additional attraction of the Islamic point of view is that such transfers come about in a dignified manner so that the poor can move about in society without any sense of shame. This satisfies the unity axiom. The free will axiom is satisfied on two counts: (a) the giver does it without any compulsion; and in the discharge of one's responsibility to society, he/she is freed from avarice and greed. (b) The recipient's substantive freedom (from poverty) is enhanced. Finally, (c) because the act of giving to the least-privileged comes about as a matter of their right, the equilibrium axiom is met. The responsibility axiom would require that the rich act out of a sense of commitment to helping the poor, even if that means a cut in their (material) welfare. The Islamic injunction is also against *capability poverty* – that is, when, because of the recipient's physical incapacity, a relief in income poverty does not get translated into a corresponding relief in capability poverty on a one-to-one basis. Thus, more resources should be transferred to the really poor people. When this happens, the *iḥsān* requirement is fulfilled *par excellence*, while other axioms are also fulfilled in the manner shown above.

b) Equality and Distributive Justice

Inasmuch as poverty is related to income and wealth inequalities, it should be clear that a move towards an *equality of economic conditions* meets all the ethical axioms. By the same token, *equality of opportunity* is not a proper objective of economic policy because it can and does normally coexist with considerable inequalities of income, and even more of capabilities. In this sense, the latter objective fails all the axioms – the unity axiom, because individuals normally act out of self-interest, so that economic and ethical considerations are not unified; the equilibrium axiom, since equalising only opportunities would imply a move *away* from social justice; the responsibility axiom, as commitment is not involved in this case as a motivational force; and the free will axiom, because substantive economic *unfreedoms* remain unrectified, though political freedoms are ensured. Thus, an *egalitarian redistribution of income and wealth* follows logically from Islamic ethical axioms. In this context, even greater urgency attaches to land reforms, i.e., one that makes own cultivation the *only* condition of land ownership. This is so because reasonably small, rather than large, land holdings are known to be generally more efficient and productive, in addition to being more equitable.

c) Economic Growth and Human Development

As shown in Chapter 4, Islamic ethics and Islamic Law must be *explicit* about the commitment to growth and human development *as a matter of individual and social moral duty*. This can be accomplished in two related ways. Firstly, one can look at the impact that growth and human development make on those variables with respect to which Islamic ethics are explicit. We know that poverty reduction on a durable basis can be achieved only if per capita income increases at a rate of 3 percent or more and if social expenditures are maintained at a high enough level over a long enough period. Whence follows that achieving the growth objective should be given as high a priority as poverty reduction on the scale of Islamic ethics. Secondly, once the moral priority of growth and development is established, the same reasoning applies to establishing the ethical nature of the factors which directly affect these objectives. Thus, high rates of physical and human capital formation and the saving rate, and increasing the share of manufacturing in GDP, the population growth rate and technological change, should be recommended on both economic and moral grounds. The same holds about the morality of ensuring the access of men and women to political and economic freedoms, literacy and health and the absence of gender bias – all of which are vital to the creation of the right motivational structure to help human development in society.

The Islamic position on achieving high rates of growth and human development can be straightforwardly established in terms of ethical axioms. Firstly, as stated above, the *moral* case of economic growth and human development rests on ensuring intergenerational equity, which requires optimal saving, investment and social spending – optimal, because a balance has to be struck between the present and the future generations, with a view to financing a dynamic Islamic economy [Naqvi (1997)]. The unity axiom is satisfied because individuals are driven by a sense of commitment to the welfare of the community. In addition to growth constraints, three more constraints must be satisfied to meet the responsibility and equilibrium requirements – namely (a) a substantial transfer of resources should take place from the rich to the poor; and (b) priority should be accorded to the welfare of the least privileged in society. And (c) the supply of wage goods must increase at the same rate as income is transferred to the poor to meet the substantial freedoms of the poor. All this should be consistent with the free will axiom. In other words, achieving maximal growth satisfies all the four ethical axioms in an intergenerational setting.

The main points that emerge from the analysis presented in this section are as follows: (a) the proposed ethical axiom system is well-placed to examine the Islamic credentials of the modern ethical philosophies. Indeed, there is *no* other analytical procedure which can do this job. (b) Insofar as the proposed ethical system rejects/accepts theories which have also been rejected/accepted on more general (secular) grounds, it demonstrates, to some extent, its "universal" character and "comprehensiveness". (c) The proposed ethical system also demonstrates the *moral* nature of achieving such purely economic objectives as economic growth, human development, poverty reduction, the egalitarian distribution of income and wealth, etc. (d) The axiom system highlights that our knowledge of things, issues, and problems is relative to the needs of society, which change with the passage of time. A ceaseless procession of non-improving ideas hardly makes a pretty sight. (This is not to deny their importance for the *history* of Muslim thought.) The melancholy fact is that intellectual obsolescence applies to all knowledge as new one is created. We should, therefore, not hesitate to discard ideas – even those propounded by great Muslim scholars and divines – which lighted the pathways to wisdom in the Middle Ages, but have since been superseded by the breathtaking advances of modern knowledge.

Notes

1. The creation of Pakistan in 1947 and the success of the Islamic Revolution of Iran in 1979 are two recent examples of revolutionary movements having been guided by Islamic ethos. The Pakistan movement gained an unstoppable momentum only when spurred on by the religious aspirations of the Muslims of the Indian subcontinent. In the case of Iran, the religious moorings of the Revolution were explicit to begin with. What moved the masses there was the Qur'ānic verse: "And We desired to show favour unto those who were oppressed in the Earth, and to make them the inheritors, and establish them on Earth" (28:5-6). This is also an example of a major reinterpretation of the Qur'ānic imperatives, and the implied moral value (i.e., the right of the oppressed to fight against oppression), which suited the needs of the 'event'. [Incidentally, Mawdūdī (1976) inferred the same moral imperative ("the right to Protect against Tyranny") from another Qur'ānic verse, "God does not love evil talk in public unless it is someone who has been injured thereby" (4:148) (p. 28).]
2. According to Fogel (2000), Christianity had to throw out its fundamental theological principles of original sin and innate human depravity "to veer towards an emphasis on the innocence of the newborn" and to pave "the way for the central doctrine that social reform was a precondition for the personal salvation of those in the grip of poverty" (p. 120). By contrast, the Holy Qur'ān emphasises that: the innate innocence of humankind is unburdened by any original sin or depravity: (a) "We created man of finest possibilities" (95:4); and (b) "Each soul earns (what it earns) for itself, and no man shall bear another's burden" (6:164).

3. Jafri (2001) correctly observes: "...if the West after centuries of slumber and moral decadence can turn to its classical period for a renewed inspiration through the movements of Renaissance, the Enlightenment and the Reformation, why cannot the Muslims...turn to the pristine Islam for inspiration...This should not, however, be confused with what today is called fundamentalism..." (p. 35).
4. For instance, Marlow (1997) has noted at length the conscious watering down of the egalitarian message of the Qur'ānic verse: "He who has more integrity has indeed greater honour with God" (49:13). He reports that most *'ulamā'* had understood this verse as conveying the idea of the equality of mankind in this world; but that there were others as well who interpreted it more ambiguously (that it only refers to the equality in the hereafter) for fear of social subversion! (pp. 96-99).
5. Gibb (1947) made a similar point: "The future of Islam rests where it rested in the past – on the insight of the orthodox leaders and their capacity to resolve the new tensions as they arise by a positive doctrine which will master the forces making for disintegration" (p.122). Obviously, this comment vastly underestimates the importance of "non-orthodox scholars" in initiating and sustaining social and economic change in Muslim societies, but there is *some* truth in it.
6. The principles given in the text are documented in [Nyazee (2000); p. 206]. However, [Kamali (1999); p. 203] states these as faith, life, intellect, property and wealth. A slightly different, but essentially the same, list is given in [Chapra (2000); p. 118]: i.e., faith, human self, intellect, posterity, and wealth. Chapra claims that these principles also provide the foundations of Islamic economics.
7. Kamali and Chapra think that the order in which these elements are listed is not an essential part of al-Ghazālī's scheme; but Nayazee (1994) thinks that it is.
8. It is important to dispel a possible confusion about al-Shāṭibī's analytical method, i.e., *istiqrā'* or induction. This method has been used to derive the stated principles from a detailed reading of the Holy Qur'ān. In other words, the principles are broadly consistent with the Holy Qur'ān though these are *not* explicitly stated there as such. However, once derived, the next step is to *deduce* specific statements about the *Sharī'ah* from these principles. This clarification is essential because the reverse procedure of reducing general (universal) statements to some elementary statements, which as Wittgenstein put it, are "pictures of reality", is known as Hume's problem of *induction* and is insoluble as *there are no universal statements about reality* [Popper (1980); p. 37]. For instance, no matter

how many white swans you observe, this does not justify a universal statement that *all* swans are white. The only valid method of creating empirically testable statements, which is probably what al-Shāṭibī used, is to deduce particular statements from general statements. Popper (1980) refers to this procedure as the deductive method of testing, i.e., that "a hypothesis can only be empirically *tested* – and only *after* it has been advanced", (p. 30; italics in the original). But regardless of what al-Shāṭibī's method was, we have used the deductive method in the text.

9. An example of the sterility of the standard reductionist procedure has been the practice among economists to reduce the variety of factors which influence the economic well-being of the people to the metric of utility alone. See, Sen and Williams (1999).
10. A basis for E_n space is a linearly independent subset of vectors from E_n which spans (i.e., generates) the entire space. The following characteristics of a (not the) *basis* are relevant for the analysis given in the text: (a) a set of vectors $a_1,..., a_n$ from E_n space is said to span E_n, if every other vector in E_n can be written as a linear combination of $a_1,..., a_n$. (b) A basis is not *unique,* in that any other set of independent vectors can also do the same job; but a representation of any vector in terms of a basis *is* unique (i.e., there is only one way of doing it). (c) The set of linearly independent vectors *cannot* be written as a linear combination of any other set of vectors in the En space. See Hadley (1961) for details.
11. *Falsifiability* of a statement is to be distinguished from its actual *falsification*. The former is used "solely as a criterion for [testing] the empirical character of a system of statements" (Popper (1980); p. 86), without insisting that each statement or a system of statements meet the (impossible) requirement of actual falsification. Thus, economics is full of not-yet-falsified (though falsifiable) statements – e.g., the Laws of Increasing (Decreasing) Returns to Scale; the timeless Cobb-Douglas production function; the assertion that producers/consumers are profit/utility maximisers, etc.
12. Two clarifications are needed about the *adequacy* of the number of axioms: (a) as pointed out in note 10, the set of chosen axioms is *not* unique. In other words, there will be an infinite number of axioms coexisting with the chosen set. Of these, we select only those which express the Islamic point of view authentically. (b) The chosen set cannot be disqualified just because someone comes up with another list of axioms which satisfies (a).
13. This requirement is adapted from Sen (1999), where it is used to highlight those aspects which characterise the kind of freedoms people value. We use this principle differently in the text.

14. The analysis presented in the text draws only very selectively on Naqvi (1994). These axioms were stated as a system in the order given in the text first in [(Naqvi (1978)]; and were then refined in [Naqvi (1981); (1994); (1997)]. In 1978 and 1981 the second axiom was stated as *al-'adl;* but in 1994 it was broadened to *al-'adl wa al-iḥsān*. (Earlier, Naqvi *et al.* (1980) and (1984) had mistakenly adopted only *al-'adl wa al-iḥsān* as the overarching principle of Islamic economics, disregarding other axioms.)
15. The Qur'ānic verse corresponding to the text is: "My service and sacrifice, my life and my death, are all of them for God, the Creator and Lord of all the worlds" (6:162).
16. The following verse from the Holy Qur'ān supports the text: "O men, We created you from a male and female, and formed you into nations and tribes that you may recognise each other" (49:13).
17. The relevant Qur'ānic verses are: (a) "He has certainly power over everything" (35:1); (b) "...He is all-wise and aware" (6:18); and (c) "To God belongs all that is in the heavens and the earth, and His is the power over everything" (5:120).
18. The Qur'ānic verses are: (a) "Verily God has enjoined justice, the doing of good..." (16:90); and (b) "Perfected are the laws of your Lord in truth and justice, and there is no changing his Laws" (6:115). The Holy Qur'ān also uses the words *al-mīzān* (balance) and *qisṭ* (equity), which convey the same meaning as *al-'adl* and *iḥsān*.
19. The Qur'ānic verses corresponding to the assertions in the text are: (a) "Each soul earns (what it earns) for itself, and no man shall bear another's burden" (6:164); (b) "It is He who made you trustees on the earth..." (6:165).
20. The Holy Qur'ān is explicit on this: "Verily God does not change the state of a people till they change themselves" (13:11).
21. The Holy Qur'ān rejects absolute individual autonomy: "And, yet man is rebellious/For he thinks he is sufficient in himself" (96:6-7).
22. The philosophical difference between the Islamic and Kantian points of view noted in the text is basic; but the relativity of human freedom does not in any way diminish its quantum or quality. Indeed, if properly interpreted, the Islamic concept of freedom may signify more, and a higher level of, freedom than Kant's absolute freedom. This is because the former flows from a deep moral conviction held by individuals, so that restrictions on it would be voluntarily accepted for the greater good of society. In addition, it also adds to freedom when one gains independence from the slavery of the self.
23. Haque (1977) has noted that Abū Dharr (651 A.D.), the distinguished Companion of the Prophet (pbuh), vigorously protested against the efforts of the government of the day to change the nomenclature of *māl al-Muslimīn* (wealth of the Muslims) to *māl Allāh* (wealth of

Allah). The strength of his conviction is shown by the fact that he himself did not own *any* property, and believed that the maximum of whatever is left over after meeting one's (modest) needs must be given away to the poor. The Qur'ānic verse he cited in support of his claim is: "And they ask you what they should give. Tell them: the utmost you can spare" (2:219).

24. The Holy Qur'ān states: "Whoever preserves himself from his own greed will be prosperous" (59:9).
25. Rahman (1979) observes: "Together [the theological] forces constitute the giant theoretical wheel of Medieval Islam revolving around the axis of Determinism" (p. 99).
26. The Holy Qur'ān is explicit on this: "Say: O men, the truth has come to you from your Lord, so he who follows the right path does so for himself, and he who goes astray errs against himself, and I am not a guardian over you" (10:108).
27. The correct doctrinal position that men/women do what Allah Wills has been widely misinterpreted in conservative circles to mean that since Allah's motives are unknown to men everything is possible, including His participation in what would be considered as an unjust act if men did it. But man's ignorance of Allah's motives does not lead to the conclusion that Allah can act arbitrarily. This possibility is ruled out by the fact that Allah would *not* Will that which is contrary to His Nature, because Allah has Himself chosen to abide by the Laws He makes. Since Allah is *Al 'Ādil* (the Just) He would not act unjustly, even though He has the power to do so. This has been emphatically stated in the Holy Qur'ān: "There is no changing of My word, nor am I unjust to My creatures" (50:29). The relevance of these arguments in the present context is that if man does evil it cannot be maintained that since he cannot do anything except what Allah wills he is not responsible for it; or, much worse, that Allah Himself is in any way responsible for these acts. This is a false induction because the Holy Qur'ān unambiguously declares: "Whatever misfortune befalls you is a consequence of your deeds" (42:30). On these issues, see Schuon (1976), esp. Ch. 5.
28. The Holy Qur'ān states: "How will you comprehend what the steep ascent is? – To free a neck (from the burden of slavery), or to feed in times of famine. The orphan near in relationship or the poor in distress" (90:12-16).
29. The relevant Qur'ānic verse is: "Each soul earns (what it earns) for itself, and no man shall bear another's burden" (6:164).
30. The Holy Qur'ān warns: "What has come upon you that you fight not in the cause of God and for the oppressed, men, women and children who pray..." (4:75).

31. The Qur'ānic condemnation on this score is unequivocal: "Woe to those who pray, but who are oblivious of their moral duties..." (107:4-5).
32. The Mu'tazilah School, founded by Wāṣil b. 'Aṭā' (d. 131/748) at Basra, was a purely theological enterprise to systematise thinking about some of the basic principles of Islam. For a brief period, during the period of al-Ma'mūn, Mu'tazilism also became an official doctrine. The "classical period" of Mu'tazilah, when it was recognised as a school of thought, lasted from the "1st quarter of the 3rd/9th century to the last quarter of the 5th/11th century". The leaders of the school in this period were al-Jubbā'ī (d. 303/933) and his son Abū Hāshim (d. 321/933), who were reverently referred to as "the two *shaykhs*". However, the Mu'tazilah School was by no means monolithic: from the very early period, there were two distinct schools, "those of al-Basra" and "those of Baghdad"; and then there were voices of dissent within each school. The two most important examples of the latter are: (i) Ḍirār b 'Amr dissented from the rest of the school by his thesis that voluntary human actions are created by God; and (ii) Bishr al-Mu'tamir contradicted one of the central Mu'tazilah doctrines – namely, that "God necessarily does for every man what is the most advantageous (*al-aṣlaḥ*) for him. The golden period of the school ended with the arrival of the *Saljuqids*; and it "disappeared altogether" with Mongol conquest. There has been a strong revival of the Mu'tazilah doctrine at the beginning of the 14th/20th century, in Egypt, Pakistan and elsewhere. For details, see Ess (1987); pp. 220-229; and Gimaret (1993); pp. 783-793.
33. The five basic tenets of Mu'tazilism – regarded as "the best manual of the *Mu'tazilī* theology" – were formalised by one of its most distinguished exponents, Abu'l Hudhayl. These are: (i) The Uniqueness of God (*al-Tawḥīd*); (ii) the Justice of God (*al-'Adl*); (iii) the promise and threat (*al-wa'd wa'l-wa'īd*); (iv) the intermediate state (*al-manzilah bayna al-manzilatayn*); and (v) command the good and forbid the evil (*al-amr bi'l-ma'rūf wa'l nahy 'an al-munkar*). However, the first two are the most fundamental. Hence, the characterisation of the school as *ahl al-'adl wa'l Tawḥīd*. For details, see Hodgson (1974); Vol. 1, pp. 437-443; Lapidus (1997); pp. 105-149; Ess (1987); pp. 220-229.
34. Al-Ash'arī Abu'l Ḥasan (260-324/874-935) known to be the best pupil of al-Jubbā'ī, the head of (Basran) Mu'tazilah, later became their principal opponent. He believed that: everything good and evil is willed by God, and He creates the acts of men by creating the power to do each act; this is his doctrine of *kasb* and lies between the doctrine of predestination and free will. In this respect, *kasb*

contrasts with the Mu'tazilah belief in the freedom of human choice and the corresponding responsibility for the acts men create themselves. Furthermore, as opposed to Mu'tazilah emphasis on Allah's justice and that He does *only* that which is beneficial for humankind, al-Ash'arī highlighted the centrality of His Omnipotence; and that His motives are not subject to human speculation. However, like the Mu'tazilah, he used *kalām* or rational argument, in defence of the prevailing orthodoxy (e.g., that God has eternal attributes; that the Holy Qur'ān is uncreated; that the vision of God on the Day of Judgement is a reality, even though one may not understand the manner of it, etc.), which the Mu'tazilah refuted. See Watt (1960); pp. 695-696; and Glassé (1989); pp. 51-52.

35. Al-Ash'arī's observations were given by way of answer to the following famous question he posed to his great Mutazilī teacher (al-Jubbā'ī) about the fate of the three brothers: one brother having a higher position in Paradise, because he lived longer and did many more good deeds than his second brother who died younger and could not do as many good actions. On the latter's complaint about his lower position God replies that He knew that had he (the second brother) lived longer he would have sinned and been worse-off. Hearing this, the third brother in Hell exclaims that, on this 'reasoning', he too could be better off if God had cut him off at an early age to prevent him from sin [cited in Hodgson (1974); p. 442]. But this analogy cannot be used to demonstrate the incompatibility of omniscience and omnibenevolence and its implied attribution of arbitrariness to Allah. This is because such an attribution clearly violates the Qur'ānic assertion: "You will not find any variation in Our line of action" (17:77). At any rate, the apparent antinomy in the Mu'tazilah position disappears once it is recognised that their principle of Divine Justice precludes Allah's arbitrariness and the principle of predestination. See also note 27.

36. The leading Mu'tazilī, al-Jubbā'ī (d. 303/933) laid down the formulae that "whoever has the power of a thing can equally well do it or not do it"; and that "every power is equally the power of an act and of its opposite", [cited in Gimaret (1993); p. 790].

37. In addition to the references in the text, see also Naqvi (1994); p. 35; Jafri (1988); Watt (1948); Boer (1970); Shahrastānī (1978); Gibb and Kramers (1961); Wensinck (1932); 'Abduh (1966) and Iqbal (1986). Chapra (2000) contains a fairly 'balanced' account of 'rationalist' and 'orthodox' positions and counsels restraint on both sides: "Reason can, thus, play a considerable role in the restructuring of Muslim society without coming into conflict with Revelation, provided that the state, the rationalists and the conservatives do not try to step on each other's toes..." (p. 104).

38. Sayyid Quṭb's (2000) remark is representative of this line of thinking: "So all creation, issuing as it does from one absolute, universal and active Will forms an all-embracing unity in which [an] individual part is in harmonious order with the remainder", and that "all creation is a unity comprising different parts; it has a common origin, a common providence and purpose, because it was deliberately produced by a single, absolute, and comprehensive Will" (p. 39).
39. For instance, Ahmad (1976) notes four basic principles of an Islamic economic order – namely, *tawḥīd* (unity); *rubūbiyyah* (Divine arrangement for nourishment, sustenance and directing things towards their perfection); *khilāfah* (God's vicegerency on Earth); and *tazkiyah* (purification *plus* growth) (pp. 178-179). Chapra (1992) gives three "fundamental principles" of Islam: *tawḥīd* (unity), *khilāfah* (vicegerency); and *'adālah* (justice) (p. 201). Nomani and Rahnema (1994) identify '*tawḥīd*', 'justice and equity', "and commanding good and forbidding evil" as the "fundamental theoretical axes" of an Islamic economic system (pp. 34-40).
40. Incidentally, Mu'tazilism would also violate the condition in the text. Of its *five* "basic principles" or axioms in modern language, only two – *tawḥīd* and *'adl* – are central to their system. For that reason, the Mu'tazilah were called, and they accepted it, as *ahl al-'adl wa al-tawḥīd*. Their third principle is derivable from the first two principles, given in note 33, especially from (ii). The remaining elements do not add up to much, from a logical point of view. Thus, theirs is really a *two*-element ethical system, because in their scheme the concepts of *ikhtiyār* and *farḍ* are seen as derived from (i.e., are *dependent* on) the principle of *'adl*.
41. As a proof of the statement in the text, let us ask the question, with reference to note 32, can *khilāfah* be added to the proposed list? The answer is in the negative because the free will axiom gives the same information – i.e., man is God's vicegerent on earth – *plus* the additional points that he is born free *and* is responsible for all his actions. Hence, adding *khilāfah* to the list is redundant. But if we substitute it for free will and responsibility then the predictive power of the axiom system will be much reduced. Can, then, we add *rubūbiyyah* to the proposed set? The answer is again in the negative because *iḥsān* gives the same information. If we substitute it for *al-'adl wa al-iḥsān* then we get much less information by omitting *'adl*. What about adding *al-'adl wa al-iḥsān* to the list? Again, the answer is in the negative because *al-'adl wa al-iḥsān* says the same thing and more; whence follows that *'adālah* cannot substitute for *al-'adl wa al-iḥsān*. And so on. However, let it be noted that this demonstration

does *not* prove that the axiom systems noted above are untrue. Indeed, as a self-contained list of principles this may well be an alternative ethical system; but then the burden of proof is on the authors.

42. As noted in endnote 40, the Mu'tazilah system (see notes 33 and 40) is *not* independent in this sense. If it is regarded as a five-element system, then it contains three 'superfluous' elements as shown in note 40. However, as a two-element system, it says too little, because contrary to their own assertion, human free will and responsibility in the fullness of their meaning stand apart (are not deducible) from Divine justice. They failed to see that the fact that the former is *consistent* with the latter is not the same thing as the *dependence* of the former on the latter, or vice versa. At any rate, on the plane of social existence, the two-element system cannot adequately generate all the relevant statements about socio-economic reality (see Section IV in the text).
43. Naqvi (1994) gives several examples of such deductions. Here in the text only a few instances are given with a somewhat different motivation.
44. There is also what is known as *utility* poverty – that is when utility is low. But this is an imprecise concept because utility is experienced only mentally, with no objective criterion of determining it. Also, it does not indicate the direction of resource transfer. Thus, a contented poor person may become mentally reconciled to bearing cheerfully what an uncontented, but a reasonably well-off, person considers an unbearable calamity. On the utility criterion the transfer of resources will, therefore, be from a very poor person to the reasonably well-off person!

CHAPTER 6

Ethical Axioms and Muslim Society

I. Introduction

In this concluding chapter, it would be instructive to start off by speculating about the influence of the axiomatised ethical system on individual behaviour and the conduct of public policy in Muslim societies. An effort in this direction has been made by Sirageldin (1995) with reference to oil-producing Muslim countries (especially Iran and Kuwait) and a non-Muslim country (Singapore). The results of this study are interesting. The hypothesis is that success on this score crucially depends on the society's commitment to working out a just and viable social contract with its people such that "the economic cost of introducing the moral filter" is "lower than the perceived benefits" flowing from it (p. 475). The data presented in Siregeldin's study suggest that, notwithstanding their apparent belief in Islamic moral ideals, public policy in oil-producing Muslim countries has apparently *not* succeeded in making such a contract with their people. Consequently, it could not produce the "right" kind of motivational structure for individuals to work for the collective good. On the other hand, a non-Muslim (Singapore) country has succeeded in doing just this by implementing its own moral ideals!

This kind of comparison, though admittedly tentative, does show that an ethics-based society can succeed *if* and *only if* it provides *moral* support to progressive forces, i.e., those which facilitate high rates of economic growth, poverty reduction, distributive justice, etc. These oil-producing Muslim countries (with the exception of Iran) seem to have failed this test. The reason is that what social contracts they have concluded with the people are *not* financially or morally viable. Profligate consumption standards of the present generation are artificially buoyed up at the expense of future generations – in gross violation of the equilibrium and responsibility axioms. Furthermore, the rental income dominates total individual income, and does *not* normally get translated into high rates of saving and productive investment; the development of non-oil production, especially that of manufacturing production is very low; the growth rates of per capita income (due both to the weakness in the growth of non-oil production as well as a higher-than-average rate of population growth) are very slow; and the system of taxation is highly under-developed. True, Iran has succeeded in lowering its fertility rate, accelerating urbanisation, increasing the literacy rate, etc; and Kuwait has had "the highest score in the United Nations Human Development Index among all the Arab countries, and has one of the highest scores in the world", (p. 471); yet the adverse verdict recorded above seems to dominate isolated success stories.

II. The Economic Challenge to Muslim Societies

The data presented in Tables 1 and 2 show, for the first time, the (weighted) average comparative performance of 53 Muslim, and 109 non-Muslim countries during the 1990/1999 period, which is measured by 13 indicators of economic and social progress. These indicators record progress in six related, but distinct, problem areas: (a) economic growth and its major determinants; (b) human development and its main components; (c) population dynamics; (d) distributive justice; (e) poverty alleviation; and (f) gender bias. The accomplishments under each of these headings also provide the material to test Sirageldin's above-noted hypothesis about the 'effectiveness' of the Islamic ethical system in terms of its effect on the economic performance of the Muslim countries, as opposed to that of the non-Muslim countries which presumably have followed *their* (religious and/or secular) ethical values. It may be noted that the achievement indicators here are somewhat 'loaded' in favour of the non-Muslim countries: while the average per capita income for Muslim countries is 5,011.06 PPP dollars, it is 7,066.25 PPP dollars for non-Muslim countries. Table 2 attempts to correct for the income differential effect by comparing the record of the six richest Muslim countries with that of the ten richest non-Muslim countries. But, the income-differential bias still remains: 14,763.17 PPP dollars in the former as opposed to 23,111 PPP dollars of the latter. Yet, some further corrections done along these lines (not reported) suggest that the data presented here do paint a fairly faithful picture of reality.

i) *The Economic Record*

a) Growth Performance

Table 1 shows that the weighted (average) growth rate of per capita income of Muslim countries is significantly *lower* than that of non-Muslim countries. Also, the growth rate in the former has been more unstable than in the latter, i.e., the ratio of standard deviation (given in parenthesis) to the mean value is higher in the Muslim countries than in the non-Muslim countries. The implications of this large differential in growth rates for the future is disturbing: it shows that if the current rates are sustained then the ratio of GDP per capita of non-Muslim countries to the GDP per capita of Muslim countries will go up from 1.5 to 2.66 in 20 years from now. Table 2 compares the top-performing six (oil-producing) Muslim countries with the ten richest non-Muslim countries (row 1). The growth rate of per capita income becomes a much more satisfactory 3.11 percent in Muslim countries, but it is still only half as high as that for non-Muslim countries (6.4 percent). The implication is still that with this differential continuing, the ratio of GDP per capita for the two sets of countries will increase in this case from the present 1.75 to 3.28 in the next 20 years.

Table 1 highlights four proximate causes for this differential in the growth rate of per capita income. (1) The investment rate for the Muslim countries is less than one half of that for non-Muslim countries (row 2). (2) The share of manufacturing in GDP is also less than half in the former than in the latter (row 3); which suggests that the rate of 'structural transformation', which is the surest indicator of the growth potential of a country, is markedly slower in the former than in the latter. This also has adverse implications for the saving and investment rates for the two groups of countries. (3) The population growth rate (which *subtracts* from the contribution that the growth rate of GDP makes to economic well-being) is twice as high in the Muslim as in the non-Muslim countries (row 4). (4) Human capital formation (the share of expenditure on education and health) in Muslim countries is only half of that in the non-Muslim countries (rows 6 and 7). Table 2 tells much the same story for the top performers. Three main causes explain the differential in their relative growth performance. (a) the investment rate is lower in rich Muslim than in rich non-Muslim countries, though the differences are much smaller between the two. The reason why a nominal differential in the investment rate is correlated with a much higher one in the growth rates is that much of the investment in the latter is in the oil-producing sector (the so-called "enclave investment"), where its pay-off is the least. Furthermore, the vagaries of oil-exports make the investment rate unstable. This is reflected in the much larger standard deviation relative to the average in the former than in the latter. (b) The share of manufacturing in

GDP is significantly less in the rich Muslim countries than in the rich non-Muslim countries (row 3). (c) The population growth rate is three times *higher* in the rich Muslim countries as compared with the rich non-Muslim countries. In this case the former, unlike the latter, breaks an important general rule – namely, that the population growth rate should be inversely correlated with the increase in income (row 4). (d) Equally deplorable is the fact that the rich Muslim countries spend on health only one-third as much as the non-Muslim countries do (row 6). This makes for a lower rate of human development. (e) All empirical evidence shows that the major contribution to growth (indeed, three-fourths of it) has come from technological change [Denison (1962)]. But this has *not* happened in Muslim countries, even though rich Muslim countries tend to spend *more* on education than rich non-Muslim countries (row 7).

b) Human Development

Table 1 (row 5) shows that the Human Development Indicator (HDI) – which averages the contributions of life expectancy, literacy rate and enrolment rate, and income to human well-being – is markedly *less* (0.22) for the Muslim countries than for the non-Muslim countries (0.49). Even *worse* is the situation in the rich Muslim countries (0.09) as compared with the much superior performance of the rich non-Muslim countries (0.59) (Table 2, row 4). The reasons are obvious: (1) a lower social expenditure (on education and health), though in rich Muslim countries the expenditure on education significantly exceeds that in rich non-Muslim countries; (2) a lower per capita income in the Muslim than in the non-Muslim countries, and (3) a much higher population growth rate in the former than in the latter, have a direct negative effect on all the three components of HDI. Thus, the Muslim countries belie two "stylised" facts of human development – namely that HDI generally gets *worse*, rather than better, as income rises; and that population growth rate rises as people/countries get richer.

Table 1: Development Indicators Across Countries (in the 1990s)

	Muslim Countries Max N=53	Non-Muslim Countries Max N=109	All Countries Max N=162
Growth Rate of GDP per capita (%)	1.87 (6.09) [53]	4.84 (4.98) [109]	3.87 (5.53) [162]
Investment-GDP Ratio (%)	8.26 (11.71) [48]	19.89 (96.01) [104]	16.22 (79.75) [152]
Share of Manufacturing in GDP (%)	6.19 (14.09) [53]	15.46 (70.23) [109]	12.43 (58.24) [162]
Population Growth Rate (%)	2.82 (1.13) [49]	1.76 (1.22) [91]	2.13 (1.29) [140]
Human Development Index (a)	0.22 (0.41) [53]	0.49 (1.80) [109]	0.40 (1.50) [162]
Share of Expenditure on Education in GDP (%)	1.21 (1.61) [53]	2.49 (7.88) [109]	2.07 (6.51) [162]
Share of Expenditure on Health in GDP (%)	0.56 (0.75) [53]	1.92 (5.79) [109]	1.47 (4.80) [162]
Gini Index (b)	22.64 (29.81) [31]	36.07 (127.79) [82]	32.39 (109.93) [113]
Ratio of Rich 10 % to Poor 10 % (b)	7.23 (9.51) [31]	13.16 (39.58) [83]	11.55 (34.18) [114]
Population below $ 1 a day	31.35 (24.60) [24]	20.94 (16.48) [35]	25.18 (20.64) [59]
Population below national poverty line	39.47 (20.39) [26]	33.82 (14.49) [33]	36.31 (17.41) [59]

Table continued overleaf

	Muslim Countries Max N=53	Non-Muslim Countries Max N=109	All Countries Max N=162
Gender Development Index (c)	0.23 (0.41) [53]	0.51 (1.83) [109]	0.41 (1.52) [162]
Gender Empowerment Measure (d)	0.029 (0.11) [53]	0.14 (0.402) [109]	0.102 (0.34) [162]

Sources: UNDP's *Human Development Report* (various issues)
World Bank's *World Development Report* (2000/01)

Note: Standard Deviation is reported in parentheses. A number of observations are reported in brackets. The figures without parentheses and brackets denote weighted averages.

a) The Human Development Index is based on the indicators of life expectancy, literacy rate, enrolment rate at various levels of education and gross domestic product per capita in real terms.
b) The Gini Index and the ratio of the richest 10 percent to the poorest 10 percent of the population are the measures of income inequality in the 1990s.
c) The Gender Development Index utilises the gender-based disaggregated data for all the indicators included in the computation of the Human Development Index.
d) The Gender Empowerment Measure measures the relative empowerment of males and females in political and economic spheres. It is unrelated to both HDI and GDI.
e) The average per capita income for Muslim countries is 5011.06 PPP Dollars; and for non-Muslim countries it is 7066.25 PPP Dollars. The PPP Dollars stand for Purchasing Power Parity Dollars.
f) Of the 53 Muslim countries, 26 belong in the low-income group; 12 in the middle-income group; and 15 in the high-income group. The corresponding figures for the non-Muslim countries are: 16, 34 and 51

Table 2: Development Indicators Across High Income Countries (in the 1990s)

	Muslim Countries (GDP per capita < PPP $ 12000) (a) AV=14,763.17	Non-Muslim Countries (GDP per capita < PPP $ 25000) (b) AV=21,111.5
Growth Rate of GDP per capita (%)	3.11 (1.83) [6]	6.41 (2.51) [10]
Investment-GDP Ratio (%)	10.67 (5.13) [3]	11.67 (28.09) [10]
Share of Manufacturing in GDP (%)	8.20 (0.70) [6]	11.35 (28.76) [10]
Population Growth Rate (%)	2.85 (2.03) [5]	0.88 (0.43) [10]
Human Development Index (1990s)	0.09 (0.07) [6]	0.59 (1.44) [10]
Share of Expenditure on Education in GDP (%)	0.90 (0.70) [6]	0.56 (1.38) [10]
Share of Expenditure on Health in GDP (%)	0.54 (0.65) [6]	3.53 (8.26) [10]
Gini Index	..(c)	30.15 (71.06) [8]
Ratio of Rich 10 % to Poor 10 %	..(c)	9.86 (26.2) [9]
Population below $ 1 a day	..(c)	..(c)
Population below national poverty line	..(c)	..(c)

Table continued overleaf

	Muslim Countries (GDP per capita < PPP $ 12000) (a) AV=14,763.17	Non-Muslim Countries (GDP per capita < PPP $ 25000) (b) AV=21,111.5
Gender Development Index	0.19 (0.01) [6]	0.56 (1.38) [10]
Gender Empowerment Measure	..(c)	0.44 (1.09) [10]

Sources: UNDP's *Human Development Report* (various issues)
World Bank's *World Development Report* (2000/01)

Note: Standard deviation is reported in parentheses. A number of observations are reported in brackets, while the figures without parentheses and brackets denote (weighted) averages.

a) The following countries are included in this group: Bahrain, Brunei, Dar us Salam, Oman, Qatar, Kuwait, and UAE.
b) The following countries are included in this group: Norway, Canada, Belgium, the United States, Iceland, Switzerland, Luxemburg, Denmark, Austria, and Ireland.
c) .. indicates missing information.
d) The average per capita income for Muslim countries during 1990/99 is 14,763.17 PPP Dollars; and for non-Muslim countries it is 23,111.5 PPP Dollars.

c) Population Dynamics

Two adverse effects of the very high rate of population have already been noted – namely, a significantly lower growth rate of per capita income and a lower level of human development. However, Table 3 (which gives forecasts of population growth till the year 2015) shows that it has had three additional adverse effects on Muslim economies: (a) notwithstanding the decline of the overall growth rate of population throughout the Muslim world (though the rate of decline here has been much slower than in non-Muslim countries), the less-than-15 years' population is expected to grow at a much higher rate of 1.33 percent in Muslim

Table 3: A Comparative Demographic Profile of Muslim and Non-Muslim Countries (1999-2015)

Variables	Muslim Countries		Non-Muslim Countries		All Countries	
	Share (%)	Growth Rate-1999-2015 (%)	Share (%)	Growth Rate (%)	Share (%)	Growth Rate (%)
Population (in millions)						
1999	25.08 (40.75)	–	41.59 (155.4)	–	36.19 (129.59)	–
2015	34.43 (53.72)	2.14	47.92 (180.55)	0.95	43.51 (151.13)	1.24
Share of Population less than 15 years (%)						
1999	40 09 (6.73)	–	29.3 (10.22)	–	32.83 (10.51)	–
2015	35.62 (9.46)	1.33	24.30 (9.94)	-0.30	28.00 (11.12)	0.17
Share of Population greater or equal to 65 years (%)						
1999	3.51 (1.55)	–	8.36 (4.92)	–	6.78 (4.68)	–
2015	4.40 (1.75)	3.71	10.43 (6.23)	0.37	8.46 (5.92)	2.75

Table continued overleaf

Variables	Muslim Countries		Non-Muslim Countries		All Countries	
	Share (%)	Growth Rate-1999-2015 (%)	Share (%)	Growth Rate (%)	Share (%)	Growth Rate (%)
Share of Economically Active Population in total Population (%)						
1999	56.4	–	62.34	–	60.39	–
	(6.24)		(5.97)		(6.66)	
2015	59.98	2.55	65.28	1.26	63.54	1.58
	(7.95)		(5.24)		(6.71)	
Dependency Ratio						
1999	79.34	–	61.97	–	67.65	–
	(18.71)		(16.51)		(19.04)	
2015	69.58	-0.87	54.26	-0.88	59.27	-0.88
	(22.10)		(13.49)		(18.22)	
Number of Countries	53	53	109	109	162	162

Source: UNDP (2001), *Human Development Report-2001*, UN.

Notes: Standard deviations are reported in parentheses.

- The share of economically active population is defined as the share of population in the age group 15-64 years old in the total population.
- The share of dependent population in total economically active is defined as a dependency ratio. The dependent population includes that population which is less than 15 years old and that population which is greater then or equal to 65 years old.

countries as compared with a *negative* growth rate of 0.30 percent in non-Muslim countries. However, since the *share* of population in this group declines, though much less than it does in non-Muslim countries (rows 5 and 6), the dependency ratio is expected to decline significantly from 79.34 percent to 69.58 percent in 2015, which will have a positive impact on the savings and investment rate. And yet, since the dependency ratio in non-Muslim countries is going to be even lower, the current disparity between the investment and growth rates of Muslim and non-Muslim countries will continue to increase in the next decade and a half. (b) A higher growth rate of economically active population in relation to the overall population growth rate presents itself as a one-time demographic gift (also referred to as a demographic window of opportunity), which *could* lower the dependency rate, increase the savings and investment rate and quality of the labour force *if* associated with a high growth rate of income and faster technological change. However, the Muslim countries have all but squandered the demographic gift (see note 15). Table 3 (row 8) shows that the growth rate of population in this group (2.55 percent) has fallen below the average population growth rate in Muslim countries (2.82 percent). However, it is only half that of the non-Muslim countries (1.26 percent), which means that Muslim countries still have an edge which, if supported by a high rate of technological advancement, *can* turn an *economic liability into an asset*; lower the unemployment and underemployment rates and the incidence of poverty. (c) There is the opposite phenomenon of population *ageing*, i.e., of the share of economically *inactive* population rising at a rate higher than the average growth rate. This is popularly known as the problem of developed countries. However, Table 3 (row 6) shows that this would be a dangerous misperception. True, in non-Muslim (mostly developed) countries, the share of population in this group will be much higher (10.43 percent) than in Muslim countries (4.4 percent); yet the population in this category, though increasing in both groups of countries, will be rising three times faster in Muslim countries (3.71 percent) than in non-Muslim countries (0.37 percent). Furthermore, the growth rate of the older cohorts will be higher than the younger cohorts within Muslim countries. The net result is that Muslim countries will have to work under a double drag – namely, the demographic window of opportunity having been closed prematurely and the onset of population ageing coming 'too early' will cumulatively lower the growth rate of GDP, investment and saving. Also, the unemployment rate will be higher; which, in the absence of a strong growth rate of per capita income, will lower the real wage rate and adversely affect the functional distribution of income (i.e., the share of wage income in total GDP declines while that of profits and rent will increase).

d) Distributive Justice

Table 1 presents a striking result. The eighth row shows that, notwithstanding their markedly low growth rate per capita income and even lower social expenditures, *the distribution of income and wealth is significantly more equitable in Muslim countries than in non-Muslim countries*: the average Gini Coefficient (22.64 percent) is much lower in the former than in the latter (36.07 percent). Also, as shown by the values of the standard deviation, the spread around the average is very much smaller in the former than in the latter. The same result is confirmed by the figures in the ninth row, which show that the differential between the rich (10 percent) and the poor (10 percent) is 7.23 in Muslim countries as compared with 11.55 for non-Muslim countries. Once again, the standard deviation in Muslim countries is much lower than in non-Muslim countries. (The corresponding figures for the top rich Muslim countries are not available.) Both the results confirm that the above-mentioned statistical finding is quite robust. It is also the more remarkable for the fact that most (26 out of 53) Muslim countries belong in the low-income countries (with less than

2000 PPP dollars) as compared with non-Muslim countries where the largest number (59 out of 109) are located in the high-income group (with 5000 PPP dollars and above). Also, the number in the middle-income category (that between 2000 – 5000 PPP dollars) is much lower in Muslim countries (12 out of 53) than in non-Muslim countries (34 out of 109). This result is somewhat unusual. The general tendency is that, even though there is no necessary *causative* link between the two, a better distribution of income is generally *correlated* both with a higher growth *rate* and *level* of per capita income [World Bank (2000)]. Yet, in the present case, greater distributive justice is associated with a lower growth rate and level of per capita income; and vice versa in non-Muslim countries. Part of the explanation for this unusual (though by no means paradoxical) result may be that, if Kuznet's hypothesis is to be believed, economies tend to be more equal at a lower level of income; but the inequality starts to grow as income rises (in the middle to high range). However, this is a rather implausible explanation, because Kuznets also hypothesised that income distribution tends to get egalitarian in the high-income range. Thus, comparing Tables 1 and 2, the Gini coefficient for *rich* non-Muslim countries is lower (30.15) than for *all* non-Muslim countries (33.07). Yet, even this lower value is so much higher than that for the (low-to-mid range) Muslim countries (22.69). Similarly, though the difference between the rich and the poor is less in rich non-Muslim countries (9.86) than in all non-Muslim countries (13.16), it is significantly higher than for all Muslim countries (7.23). This is *not* explained by Kuznet's hypothesis. It is, therefore, not far-fetched to hypothesise that a superior achievement of the Muslim countries may have been attributable, at least in part, to the greater strength of their moral message.

e) Poverty

Rows 10 and 11 of Table 1 depict the average incidence of poverty to be greater in Muslim countries than in non-Muslim countries, with a higher variation around the average in the former than in the latter: the percentage of population earning less than $1 per day is 31.35 percent in the former as compared with 20.94 percent in the latter. 39.47 percent of the population in Muslim countries lives below the national poverty line whilst 33.82 percent in non-Muslim countries do so. This result, though contrary to the Islamic ethical message, should be expected for several reasons: (a) as noted above, the number of countries in the low-income and middle-income groups is so much larger in Muslim countries (26) than in non-Muslim countries (12). (b) The growth rate of per capita income in Muslim countries is much lower than the critical growth rate (3 percent per annum) required for poverty reduction; it is also significantly less than that in non-Muslim countries. (c) The population growth rate is much higher in Muslim than in non-Muslim countries; which, given the low growth rate of per capita income, increases the unemployment rate and lowers the real wage rate and the share of wage income in total income. (d) Social expenditures are much lower in Muslim than in non-Muslim countries. These adverse causative factors enhance the effect of a dismal failure of public policy in Muslim countries – a failure that has more than offset Islam's strong and unequivocal position on reducing poverty as well as the number of poor.

Yet, the poverty differential between Muslim and non-Muslim countries is *not* as large as one would expect from the differences in their respective average level of per capita incomes – i.e., 5011.6 PPP dollars for Muslim countries as compared to 7066.25 PPP dollars for non-Muslim countries – and the much larger differential in the growth *rate* of per capita income. At least, a part of the reason may be the better distribution of income and wealth in Muslim countries, which converts a lower level and growth rate of income into a larger-than-normal rate of poverty reduction [World Bank (2000); p. 55]. There is yet another implication of better distributive justice for the intensity of poverty: it is that the "capability deprivation" – measured, among other factors, by the absolute reduction in the capability to take part in the life of the community – is lower when the income differential is small than when it is large, and that it is greater in rich than in relatively less affluent societies [Sen (1992)]. This implies that capability deprivation in Muslim countries, as opposed to that in non-Muslim countries, should be much less than the income poverty figures would suggest. This has considerable social and political implications as well because a society with greater social justice and a lower sense of deprivation will be more "stable".

f) Gender Disparity/Bias

Two important indices have been developed by the UNDP to adjust the HDI by gender economic and political inequalities. The Gender Development Index (GDI) adjusts achievements in all the three components of HDI – i.e., life expectancy, educational attainment, and income – for gender inequality. Thus, GDI < HDI shows gender inequality with respect to the components of HDI noted above; GDI = HDI shows no gender bias, and GDI > HDI suggests a more equitable pattern. The other indicator is the Gender Empowerment Measure (GEM), which records gender bias in regard to the respective achievements of males and females in political and economic spheres. However, GEM does not have any direct causal relationship with the HDI or the GDI; though some kind of a correlation may be observed. Thus, countries with a better HDI and GDI are expected to do better with respect to GEM than those with a worse record

The GDI

As one would expect, like the HDI, the GDI in Muslim countries is much lower than in non-Muslim countries (Table 1, row 12). But some more interesting aspects of it must be noted. Firstly, *within* Muslim countries GDI_M (0.23) > HDI_M (0.22). This suggests that, on average, there is an equitable distribution of economic opportunities between sexes in Muslim countries. The same is the case with non-Muslim countries: GDI_{NM} (0.51) > HDI_{NM} (0.49).

Secondly, notwithstanding the absence of gender bias in both, the level of accomplishment on the HDI scale is much lower in Muslim countries than in non-Muslim countries. Thus, as one would expect, GDI_{M} (0.23) < GDI_{NM} (0.51), which shows that non-Muslim countries distribute economic opportunities among their people significantly better than Muslim countries do. Thirdly, Table 2 shows a similar pattern for the top (oil-producing) rich Muslim and non-Muslim countries. However, with respect to GDI, rich Muslim countries once again break a general rule: they have done *worse* (0.19) than the relatively less prosperous Muslim countries (0.23). By contrast, rich non-Muslim countries have done *better* (0.56) than the rest of non-Muslim countries (0.51) with respect to GDI. In other words, rich Muslim countries have *not* used their riches to enhance gender equality when compared with the rest of Muslim countries.

Fourthly, Table 2 shows the surprising result that *within* non-Muslim *rich* countries GDI_{NMR} (0.56) < HDI_{NMR} (0.59). By contrast, among Muslim rich countries GDI_{MR} (0.19) > HDI_{MR} (0.09). In other words, *for all their high accomplishments with respect to both GDI and HDI, non-Muslim rich countries exhibit a distinct gender bias*. On the contrary, Muslim countries, notwithstanding their miserable record with respect to both GDI and HDI, do *not* exhibit a gender bias – which can be attributed to Islam's unequivocal emphasis on the equality of humankind.

The GEM

Table 1 (row 13) shows that, with respect to The Gender Empowerment Index (GEM), Muslim countries (0.029) have done much worse than non-Muslim countries (0.14). Also, Table 2 shows that, in rich non-Muslim countries GEM_{NMR} (0.44) > GEM_{NM} (0.14). No corresponding figures are available for Muslim countries; but presumably they must have done worse on this score than rich non-Muslim countries – in violation of Islam's teachings.

III. Economic Reality Versus Islamic Morality

A cursory look at the empirical information presented in Section II-(i) seems to confirm Sirageldin's (1995) conjecture – namely that, with the exception of distributive justice and a lack of gender bias, Islamic ethical values have not had a significant effect on the economic performance of Muslim societies. Yet, it *cannot* be logically inferred (as Hume's Law instructs us) from the instances of the poorer performance of Muslim societies as opposed to non-Muslim societies that Islam's moral message is either weak, indecisive or plainly irrelevant to meet the challenges of a modern Muslim society. Also, the constraining authority of accumulated facts qualifies this negative impression in several ways. Firstly, Islamic morality, or any other, can make the difference only when it is most *explicit* and compelling. Thus, even amidst a generally unfavourable economic climate of low economic growth and unsatisfactory human development, the fact is that the Gini coefficient in Muslim societies and the differential between the rich and the poor is lower than in non-Muslim ones, the difference between the rich and the poor is much less in the former than in the latter, and the gender bias is absent. This is an eloquent tribute to the clarity of Islamic egalitarianism, which has managed to shine through layers of casuistic misinterpretations. How does one, then, explain the rampant poverty in Muslim societies where the Islamic moral values are equally emphatic, explicit, unequivocal and free from any misinterpretations? The answer to this apparent 'paradox' is that, but for the Islamic moral values, which have duly modified the Muslim individual's economic behaviour, poverty in the Muslim countries would have been higher still! The AKDN's (2000) study, referred to in Chapter 4, shows that private philanthropy in Pakistan, motivated by religious conviction, has been large, even by international standards; and that it must have significantly moderated the incidence of poverty and prevented starvation and famine. These results are typical of Muslim countries in general. Even the empirical evidence of Table 1 shows that the differential in poverty figures is not as large as one would expect from the large observable differential between the income levels, the growth rates of income and population between Muslim and non-Muslim countries. But, morally-motivated private behaviour can only make a limited impact on poverty outcomes. Thus, private (voluntary) beneficence alone will normally fail to generate a sizeable transfer of resources to the poor because of the free-riding and assurance problems. Generally speaking, society-level welfare and education programmes cannot be supported by private charity alone. The generally adverse economic outcome of the Muslim countries is, therefore, largely attributable to their extremely inefficient public policies. This brings us back to Sirageldin's observation that the (oil-producing) Muslim countries have generally failed to devise a proactive egalitarian and financially viable public policy.

Secondly, the empirical evidence demonstrates the truth of the observation made several times in this book – namely, that religious values will *not* affect individual behaviour if stated only *implicitly* and *indirectly*. This shows up most convincingly in the very inferior performance of Muslim countries with respect to growth and human development. As observed in Chapter 4, while there is nothing obviously anti-growth in Islamic ethical values, yet the importance of high rates of growth and development has seldom, if ever, been stated as a *moral obligation* of Muslims. Here the *'ulamā'* have not matched Calvin's audacious reformation of Christian ethics to meet the challenge of the Industrial Revolution. This is unfortunate because the much emphasised Islamic moral obligation to reduce poverty *and* the number of poor cannot be achieved without achieving high rates of growth and development on a sustained basis for several decades.

Thirdly, the unfavourable comparative performance of Muslim countries with respect to the growth rate of the population is a prime illustration where (ill-informed) conservative interpretations of Islamic moral values have *misguided* individual behaviour. Indeed, a complete lack of understanding by the *'ulamā'* and even many Islamic economists and scholars of population dynamics and its extremely adverse impact on growth, human development, unemployment rates and poverty has directly contributed to pro-natalist policies in the majority of Muslim countries. Another unfortunate victim of unhelpful interpretation is gender discrimination in political and social spheres (as reflected in GEM), which has led to downplaying the agency aspect of women as an independent force for social change. Yet another is the failure to lend religious support to scientific education, innovation and technological change.

Three general observations follow from the analysis presented in this chapter so far. (a) The potential of an ethics-based society to internalise a sense of social obligation and commitment in individuals and contribute to economic progress is large; but it can be completely frustrated by myopic, inefficient, and amoral public policy. (b) The mere introduction of an ethics-based society – even when a Divine origin of the ethical values is claimed – does *not* guarantee its success. Its efficiency and equity will rather be determined by society's ability to implement an economically viable social contract with its people to win their voluntary support for its programmes and policies. (c) The traditional ethical value system, articulated more than a thousand years ago by great Muslim luminaries like al-Ghazālī at a time of the intellectual and moral decline of Muslims is, to put it mildly, of limited relevance today. Islamic ethics must shake off the shackles of anachronism to play a leadership role in guiding Muslim societies towards greater material prosperity and inner peace. It needs to be replaced by one which helps it to address modern challenges. This is what Chapter 5 has attempted to do.

IV. The Taxonomy of Policy Objectives and Policy Instruments

It follows from the preceding analysis that there is an urgent need to refocus Islamic moral values to suit the needs of Muslim societies – and in particular to pull them out of the morass of economic stagnation. Equally important is the task of integrating public policy with the true Islamic moral imperatives with a view to accelerating economic growth, human development, and poverty reduction in Muslim societies, and deepening its egalitarian character. A key element of success on this score is to clearly spell out the basic policy objectives and the policy instruments to achieve these objectives – while ensuring that both remain within the broad parameters of the Islamic ethical principles explained in Chapter 5.

i) *The Choice of Objectives*

The *objectives* of a typical Muslim society, derivable from the ethical axioms, must help devise and implement a dynamic and just *social contract*. The flow of its benefits must be perceived by the people to exceed its cost, and both the costs and the benefits equitably shared between them – that is, in proportion to their respective economic conditions. The analysis presented so far suggests that the following *three* objectives should form an irreducible set: (a) a high rate of growth of *per capita* income and human development; (b) a stronger accent in Muslim societies on ensuring the equality of the human condition; and (c) a reduced incidence of poverty and the number of poor. However, the Islamic ideal of equality of mankind in the Eyes of Allah *cannot* be accomplished if women, who make up more than fifty percent of the Muslim population, are reduced to a secondary place in society, and if they cannot make their own decisions freely. The free will axiom implies *a free agency of both men and women as active promoters of social change*. An emphasis on human freedom for both men and women is, therefore, the basic point of reference for the realisation of its basic objectives and their link with its moral values. It is in the sunshine of political and economic freedoms that men and women live fuller lives and take greater responsibilities to achieve the basic objectives of Islamic economic policy – namely, a high rate of economic growth and human development, the equality of the human condition, and poverty reduction. These are also the areas where the force of Islamic morality can greatly strengthen public policy in contributing to social welfare at minimum policing and monitoring costs, i.e., by checking the incidence of free-riding in the society. It may, therefore, be instructive, even at the risk of some repetition, to recapitulate the highlights of the discussion in the preceding chapters about the Islamic position on the basic Islamic objectives.

a) Economic Growth and Human Development

The issues of poverty and distributive justice are directly related to economic growth and human development. A high rate of growth of per capita income (of 3 percent per annum plus) plus a high level of social spending on education and health, *especially of women*, are the essential building blocks of a successful anti-poverty policy. And yet, the extant interpretations of Islamic ethical values, though not inimical to growth in principle, do not emphasise these matters enough. The question is: might not the lack of explicit emphasis in the traditional interpretation of Islamic ethical values on growth related issues be *one* of the reasons for the lacklustre growth performance of Muslim societies? As noted above, the answer to the question must be positive, if the main hypothesis presented in this book – namely that *only* explicitly stated religious moral values make a decisive impact on human motivation to work for social good – is accepted. A lack of understanding of the problems of growth and development in Muslim societies when the whole world is talking about its vital importance to human well-being, is truly tragic.[1] This historical anti-growth bias must be undone – especially because, as Rodinson (1978) notes, there is nothing adverse in Islamic values which could have prevented the onset of the Industrial Revolution – contrary to Weber's thesis – or hold it back now in the Muslim world.[2] The religious ethical values that seem to have motivated capitalist growth in the West, i.e., (a) truthfulness, (b) honesty in public dealings, (c) honouring of contracts, are emphasised at several places in the Holy Qur'ān as well with great clarity.[3] That being the case, among other measures taken to promote economic growth and human development in Muslim countries (which are discussed briefly in Section IV of this Chapter), the moral values favourable to these phenomena should be given a starring role. It is understandable why this could not be done one thousand years ago; but there is no justification for neglecting this vital aspect of human well-being now.[4] A related issue vital to economic growth and human development that must be attended to on an *urgent* basis are the very low saving and investment rates in Muslim countries. True, some countries may have been able to invest without growing and grow without investing a lot; yet the mitigating factor has been the inefficiency of investment in the former and superior efficiency in the latter. In general, high saving rates are vital to growth. In this context, an extremely important role can be played by mobilising public opinion against wasteful consumption rife in Muslim societies (especially, in oil-producing countries). And yet there is a tendency among many *'ulamā'* to condone, even praise, luxury consumption as a "sign of good economic judgment" [Kuran (1995b); p. 166] – even though free spenders have been declared as Brothers of the Devil in the Holy Qur'ān.

Yet another anti-growth factor is that – with the exception of Bangladesh and Iran – the population growth rates are still too high in Muslim countries. Now, this may not be the only, or even the most important, impediment to growth, yet it would be dangerously naive to ignore that it adversely affects practically every key economic variable.[5] Human development suffers because of the much greater investment rates required to provide for child care, literacy and education. Equally urgent is paying serious attention to scientific and technological advancements – the lack of which has historically been the single-most reason why the Industrial Revolution never arrived in Muslim countries. In this context, the misinterpretation of education as merely traditional religious education must be urgently removed because it has led to an open hostility towards modern scientific education in conservative circles.

b) The Equality of Economic Condition

The equality of the human condition is perhaps one of the most potent ideas which have helped catalyse societies. And "Islam is probably the most uncompromising of the world's religions in its insistence on the equality of all believers before God" [Marlow (1997; p. XI]. This essentially religious idea flows with equal force on the socio-economic plane. The highly original Islamic approach to human equality with respect to the distribution of income and wealth is determined by the following considerations: (a) the right to private ownership is neither absolute nor unlimited but is relative to Allah's ownership of all wealth; and for this reason there is a share for the poor in the rich man's wealth. (b) Being essentially trustees, people are not absolutely free to do whatever they like with the wealth they own; nor are they free to hoard it. (c) The concentration of wealth in a few hands is undesirable and immoral. (d) People are equal in the use of wealth, though there may be inequality in earning it. The data in Table 1 show that moral values have led to greater egalitarianism in Muslim societies. This happy state of affairs must be preserved and strengthened. In this context, it is important to interpret properly Islamic egalitarian ideals. In particular, the following statements must be qualified: that Islam "does not require equality but only equity in the distribution of wealth" [Mawdūdī (1970); p. 149]; and that "...economic equality is, to be precise, equality of opportunity..." [Sayyid Quṭb (2000)]. These opinions are widely shared by *'ulamā'* and Islamic economists. In the first case, the distinction between 'equality' and 'equity' begs the question as to what good is equity if it does not mean some sort of equality, which is really the foundational principle of Islamic moral philosophy. If it means that Islam does not aim at *perfect* equality, then this is a self-evident statement, because *no one* (including Karl Marx) has ever advocated it. However, if whatever is earned by *legitimate* means is regarded as equitable, then by this definition equity can co-exist with *any* degree of inequality which, however, contradicts the Islamic injunction against the concentration of wealth in the hands of a few.[6] The second opinion is also open to misinterpretation because equality of opportunities to all can be Islamically justified if and only if it guarantees equality of outcomes. This, however, is never a sure thing because equality of opportunity to people with different starting points in life – especially, due to unequal circumstances of birth or early nurture or to the large initial differences in income and wealth – is more likely to *increase*, rather than decrease, existing inequalities of income and wealth. Yet, this is an unacceptable outcome because rising inequalities of income and wealth tend to aggravate poverty, which is clearly a violation of the Islamic ethical principles. This means that, judged by its actual or expected consequences, the principle of equality of opportunity is false. True, "there is no point in denying that natural endowments of individuals are not equal" [Sayyid Quṭb (1976); p. 48]; but it does *not* follow that either (a) the 'natural' endowments are also just; or (b) that society should perpetuate the 'natural' state.[7] In fact, the correct interpretation of the Islamic principle is that people should *not* be compensated for advantages that they have not worked for (or, as Dworkin (1981a; 1981b) put it, for which they are not "responsible"). This observation is strictly consistent with the Qur'ānic principles that: (a) one should get only that which one has worked for; and that (b) individuals are not punished/rewarded for what others do.[8] This lack of clarity on the question of equality has been partly responsible for creating a misconception that egalitarianism is not necessarily a property of the Islamic system [Khadduri (1971); Kuran (1992); Behdad (1992)]. True, this observation is logically erroneous because a general principle cannot be derived from isolated empirical observations; yet it cannot be denied that misinterpretations of the Islamic moral principles on this count (e.g., that inequality is ordained by God) are still common currency in ultra-conservative circles.

c) Poverty Reduction

Islamic values on poverty alleviation are both emphatic and original. They lay down, as no other ethical system does, that: (a) the poor have a *right* in the wealth of the rich; which implies that the latter's right to private property is neither absolute nor unlimited. (b) The act of giving, for that reason, amounts to "returning" to the poor what was in fact theirs in the first place, which means that giving to the poor is not charity but an act of justice. (c) Helping the poor is the *most* important means of attaining spiritual bliss, which instils into individuals (those who are rich) a *commitment* to work for the social good – i.e., even when giving means accepting a cut in one's welfare. And (d) *not* giving to the poor (i.e., hoarding and/or spending excessively on luxuries while the needs of the poor are neglected) amounts to a denial of one's faith. As a matter of comparison, the Islamic moral values on poverty alleviation would motivate individuals to work for the common good with greater commitment than any other ethical system. Thus, for instance, Christian moral values encourage charity, but not as a matter of the right of the poor, or of doing justice to them. In Jewish moral values charity is essentially 'stratified', giving more to persons who were rich but then fell on the thorns of life than to one who has always been poor [Wilson (1997); see also Chapter 3 of the present book for details].

The impact of clarity in Islamic moral values on human motivation in Muslim societies has also been quite noticeable. There is a very significant amount of private philanthropic activity *on strictly religious grounds*. Also, to a considerable extent, this activity, has for centuries, been institutionalised in the form of charitable trusts (*Awqāf*) in almost all the Muslim countries, which are early examples of non-government organisations (NGOs). These institutions have greatly broadened the scope of charitable giving to education and health services, in addition to helping a much larger number of those who do not ask for help. Even some financial institutions in Muslim countries strengthen charitable activity. Thus, the Islamic Development Bank (1993) has allocated a substantial part of its resources to helping the least-developed Muslim countries.[9] It is, therefore, nothing less than a violation of the clear Islamic position that more than a third of the Muslim population lives below the poverty line, even though of the 54 Muslim countries, 4 countries belong to the high-income (non-OECD), 6 to the high middle-income group and 21 to the low-middle income group.

That being the case, a viable poverty-reduction programme must be one of the top priorities in Muslim societies. Such a programme must consist of the following elements: (a) the governance standards must be raised significantly. This is because if budgetary deficits are large public spending on poverty alleviation is universally cut first. In this connection, the substantial waste of resources in Muslim countries, especially in oil-producing countries, must be stopped. (b) The growth rates of per capita income (with the exception of three or four countries) should be substantially increased to at least the 3 percent per annum required for sustained poverty reduction on a durable basis. (c) Although inequalities of income and wealth are on average moderate in Muslim countries, these should be reduced wherever they are significantly higher than the average.[10]

ii) *The Choice of Policy Instruments*

Achieving the stated policy objectives requires making an optimal choice of policy instruments as well. The general principle here is that, to avoid implementational contradictions, there be as many policy instruments as there are objectives because a shortage of effective policy instruments impedes achieving the desired policy objectives [Tinbergen (1958)]. However, considerable lack of clarity exists in the literature on Islamic economics about the kind of policy instruments available to achieve Islamic objectives. The general approach is to cite traditional policies – e.g., the substitution of a profit-based system for an interest-based system, the imposition of *zakāt*, a faithful implementation of the Islamic Law of Inheritance, etc. These are important policy instruments but it would be misleading to exaggerate their effectiveness in a modern Muslim economy. It is an area where the need to break out of 'traditional' modes of thought is the most urgent. This is because the priority of objectives has changed (e.g., growth and human development now receive top priority) in modern times, *and* that these objectives *cannot* be achieved by traditional policies.

This subject is explored in greater detail in Naqvi (1994), but here only a few of the key policy instruments are explained briefly.

a) Structural Transformation

The share of manufacturing in GDP must steadily rise along with a substantial increase in physical and human capital. This is referred to as structural transformation.[11] This is especially the case in oil-producing Muslim countries. Here a very substantial increase in non-oil manufacturing and a decrease in their dependence on oil production and exports (i.e., decreasing their share in total production and total exports respectively) is the *only* way to sustain long run economic and human development. In non-oil countries, the corresponding strategy is to help transfer labour and capital from agriculture to manufacturing sectors, while maximising the growth of the former. Since substantial investable resources are available with these countries, a high rate of investment in non-oil production is an entirely feasible proposition. As noted above, this will require, among other measures, a substantial curtailment in luxury consumption, which has sapped the economic and moral foundations of (Muslim) oil-producing countries.

b) The Abolition of Feudalism and Rent Dependence

Muslim countries must build on their superior (average) performance with respect to distributive justice by an even better distribution of income and wealth and a reduction in the differential between the very rich and the poor. In non-oil producing Muslim countries the extant feudal systems have been parent to grave social, economic, and moral problems. These must be abolished and replaced by owner-cultivated and cooperative farming organised on a scientific basis. In oil-producing countries, the current dependence on the rental income of a few rich individuals has led to socially irresponsible behaviour, involving a colossal waste of resources on trivia, in clear violation of Islamic moral principles. Thus, unearned income should be sharply reduced and eventually eliminated. However, this will happen when, as noted above, the share of non-oil production is very significantly increased. Both these steps – the abolition of feudalism and rental income – will greatly raise agricultural productivity in the former case and increase profit-seeking activities in the latter. In both cases, the distribution of income will improve. Yet another step in this direction is the imposition of progressive taxation on income, which should fall especially heavily on the large rental income sector, which only encourages wasteful consumption. This is essential "not just to reduce debt [in oil-producing countries] but to make revenues less dependent on volatile oil prices" [*The Economist* (2002); p. 17]. In this context, the current thinking among Muslim scholars, especially in oil-producing countries – that the imposition of any tax other than *zakāt* is not Islamically permissible – is germane to fiscal irresponsibility. It should be clear that *zakāt* is a religious obligation and an invaluable element of private philanthropy; but it alone is neither an effective redistributive device nor is it sufficient to reduce poverty on a durable basis. Fortunately, there is now a growing consensus that the government can, and should, levy taxation in addition to *zakāt* if the need arises. Yet another mistaken, but widespread, notion is that the Islamic Law of Inheritance is sufficient to solve the problem of distributive justice. Now this Law is certainly a just system of distributing the deceased's wealth among his legal heirs within the family, but it is certainly *not* an instrument for achieving an egalitarian redistribution of wealth. That job must be done by a carefully crafted system of death duties and other taxes, and land reforms, to diffuse the extant concentration of wealth within a few family oligarchies. Doing this should be an easier task now because the overwhelming opinion (of religious scholars) favours the abolition of the feudal system of land ownership to improve the efficiency and equity of agricultural production.

c) The Profit-and-Loss Sharing (PLS) System

Nearly all treatments of social justice in the literature on Islamic economics assign a starring role to the abolition of interest *and* its replacement by profit-and-loss sharing arrangements for radically altering the distribution of income and wealth and in achieving Islamic social justice [e.g., Sayyid Quṭb (2000); Shafī' (1968); Mawdūdī (1970)]. Now this is an example of *faith-based* reasoning, the limitations of which should be carefully noted.[12] While every society has a right to prescribe the ground rules on how it wishes to conduct its economic affairs; yet, within the constraints of these rules, efforts must be made to make the best of what can be achieved. True, one of the defining characteristics of an Islamic economy is that interest will be abolished in it. This part is uncontroversial. However, the other part of this prescription that the Islamic system can be run *exclusively* on the PLS-only (profit-and-loss sharing) system is no longer so uncontroversial. At any rate, the PLS-*only* alternative to interest is a juristic opinion about which debate is possible; and where the consequences of the proposed scheme must be evaluated. This is a large issue which has been discussed elsewhere [Naqvi (2000)]. Here the focus is only on the *redistributive effects*, beneficial or otherwise, of the substitution of profit for interest on an economy-wide basis. Table 4 shows that, at least in Pakistan, the effect of the proposed reform is most likely to make the distribution of income worse.[13] The Table clearly shows that: (a) when income is unequally distributed (21.09 percent of households receive 64.02 percent of the total income), the high income groups

TABLE 4: The Distribution of Various Types of Incomes Among Households and Their Relative Shares in Total Household Income (1996-97)

% of Total *		Types of Income (In Percentages)					
Income	Number of Households	Household Income in Rs.	Interest	Profits and Salaries	Wages	Others	Total Income (%)
1.63	9.46	Up to 1000	0.00 (0.0)	1.02 (22.89)	1.14 (26.40)	3.29 (50.71)	(100)
12.14	45.19	1001-2500	7.53 (0.06)	5.89 (17.88)	16.59 (51.79)	14.58 (30.27)	(100)
22.21	24.26	2501-4000	18.55 (0.08)	16.85 (27.94)	28.44 (48.49)	20.71 (23.49)	(100)
64.02	21.09	4001 & above	73.92 (0.11)	76.24 (43.86)	53.83 (31.85)	61.42 (24.18)	(100)
100.00	100.00	100.00	100.00	100.00	100.00		

Source: Reproduced from Naqvi (2000). Computed from the Federal Bureau of Statistics (1996-97) *Income and Household Survey* (unpublished); and Rizwana Siddiqui and Zafar Iqbal (1999).

Notes: * Columns 1 and 2 are taken from 1989/90 in Rizwana Siddiqui and Zafar Iqbal (1999). It is reasonable to assume that these variables have not changed much in the short span of five years.

1. Figures in parentheses show the relative share of each income type in total household income (read horizontally); whereas the figures without parentheses denote the distribution of each income type in different households (read vertically).
2. Income from profits in the low-income groups derives from crop farming, livestock, and self-employment; while that of "others" comes from commercial and industrial activities, including rent from buildings, etc.

receive most of both interest income (73.92 percent) and profit income (76.24 percent). On the other hand, the lowest income group receives the least of *both* types of income (nothing of the former and next-to-nothing of the latter). (b) The share of interest income in total income is, by and large, *inversely* related to the increase in total income. (c) The share of profit income in total income is positively related to an increase in total income. Whence follows that an economy-wide substitution of profit income for interest income is more likely to make the distribution of income more skewed than to improve it.[14] The policy implication is *that those who lose from the reform (the fixed-income group) must be compensated by those who gain from it (the profit-earning class)*; and that depositors' savings must be saved from the rapacity of profit-maximising bankers. Fortunately, there is a growing opinion that the aim should be to combine the PLS system with Islamically approved debt-creating policy instruments [Al-Jarhi (1999); Khan (1994); Naqvi and Qadir (1986)]. In addition, it is now understood that, contrary to the earlier opinion that the rate of return on bank deposits must be totally *unguaranteed*, some credible guarantees about giving at least as high a rate of return on private savings as those offered by traditional banks must be provided. In fact, Islamic banks do, in fact, provide such guarantees both in Pakistan and Iran [Iqbal and Mirakhor (1987)].

d) Population Planning

Table 3 should make it clear that the population problem facing Muslim countries is rather daunting. The difficulty is that it is *not* going to be solved in the next 25 years even if the growth rate of the population is brought down to the replacement level *now* by a simultaneous reduction in fertility rates and death rates. This is because, with a large proportion of the population below the age of fifteen (40 percent), the overall population will still continue to grow in the years to come as before. (By the Law of Demographic Momentum, a fall in the population growth rate *now* reduces the growth of employable labour only after a generation.) This adds urgency to reducing both rates now. Indeed, the two are, to some extent, inter-related: a reduction in death rates (especially, the under-5 year infant mortality rate) to very low levels lowers the fertility rates as well. Then, an increase in female literacy and labour force participation rates also works in the same direction. Thus, the current restrictions in many Muslim countries on female education and labour force participation should be done away with. This will simultaneously help remove the large gender bias (measured by GEM) in Muslim countries, increase human freedom, and move them towards egalitarian ideals – all three of which are emphasised by the Holy Qur'ān, but *not* practiced by Muslims on a significant scale. A lowering of population growth rates will itself contribute to raising the growth rate of per capita income directly and indirectly – by reducing the current consumption of the increments in Gross National Product; and, as Coale and Hoover (1958) show, by making a positive impact on saving and investment rates.

Above all, it will bring down poverty, reduce unemployment rates, and increase the real wage rate – which together make functional distribution more equitable as the share of wages in Gross Domestic Product rises. The real challenge is, however, not just to reduce population growth but to do it within the framework of a fast-increasing growth rate of GDP, and on the back of high literacy rates, a universal access to health care, and an acceleration of technological change – all of which are crucial to improving the quality of the labour force before the one-time Demographic Gift is irreversibly withdrawn and population ageing takes a firmer foothold in the overall demographic structure of Muslim countries.[15] Fortunately, many empirical studies [e.g., Gavin (2000); Karim (1997)] show that (a) there is no such thing as a (high) *Muslim* pattern of fertility. (b) Excluding the oil-producers, Muslim countries (especially Iran, Algeria, Tunisia, Syria and Bangladesh) have experienced sharp fertility declines in relatively short periods of time. And (c) that, once the demographic transition sets in, fertility rates can be expected to decline very rapidly. This process must become universal in Muslim countries to improve the level of economic well-being of the people on a durable basis.

e) Social Expenditure

A very significant increase in expenditure on education *and* its effective use is essential for several reasons. Firstly, an increase in primary education reduces poverty directly; and greater secondary and tertiary education contributes to technological advances and scientific sophistication. Secondly, it tends to accelerate economic growth by adding to human capital formation and a scale down of production costs to make Muslim countries more competitive in international markets, increases consumer welfare, and upgrades the labour force. Thirdly, as noted above, greater social expenditure reduces fertility rates. Indeed, in all episodes of rapid fertility decline in Muslim countries (e.g., Iran, Bangladesh, Indonesia), improved education and health (*especially* of women) figures prominently among the causative factors [Gavin (2000); pp. xvii-xviii].

V. The Sway of Islamic Morality

The analysis presented in this book has highlighted the foundational role of religious moral values in improving human well-being. However, as noted above, this general proposition is subject to two important limitations: firstly, voluntary individual behaviour cannot *all by itself* maximise social welfare; it must be supplemented by an activist public policy. In other words, moral ideals must be reflected both in individual behaviour *and* in public policy. Secondly, religious moral values *if not properly interpreted*, can become a positive obstacle to economic progress. It is, therefore, apt to conclude this book by emphasising the need for a public policy with an ideological compass that gives 'true' morality a chance to brighten up the face of Muslim societies.

i) *Public Morality*

It has been emphasised in this book that public policy in an Islamic economy can work more effectively if it mobilises the individual commitment to its basic objectives. The following considerations are important in this context. Firstly, Muslim societies should agree on a broad division of social responsibility between the public domain and the private domain. This is because, like *any* other properly structured economy, Islam's must also be a "mixed economy", in which public policy enters where private action is hesitant, missing or wrong-headed. In general, the level of state intervention will decline, though *never* become 'minimal' (in the Nozickian sense), as a Muslim society attains a higher stage of economic and human development.[16] The reasons why it will never become minimal are both economic and moral. Both of these reasons have been discussed at length in this book (especially in Chapter 4); but it may be useful to briefly recapitulate them here. The *economic case* for public policy rests on the success achieved in breaking the hold of selfishness on economic behaviour and to bring it in line with the needs of society. Without such (selective) intervention by the government, it will not be possible to take even the first step towards resolving the "perennially unfinished agenda" of human existence – e.g., slow growth, inequities of the human condition, poverty, and human deprivation. And yet, it is this agenda which Muslim societies must address on an urgent basis in order to avoid economic *extinction* in an increasingly globalised world. The *moral* case for public policy flows from the inherent limitations of altruism and voluntary individual action to achieve social goals in any society. Thus, Olson (1971) points out: "despite the force of patriotism, the appeal of the national ideology, the bond of common culture, and the indispensability of system of law and order, no major state in modern history has been able to support itself through voluntary dues or contributions", (p. 13).

Secondly, as noted several times in this book, free-riding and assurance problems to a large extent dilute the potential of private morality to achieve social goals and aspirations. True, religious morality, especially when it takes the form of commitment, does minimise free-riding, but the assurance problem and that of coordinating private philanthropic activities still remain.

Furthermore, it would be unrealistic to assume that the elite in society, whose interests are best served by perpetuating existing institutions and who are the ones *least* susceptible to the call of morality, will voluntarily consent to change them. Thus, almost *any* public policy that seeks to change unjust social institutions is beneficial to the individual and to society.[17] The fact is that morality and public policy are complements rather than full substitutes. Without morality, public policy will become much too extensive as the policing and monitoring costs of an amoral individualist system rise exponentially. Conversely, in the absence of an effective public policy, the demands of an ethically motivated economic system on scarce moral resources can increase rapidly; and an overload of morality can make carefully crafted public policy implementationally dysfunctional.[18] It is for this reason that, as noted in Chapter 5, we need minimum, *not* maximum, moral controls even in an ideal Islamic economy – much less in a real-life Muslim society. On the other hand, an inept public policy will blunt the intensity of moral motivation by eroding the commitment of the people to an economic and social system which they do not perceive to be just. Thus, we have the paradoxical situation that while Islamic ideals (when properly interpreted) have moved individuals to laudable charitable acts, the governments in these countries have failed spectacularly in providing effective governance to implement a morally correct and economically viable social contract to resolve the many difficult economic problems noted above [Sirageldin (1995; 2000)]. In particular, large budgetary deficits, caused by profligate non-development expenditure and the inability to impose (and collect) just and effective taxation, have left very little money for growth-promoting and poverty-reducing policies in Muslim societies. Even more important, the power of vested interests has generally obstructed – sometimes in the name of Islam – sustainable egalitarian policies in Muslim societies.

ii) *Private Morality*

Public policy can reinforce morality by influencing the reaction patterns of the individual, and *through them*, of the society. This is important because society does *not* stand apart from the individual. As Marx (1844; 1959) noted, "What is to be avoided above all is re-establishing 'Society' as an abstraction *vis-à-vis* the individual" (p. 104). In the present context, there are two reasons for keeping this in mind. Firstly, as noted in Chapter 2, for all the demands of self-interest in matters of mutually beneficial exchange, moral considerations *dominate* individual behaviour in matters of public weal. For if this were not so, and if the economic universe were afflicted by undiluted selfishness and greed, then a reasoned dialogue among the members of society about the vital problems of human existence would become an impossibility. The fact is that rationality is seldom antiseptically amoral and moral judgements are never entirely irrational. This is the reason why truculent vested interests have never been able to prevent the forces of change, even of cataclysmic proportions, from doing good. Secondly, since society represents individuals, forging mutually beneficial links between *individuals* is essential when their interests clash. Such is the essential interconnectedness of human societies that neglecting it can lead to social breakdown. Thus, it is sheer romanticism to take an overly melioristic view of human nature and assume that 'rational' self-interest always maximises social welfare. Similarly, one should not be misled into believing that humans are all starry-eyed altruists and *always* look beyond their self-interest for the collective good.

Secondly, while recognising the reality of selfishness, it is morality that prompts individuals to work for the common good. A commitment to human well-being becomes the necessary condition of social progress when the existing institutions are unjust – which, unfortunately, is the case in Muslim societies. This is our main theme: morality moulds individual behaviour; that religious morality does it even more effectively; and that in Muslim societies this happens decisively because they take religion more seriously than other societies do. The ubiquity of morality in human motivation carries with it a splendid opportunity because it can undo obstructions to social progress.[19] But there is also the risk that this may not happen if, for all its powerful appeal, religious morality is not correctly presented before individuals. Great economic changes have succeeded in changing the course of history and transforming human lives *only* when moral values did not stand in their way. Muslim societies too must learn to canalise the rush of the informational tide into economic progress and human happiness.

Islam need not be sitting listlessly under the shadow of its own lofty ideals, as it has for centuries now. To climb to great heights, the Islamic ideals, arrayed in their 'native' purity, must be faithfully reflected in Islamic ethics and Islamic law. To this end, both must be refocused and updated to perform their historic mission – to bring material and spiritual strength to themselves, and also to the majority of humankind stuck in the quagmire of want, poverty, and material and moral degradation. This is because, while right morals *guide*, wrong morals (or even a conservative interpretation of right ideals) can *misguide*. Unfortunately, the latter has nowhere done more damage than in the heartlands of Islamic beliefs where human freedom has been suppressed, and egalitarian impulses have been aborted to meet the exigencies of politics and privilege. Misconceptions about Islam's soaring idealism have ensnared the Muslim mind and the soul into believing that the future is nothing but an unchanging extension of the past and that enlightenment and new ideas are useless. In particular, a non-recognition of the agency of the human being (especially women), in the name of the false doctrine of predestination, has done incalculable damage both to human freedom and human well-being. It is high time, therefore, that such dangerous misconceptions and superstitions, which blur the hard edge of actual Muslim ideas and strip words of their meaning, were cleared out of the way. Circumstances have changed from what they were in the Middle Ages, and so have the demands for presenting Islam's moral ideals in a new light.

Muslim societies, weighed down for centuries by the conservative spirit, must finally come to terms with change and free human reason from the chains of antediluvian ideas. They must conquer the fear of the unattempted and progress from the frost-bitten wilderness of economic and moral stagnation to a glorious spring of prosperity. They have the knowledge of Divine Assurance that humankind has limitless possibilities of evolution: "So indeed I call to witness the evening twilight/And the night and all it gathers/And the moon when at the full, that you will climb from stage to stage" (84:16-19). This is the challenge to which the Muslims must respond in order to survive and prosper in the twenty-first century and beyond.

Notes

1. Growth appears only by implication as the last of the five moral values accepted by the *'ulamā'* as of primary importance to the *Sharī'ah* – i.e., faith, life, progeny, intellect, and wealth. True, the preservation of wealth includes its growth, yet this must be stated explicitly and given a starring role in the ethical scheme. However, this omission is not surprising – especially because growth is relatively a recent phenomenon and fast growth has occurred only in the last 50 years or so. The *'ulamā'* could not be explicit about a moral value which they could neither observe nor speculate about. Yet this does not explain why the situation has not changed in modern times as well. It is an interesting historical footnote that Ibn Khaldūn (d. 1406); [Rosenthal (1967)], not only observed the phenomenon of growth and development but also explained the many determinants of growth. See Chapra (2000), Ch. 5. It is, thus, surprising that the findings of even such a great scholar did not find an echo in *fiqh*, or even in what Chapra calls "Classical Islamic Economics".
2. Among the factors that facilitated the Industrial Revolution was, according to Tawney (1937) that Puritanism "insisted...that money making, if not free from spiritual dangers was not a danger and nothing else, but that it could be, and to be carried on for the greater glory of God" (p. 238). Islam, as has been noted several times in the book, explicitly links legitimate material activity to the glory of man's soul.

3. The Qur'ānic verses in support of (a), (c), and (e) are given in Chapter 4. Those which state the remaining principles are: (b) "Shu'aib, does your piety teach we should abandon what our fathers worshipped, or desist from doing what we like with our goods?..." (11:87); (d) "...so that it [i.e., wealth] does not concentrate in the hands of those who are rich among you" (59:7).
4. Unlike the *'ulamā'*, Islamic economists have consistently written on the Islamic concept of development. For instance, see Ahmad (1976) and Chapra (1993). Siddiqi (1976; 1981) devotes a whole section to "Development and Growth" issues.
5. Though not shown in Table 3, the situation is worse in *rich* (oil-producing) Muslim countries, which seem to take pride in being the champions of procreation! Thus, during 1960–2000, the populations in these countries grew at phenomenal rates: UAE (8.8 percent), Qatar (6.5 percent), Kuwait (4.9 percent), Saudi Arabia (4.1 percent), Oman (3.9 percent), Bahrain (3.6 percent). This myopic policy (unfortunately followed in the name of Islam) will have, as it already has, disastrous consequences for their growth rates and human development [*The Economist* (2002)].
6. And, yet this appears to be the opinion of some *'ulamā'*. For instance, Mawdūdī (1970) clearly states that as long as wealth is acquired by legal means, "there is no restriction on how much an individual can earn (accumulate). However, there are restrictions on the manner of spending it" (p. 151).
7. Sayyid Quṭb's (1953; 2000) classic exposition of Islam's social justice philosophy contains the following erroneous statement: "Economic equality is, to be precise, equality of opportunity, combined with the freedom to develop one's talents within the boundaries set by the higher purposes of life" (p. 47). He goes on to strengthen this argument: "Accordingly, to deny the existence of outstanding endowments of personality, intellect and spirit, is a piece of nonsense not worth pursuing" (p. 48). But then who denies this obvious fact; what is denied is that this cannot be an excuse for justifying large differences in income and wealth on moral grounds.
8. The corresponding Qur'ānic verses are: (a) "That a man receives but only that for which he strives" (53:39); (b) "Each soul earns (what it earns) for itself, and no man shall bear another's burden" (6:164). In this context, Sadr's (1982) dual principles of social justice – Social Balance and Reciprocal Responsibility – state the Islamic position accurately and lend support to the general principle that social justice means equality of economic condition, from which departures can be allowed only if it is demonstrated that these work to everybody's advantage.

9. Of the 45 member countries of the Islamic Development Bank, 20 are least-developed, mostly located in Africa, which receive interest-free loans with only a modest service charge. The repayment period is 15-25 years, with a grace period of 3-7 years. Also, about 71 percent of its technical assistance goes to these countries [Islamic Development Bank (1993); pp. 13-14].
10. As a general rule, growth tends to be more pro-poor in egalitarian societies than in non-egalitarian ones [World Bank (2000)].
11. A rising share of manufacturing production, known as structural transformation, can be regarded as the Fundamental Law of Economic Development. It lies at the centre of Arthur Lewis's two-sector model of Economic Development (1954) in which the agriculture sector is too large in relation to the manufacturing sector. The transfer of labour and capital from the former to the latter holds the key to initiating and sustaining the development process. The unlimited supply of (agricultural) labour at a fixed real wage rate to manufacturing activity explains a rising savings rate to finance capital formation. The accumulation of capital in this model performs a double role: it increases the level of national output *and* also moves the composition of output towards a greater efficiency (from less productive agriculture towards high-productivity manufacturing). See, Naqvi (2002).
12. However, it may be noted that this is not the *only* example of faith-based reasoning. Thus, for instance, the liberalist philosophy (which draws strength from the dominant paradigm of neo-classical economics), described in Chapter 2, is yet another such example. It has unlimited *faith* in the unfettered markets' capacity to bring great economic benefits to *all* economies, irrespective of their stage of economic development and regardless of any adverse empirical findings. Also, this philosophy assigns *priority* to individual's (political) liberty over all social objectives. It is on this ground alone that *any* state intervention (including that which aims to help the poor) is opposed [Hayek (1960); Friedman (1962); Nozick (1974)]. But this 'fact' does not justify this kind of reasoning in Islamic economics, nor does it diminish its adverse effect on rational thought in our discipline.
13. It is interesting to note that even the Islamic Ideology Council (1992) argues that "if interest is abolished, without taking other complementary steps to make the economy truly Islamic, then it will most likely benefit the capitalistic class...and hurt the poor and the middle income groups who depend on fixed deposit small saving schemes...However, this is not an excuse for continuing the interest based system even for a minute; but only to argue for the

introduction of a full-fledged Islamic system" (p. 87; English translation is mine). Note: This quote is from Maulana Irshadul Haq Thanvi's note which is (approvingly) appended to the Council's main report. For an earlier statement of this position, see Naqvi *et al.* (1980; 1984).

14. Empirical evidence on the working of the 177 Islamic Banks shows that the rate of return offered by them has been typically *lower* than that offered by traditional banks where both types are operating together. The same is the case where (Pakistan, Iran, Sudan) Islamic Banking has replaced traditional banking on an economy wide basis [see Iqbal *et al.* (1998); Naqvi (1994; and many other references cited in Naqvi (2000)].
15. The one-time demographic window of opportunity is that as Demographic Transition from a high fertility-high mortality sequence takes place, the labour force increases at a faster rate than the overall growth of population; which means a lower dependency rate and a potential for a higher rate of saving. If this potential is mobilised by high rates of physical and human capital formation, the growth rates of per capita income can be increased. However, as is the case in Muslim countries, if this opportunity, which will last for about a generation (of about 25 years or so), is not utilised the dependency rates will again start to rise as the proportion of the old age population increases at the end of this period, which would mean lower savings, investment and growth rates and higher poverty. The tragedy is that once this opportunity is wasted, the loss will be irreversible because such opportunity comes *only* once in the life of a nation, from here to eternity! [Sirageldin (2000)].
16. The statement in the text implies that the following description of the Islamic Economic System is *invalid*: "it can be argued that perfect competition, operating through its own self-adjustment mechanisms, constitutes the primary coordinating mechanism of the Islamic economic system, providing it fulfils the Islamic economic system's first-order priorities", [Nomani and Rahnema (1994)]. This statement is invalid for three reasons. First, by the First Fundamental Theorem of Welfare Economics, a competitive equilibrium is "unimprovable" and morally neutral. Whence follows that it, by itself, *cannot* fulfil Islam's first-order (moral) priorities. Secondly, by the same token, a state of equilibrium cannot be improved by public policy – say, with respect to reducing poverty, narrowing inequalities of income and wealth, etc. This, again, makes a regime of perfect competition irrelevant for an Islamic economy. Thirdly, the link between competitive equilibrium and Pareto optimality (efficiency) is broken when markets are missing, non-

universal and prone to complete collapse, which is almost always the case in the real world. See, Naqvi (2002).

17. Rodinson (1978) notes that force of Islamic morality in the Middle Ages was, by and large, ineffective to bridle the rich from abusing the power and wealth they possessed: "On the whole, the traditional Muslim states offer throughout history the spectacle of a poignant contrast between astonishing luxury that prevails at the courts and among the rich, and the most abject misery in which the mass of the people are sunk", (p. 73). The reality is no different in the present age, when rich governments and elites lord it over the poor in many Muslim countries. Yet this 'fact' only highlights the need for a proactive public policy, as noted in the text.
18. Indeed, as Arrow (1972) points out, "ethically motivated behaviour may even have a *negative* value to others if the agents act without sufficient knowledge of the situation", (p. 355).
19. That, for better or worse, religious values have a decisive influence on individual behaviour can be illustrated by only two examples: on the *negative* side, the opposition by most religious scholars to family planning programmes, has undermined the government efforts in this direction. As a result, Muslim societies (with few exceptions like Bangladesh and Iran where religious leaders have supported family planning) are burdened with high rates of population growth. On the positive side, the opposition to *ribā* has resulted in the establishment of Islamic Banks in nearly all Muslim countries.

References

'Abduh, Shaykh, Muḥammad (1966, original 1908), *The Theology of Unity* (*Risālah al-Tawḥīd*), translated by Isḥāq Musa'ad and Kenneth Cragg, Allen & Unwin (translation of the 18th edition, 1957).

Aga Khan Development Network (2000), *Philanthropy in Pakistan*, Pakistan: Aga Khan Foundation.

Ahmad, Khurshid (1975), *Islam: its Meaning and Message*, London: Islamic Council of Europe.

__________ (1976), "Economic Development in an Islamic Framework", in Khurshid Ahmad (ed.), *Studies in Islamic Economics*, Leicester: The Islamic Foundation.

__________ (1981), "Foreword to Syed Nawab Haider Naqvi, *Ethics and Economics, An Islamic Synthesis*", Leicester: The Islamic Foundation.

__________ (1994), "Foreword to Syed Nawab Haider Naqvi's (1994) *Islam, Ethics and Society*", Kegan Paul International, London, UK.

Ali A. Ali and Ibrahim A. Elbadawi (1999), "Poverty in the Arab World: The Role of Inequality and Growth", Paper Presented at ERF Sixth Annual Conference on "Regional Trade, Finance and Labor", Cairo, 23-31 October 1999. Forthcoming in Ismail Sirageldin (ed.), *Population and Development Challenges in the Middle East and North Africa: Towards the 21st Century*.

Ali, Ahmad (1994), *Al-Quran* – A Contemporary Translation: New Jersey: Princeton University Press (Reprinted in 1995 by Karachi: Akrash Publishing).

Ali, Syed Ameer (1988), *The Spirit of Islam*, Karachi: Elite Publishers Pvt (First published in 1922, London: Christophers).

Arrow, Kenneth (1951), *Social Choice and Individual Values*, New York: John Wiley & Sons (2nd edition in 1963).

__________ (1973), "Some Ordinalist Notes on Rawls, Theory of Justice", *Journal of Philosophy*, May 70 245-63.

__________ (1972), "Gifts and Exchanges", *Philosophy and Public Affairs*, 1:4, 343-362.

__________ and F.H. Hahn (1971), *General Competitive Analysis*, San Francisco: Holden-Day; republished Amsterdam: North Holland (1979).

Augustine, Saint (1878), *The City of God*, translated by Rev. Marcus Dods, Edinburgh: T. and T. Clark.

Barry, Brian (1973), *The Liberal Theory of Justice*, Oxford: Clarendon Press.

Behdad, Sohrab (1989), "Property Rights in Contemporary Islamic Thought, A Critical Perspective", *Review of Social Economy*, 47, 185-211.

__________ (1992), "Property Rights and Islamic Economic Approaches", in Jomo, S.K. (ed), *Islamic Economic Alternatives*, London: Macmillan Academic and Professional Ltd.

Bell, Richard (1953), *Introduction to the Qur'ān*, Edinburgh: Edinburgh University Press.

Bergson, Abram (1938), "A Reformulation of Certain Aspects of Welfare Economics", *The Quarterly Journal of Economics*, 52 (Feb.), 314-44.

Birdsall, N. and Londono, J.L. (1997), "Asset Inequality Matters: An Assessment of the World Bank's Approach to Poverty Reduction", *The American Economic Review*, 87:2, 32-37.

Boer, De (1970), *The History of Philosophy in Islam*, London: Luzac & Company Ltd.

Boisard, Marcel A. (1987), *Humanism in Islam* (English Translation) Indianapolis: American Trust Publications (originally published in French in 1979).

Boulding, Kenneth (1966), "The Economics of Knowledge and the Knowledge of Economics", *The American Economic Review*, 56:2, 1-13.

__________ (1973), *The Economy of Love and Fear*, Belmont; Calif: Wadsworth Publishing Co.

Buchanan, Allen (1985), *Ethics, Efficiency and the Market*, Totowa, N.J.: Rowman and Allenheld.

Buchanan, James (1975), *The Limits to Liberty: Between Anarchy and Leviathan*, Chicago: University of Chicago Press.

__________ (1985), *Liberty, Market and the State: Political Economy in the 1980s*, Sussex: Wheatsheaf Books Ltd.

__________ and Gordon Tullock (1962), *The Calculus of Consent*, Ann Arbor: The University of Michigan Press.

Calder, N. (1997), "Sharī'ah", in C. E. Bosworth, E. Van Donzel, W. P. Heinrichs and G. Lecomte (eds.), *The Encyclopaedia of Islam*, Vol. IX, Leiden: Brill, Vol. (pp. 320-326).

Chapra, M. Umer (1992), *Islam and the Economic Challenge*, Leicester: The Islamic Foundation.

__________ (1993), *Islam and Economic Development*, Islamabad: Islamic Research Institute.

__________ (2000), *The Future of Economics: An Islamic Perspective*, Leicester: The Islamic Foundation.

Choudhury, M.A. (1995), *The Epistemological Foundations of Islamic Economic, Social, and Scientific Order*, Ankara: Statistical, Economic, and Social Research and Training Centre for Islamic Countries.

Coale, Ansley J. and Edgar M. Hoover (1958), *Population Growth and Economic Growth in Low-income Countries*, Princeton N.J.: Princeton University Press.

Coats, A.W. (ed.) (1971), *The Classical Economists and Economic Policy*, London: Methuen.

Collier, Laurence (1947), *Flight from Conflict*, London: C. A. Watts & Co.

Denison, Edward F. (1962), *The Sources of Economic Growth in the United States and Alternatives before the US*, New York: Committee for Economic Development.

Dworkin, R. (1981a), "What is Equality? Part I: Equality of Welfare," *Philosophy and Public Affairs*, 10:3, 185-246.

__________ (1981b), "What is Equality? Part II: Equality of Resources," *Philosophy and Public Affairs*, 10:4, 283-345.

Eaton, Charles le Gai (1987), "Man" in Nasr, S.H. (ed.), *Islamic Spirituality: Foundations*, London: Routledge & Kegan Paul Ltd.

Edgeworth, F.Y. (1881), *Mathematical Physics: An Essay on the Application of Mathematics to Moral Sciences*, London: Kegan Paul.

Ess, Joseph Van (1987), "Mu'tazilah", in Eliade, Mircea (1987), *The Encyclopaedia of Religion* (Vol. 10), London: Macmillan Publishing Company, pp. 220-229.

Feldman, Allan, M. (1991), "Welfare Economics", In John Eatwell, Murray Milgate, and Peter Newman, *The World of Economics (The New Palgrave)*, London: Macmillan.

Fogel, R.W. (2000), *The Fourth Great Awakening and Future of Egalitarianism*, Chicago: The University of Chicago Press.

Friedman, Milton (1962), *Capitalism and Freedom*, Chicago: Chicago University Press.

Gauthier, David (1986), *Morals by Agreement*, Oxford: Clarendon Press.

Gavin, W. Jones (2000), "Population Issues for Pakistan: Perspectives from the Wider Muslim World", in *Pakistan Population Issues in the 21st Century* (Conference Proceedings, Oct. 24 – 26), Karachi: Population Association of Pakistan.

Gibb, H.A.R. (1947), *Modern Trends in Islam*, Chicago: Chicago University Press.

__________ (1975), *Islam*, London: Oxford University Press.

__________ and J.H. Kramers (1961), *The Shorter Encyclopaedia of Islam*, Ithaca, N.Y.: Cornell University Press.

Gibbon, Edward (1984), *The Decline and Fall of the Roman Empire*, Edited by Dero A. Saunders, Harmondsworth: Penguin Books (original work published from 1776 to 1788).

Gimaret, D. (1993), "Mu'tazila", in C. E. Bosworth, E.Van Donzel, W. P. Heirichs and Ch. Pellat (eds.), *The Encyclopaedia of Islam* (new edition) (Vol. VII), Leiden – New York, E.J. Brill, pp. 783-793.

Glassé, Cycril (1989), *The Concise Encyclopaedia of Islam*, London: Stacey International.

__________ (1989), "al-Ghazālī, Abū Ḥāmid Muḥammad (450-505/1058-1111)", *The Concise Encyclopaedia of Islam*, London: Stacey International.

Graff, J. Dev (1991), "Social Cost", In John Eatwell, Murray Milgate, and Peter Newman, *The New Palgrave: The World of Economics*, United Kingdom: Macmillan Press Ltd.

Hadley, G. (1961), *Linear Algebra*, London: Addison-Wesley Publishers.

Hall, Herbert (1973), "Rawls on Liberty and its Priority", Reprinted in Norman Daniels (ed.) (1975), *Reading Rawls*, New York: Basic Books.

Haque, Ziaul (1977), *Landlord and Peasant in Early Islam*, Islamabad: Islamic Research Institute.

Harsanyi, John (1955), "Cardinal Welfare, Individual Ethics and Interpersonal Comparisons of Utility", *Journal of Political Economy*, 63 (Aug.), 309-321.

__________ (1977), "Morality and the Theory of Rational Behaviour", *Social Research* (Winter) 44:4, 623-656.

__________ (1991), "Value Judgements", In John Eatwell, Murray Milgate, and Peter Newman, *The World of Economics (The New Palgrave)*, London: Macmillan.

Hausman, Daniel, M. and Michael S. McPherson (1993), "Taking Ethics Seriously: Economics and Contemporary Moral Philosophy", *Journal of Economic Literature*, 31; 671-731.

Hayek, F.A. (1960), *The Constitution of Liberty*, Chicago: University of Chicago Press.

__________ (1967), *Studies in Philosophy, Politics, and Economics*, Chicago: University of Chicago Press.

Hirsch, Fred (1977), *Social Limits to Growth*, London: Routledge & Kegan Paul. (Reprinted with a new foreword by Tibor Scitovsky, 1995).

Hochman, Harold. M., and James D. Rogers (1969), "Pareto-optimal Redistributions", *The American Economic Review*, 59:4, 542-557.

Hodgson, Marshall, G.S. (1974a), *The Venture of Islam*, (Vol. 1), Chicago: The University of Chicago Press.

__________ (1974b), *The Venture of Islam* (Vol. 2), Chicago: The University of Chicago Press.

__________ (1974c), *The Venture of Islam*, (Vol. 3), Chicago: The University of Chicago Press.

Iqbal, Mohammed (1986), *The Reconstruction of Islamic Thought in Islam*, M. Saeed Sheikh (ed.), Lahore: Institute of Islamic Culture (First published in 1932 by Oxford University Press).

Iqbal, Munawar, Ausaf Ahmad, Tariqullah Khan (1998), *Challenges Facing Islamic Banking*, Jeddah: Islamic Research Institute, Islamic Development Bank.

Iqbal, Zubair and Abbas Mirakhor (1987), *Islamic Banking*, Washington D.C.: International Monetary Fund.

Islamic Development Bank (1993), *Nineteen Years in the Service of Development*, Jeddah: Islamic Development Bank.

Islamic Ideology Council (1992), *Report on Islamic Economic System* (Urdu), Islamabad: Islamic Ideology Council, Government of Pakistan.

Issawi, Charles (1969), *An Arab Philosophy of History*, London: John Murray (Publishers) Ltd.

Jafri, Syed Hussain (1988), *A Historical Review of the Development of Islamic Thought*, in S.H.M. Jafri (ed.), *Iqbal, the Reconstruction of Islamic Thought* (Text in Urdu), Karachi: Pakistan Area Study Centre.

___________ (2001), *A Political and Moral Vision of Islam*, Lahore (Pakistan): Institute of Islamic Culture.

Al-Jarhi, Mabid Ali (1999), "Islamic Banking and Finance in the 21st Century", Keynote Address presented at the *International Conference on Islamic Economics*, Kuala Lumpur, Malaysia.

___________ and Iqbal, Munawar (2001), *Islamic Banking: Answers to Some Frequently Asked Questions*, Jeddah: Islamic Research Institute, Islamic Development Bank.

Jauhri, Talib (1984), *Islamic Economics* (Urdu), Karachi: Mass Printers.

Jomo, K.S. (1992), *Islamic Economic Alternatives*, London: Macmillan Academic and Professional Ltd.

Kamali, Mohammed Hashim (1999), "Maqāṣid al-Sharī'ah: The Objectives of Islamic Law", *Islamic Studies*, Vol. 38, No. 2, pp. 193-208.

Kant, Immanuel (1948), *Groundwork of Metaphysics of Morals*, Trans (1948) by H. Paton, New York: Harper & Row (First published in 1785).

Karim, Mehtab (1997), Reproductive Behaviour in Muslim Countries: DHS Working Papers, No. 23, New York: Macro International Inc., and the United Nations Population Fund.

Keynes, John Maynard (1932), *Essays in Persuasion*, New York: Harcourt Brace.

Khadduri, Majid (1971), *The Islamic Concept of Justice*, Baltimore: Johns Hopkins University Press.

Khan, Fahim M. (1994), "Comparative Economics of Some Islamic Financing Techniques", *Islamic Economic Studies*, 2:1, 35-68.

Khan, Mohsin S. and Abbas Mirakhor (1992), "Islamic Banking", In Paul Newman, Murray Milgate, and John Eatwell, *The New Palgrave Dictionary of Money and Finance*, London: Macmillan, pp. 531-533.

Klein, Issac (1979), *Mishna Torah – Book of Agriculture*, US: Yale University Press.

Klein, Lawrence R. (1985), "Reducing Unemployment without Inflation", *America*, 4 May, 362-365.

Kuran, Taimur (1992), "Economic Justice in Contemporary Islamic Thought", in Jomo, S.K. (ed.), *Islamic Economic Alternatives*, London: Macmillan Academic and Professional Ltd.

___________ (1995a), "Economic Theory", in Esposito, J.L. (ed.), *The Oxford Encyclopaedia of the Modern Islamic World*, New York: Oxford University Press.

___________ (1995b), "Islamic Economics and the Islamic sub-Economy", *Journal of Economic Perspectives*, 9:4, 155-173.

Lapidus, Ira. M. (1982), *"The Arab Conquests and the Formation of Islamic Society"*, in G.H.A. Juynboll (ed.), *Studies in The First Century of Islamic Society*, Carbondale: Southern Illinois University Press.

___________ (1997), *A History of Islamic Societies*, Cambridge: Cambridge University Press.

Latimer (1848), The Fifth Sermon on the Lord's Prayer, In *Sermons*, London: Everyman.

Lewis, Arthur W. (1954), "Economic Development with Unlimited Supplies of Labour", *Manchester School of Economics and Social Studies*, 22, 139-191.

Little, Ian (1957), *A Critique of Welfare Economics* (2nd Edition), Oxford: Oxford University Press.

Locke, J. (1952), *Second Treatise of Civil Government*, edited by P. Laslett (2nd Rev. Ed.) Indianapolis: Bobbs-Merrill.

MacIntyre, Alasdair (1971), *Marxism and Christianity*, Harmondsworth: Penguin (First published in 1951).

Marlow, Louise (1997), *Hierarchy and Egalitarianism in Islamic Thought*, Cambridge: Cambridge University Press.

Marx, Karl (1959), *Economic and Philosophic Manuscript of 1844*, Moscow: Foreign Languages Publishing House (First published in 1844).

Mawdūdī, Abul A'lā (1970), *Islamic Economics* (Urdu), Lahore: Islamic Publications Co.

__________ (1976), *Human Rights in Islam*, Leicester: The Islamic Foundation.

McCord, C. and Freeman, H.P. (1990), "Excess Mortality in Harlem", *New England Journal of Medicine*, 322 (Jan.).

Mill, John Stuart (1874), "The Utility of Religions", *Collected Works*, X, Toronto: University of Toronto Press (Reprinted 1969).

Morishima, M. (1982), *Why Has Japan Succeeded? Western Technology, Japanese Ethos*, Cambridge: Cambridge University Press.

Mueller, Dennis, C. (1979), *Public Choice*, Cambridge: Cambridge University Press (2nd edition published in 1989).

Murata, Sachiko and William C. Chittick (2000), *The Vision of Islam*, London: I.B. Tauris.

Murphy, J.G. (1970), *The Philosophy of the Right*, London: Macmillan.

Musgrave, Richard (1959), *The Theory of Public Finance*, New York: McGrawHill.

Nagel, T. (1975), "Libertarianism Without Foundations", *Yale Law Review*. Reproduced in Jeffrey Paul (ed.) (1981), *Reading Nozick*, Oxford: Basil Blackwell.

Naqvi, Syed Nawab Haider (1978), "Ethical Foundations of Islamic Economics", *Islamic Studies*, 17:2, 105-136.

__________ (1981), *Ethics and Economics: An Islamic Synthesis*, Leicester: The Islamic Foundation.

__________ (1993), *Development Economics: A New Paradigm*, New Delhi, London: Sage Publications.

__________ (1994), *Islam, Economics, and Society*, London: Kegan Paul.

__________ (1995), "The Nature of Economic Development", *World Development*, 23:4, 543-556.

__________ (1997), "The Dimensions of an Islamic Economic Model", *Islamic Economic Studies*, 4:2, 1-19.

__________ (2000), "Islamic Banking: An Evaluation", *IIUM Journal of Economics and Management*, 8:1, 41-70.

__________ (2002), *Development Economics: Nature and Significance*, London: Sage Publications.

__________, H.U. Beg, Rafiq Ahmed and Mian M. Nazeer (1980), *The Agenda for Islamic Economic Reform*, Islamabad: Pakistan Institute of Development Economics.

__________, __________, __________and __________ (1984), *Principles of Islamic Economic Reform*, Islamabad: Pakistan Institute of Development Economics.

__________ and Asghar Qadir (1985), "Incrementalism and Structural Change", *The Pakistan Development Review*, Vol. 24, No. 2, pp. 87-102.

__________ and __________ (1986), *A Model of a Dynamic Islamic Economy and the Institution of Interest*, Islamabad: Pakistan Institute of Development Economics.

Nasr, Seyyed Hossein (ed.) (1987), *Islamic Spirituality – Foundations*, Routledge and Kegan Paul Ltd.

Neusner, Jacob (1990), *The Economics of Mishnah*, Chicago: University of Chicago Press.

Nomani, Farhad and Ali Rahnema (1994), *Islamic Economic System*, London: Zed Books Ltd.

Nozick, Robert (1974), *Anarchy, State and Utopia*, New York: Basic Books.

Nyazee, Imran Khan (1994), *Theories of Islamic Law*, Islamabad (Pakistan): International Institute of Islamic Thought and Islamic Research Institute.

__________ (2000), *Islamic Jurisprudence*, Islamabad (Pakistan): International Institute of Islamic Thought and Islamic Research Institute.

O'Rahilly, Alfred (1948), *Aquinas Versus Marx*, Oxford: Oxford University Press.

Olson, Mancur (1971), *The Logic of Collective Action*, Cambridge Mass.: Harvard University Press.

Parfit, Derek (1984), *Reasons and Persons*, Oxford: Clarendon Press.

Pastoral Letter on Catholic Social Teaching and the U.S. Economy (1985), Washington D.C.: National Conference of Catholic Bishops.

Popper, Karl (1980), *The Logic of Scientific Discovery*, (10th revised edition), London: Hutchinson.

Quṭb, Sayyid (1976), "Islamic Approach to Social Justice", In Khurshid Ahmad (ed.), *Islam: its Meaning and Message*, London: Islamic Council of Europe.

__________ (2000), *Social Justice in Islam*, New York: Islamic Publications International (First published in 1953; English translation by Hamid Algar).

Rahman, Fazlur (1979), *Islam*, Chicago: University of Chicago Press.

__________ (1980), "Islam: Legacy and Contemporary Challenge", *Islamic Studies*, 19:4, 235-246.

Rapoport, Anatol (1991), "Prisoner's Dilemma", In John Eatwell, Murray Milgate, Peter Newman, *The World of Economics (The New Palgrave)*, UK: The Macmillan Press Ltd.

Rawls, John (1971), *A Theory of Justice*, Cambridge, Mass.: Harvard University Press.

__________ (1985), "Justice as Fairness: Political Not Metaphysical", *Philosophy and Public Affairs*, 14:3, 223-251.

__________ (1999), *A Theory of Justice* (Revised Edition), London: Oxford University Press.

Reder, Melvin (1979), "The Place of Ethics in the Theory of Production", in Michael Boskin (ed.), *Economics and Human Welfare: Essays in Honour of Tibor Scitovsky*, New York: Academic Press, pp. 133-146.

Robbins, Lionel (1935), *An Essay on the Nature and Significance of Economic Science* (2nd Edition), London: Macmillan.

Robinson, Joan (1973), *Economic Philosophy*, England: Pelican Books.

Rodinson, Maxime (1978), *Islam and Capitalism* (English Translation), New York: Pantheon Books (The original French edition in 1966).

Roemer, John E. (1996), *Egalitarian Perspectives*, Cambridge: Cambridge University Press.

Rosenthal, Franz (1967), *Ibn Khaldūn: The Muqaddimah, An Introduction to History*, London: Routledge & Kegan Paul (First published in 1958).

Rousseau, J.J. (1964), *A Discourse on the Origin of Inequality*, in the *First and Second Discourses*, (ed.) by R.D. Masters, New York: St. Martin's Press.

Russell, Bertrand (1954), *Human Society in Ethics and Politics*, London: George Allen & Unwin.

Sadr, Mohammed Baqir (1982), *Our Economics* (Arabic), English Translation, Vol. 1, Part II, Tehran: World Organization of Islamic Services.

Samuelson, Paul A. (1947), *Foundations of Economic Analysis*, Cambridge, M.A.: Harvard University Press.

Scanlon, T (1986), "Equality of Resources and Equality of Welfare: A Forced Marriage", *Ethics*, Vol. 97, pp. 111-118.

__________, (1999), "Utilitarianism and Contractarianism", In A.K. Sen and Bernard Williams, *Utilitarianism and Beyond*, Cambridge: Cambridge University Press.

Schuon, Frithjof (1976), *Islam and the Perennial Philosophy*, London: World of Islam Festival Publishing Company Ltd.

__________ (1987), "The Spiritual Significance of the Substance of the Prophet", in S.H. Nasr (ed.), *Islamic Spirituality*, London: Routledge & Kegan Paul Ltd.

Sen, Amartya K. (1970), *Collective Choice and Social Welfare*, Cambridge, M.A.: Holden-Day, Inc.

__________ (1973), "Behaviour and the Concept of Preference", *Economica*, 40:159, 241-259.

__________ (1977), "Rational Fools", *Philosophy and Public Affairs*, 6:4, pp. 317-344.

__________ (1981), *Poverty and Famine: An Essay on Entitlement and Deprivation*, Oxford: Clarendon Press.

__________ (1987), *Ethics and Economics*, London: Basil Blackwell.

__________ (1992), *Inequality Re-examined*, New York & Oxford: Clarendon Press.

__________ (1997), "Maximization and the Act of Choice", *Econometrica*, 64:4, 745-779.

__________ (1999a), "The Possibility of Social Choice", *The American Economic Review*, 89:3, 349-378.

__________ (1999b), *Development As Freedom*, Oxford: Oxford University Press.

__________ and Bernard Williams (1999), *Utilitarianism and Beyond*, Cambridge: Cambridge University Press (First Published in 1982).

Al-Shakaa, Moustafa (1994), *Islam without Factions* (Arabic), Cairo: Al-Dar Al-Miṣrīyah Al-Lubnānīyah.

Shafī', Muftī Muḥammad (1968), *Distribution of Wealth in Islam* (Urdu), (English translation by Muhammad Hasan Askari and Karrar Hussain), Karachi: Ashraf Publications.

Shahrastānī, 'Abd al-Karīm (1978), *Al-Milal wa al-Niḥal* (Arabic), Cairo: Muṣṭafā al-Bābī al-Ḥalabī.

Sherwin, Byron (1989), "The US Catholic Bishop's Pastoral Letter on the Economy and Jewish Tradition", in Charles R. Strain (ed.), *Prophetic Visions and Economic Realities: Protestants, Jews and Catholics Confront the Bishop's Letter on the Economy*, Grand Rapids, Michigan: William B. Erdman's Publishing House.

Siddiqi, Muhammad Nejatullah (1976), "Muslim Economic Thinking: A Survey of Contemporary Literature", in Khurshid Ahmad (ed.), *Studies in Islamic Economics*, Leicester: The Islamic Foundation.

___________ (1981), *Muslim Economic Thinking: A Survey of Contemporary Literature*, Leicester: The Islamic Foundation.

Sirageldin, Ismail (1995), "Islam, Society and Economic Policy", *The Pakistan Development Review*, 34:4, 457-478.

___________ (2000), "Elimination of Poverty: Challenges and Islamic Strategies", *Islamic Economic Studies*, 8:1, 1-16.

Smith, Adam (1776), *An Enquiry into the Nature and Causes of the Wealth of Nations*, Reprinted R.H. Campell and A.S. Skinner (eds.), Oxford: Clarendon Press (1976).

___________ (1790), *Theory of Moral Sentiments*, Reprinted D.D. Raphael and A.C. Macfie (eds.), Oxford: Clarendon Press (1975).

Smith, Charles D. (1962), "Secularism", in *The Encyclopaedia of Modern Islamic World*, New York: Oxford University Press.

Stephen, J. Fitzjames (1967), *Liberty, Equality, Fraternity*, Reprinted Cambridge, England: Cambridge University Press (First published in 1873).

Stigler, George J. (1975), "Smith's Travel on the Ship of the State", in Skinner, A.S and Wilson, T. (1975), *Essays on Adam Smith*, Oxford: Clarendon Press.

___________ (1981), "Economics or Ethics?" in McMurrin, S. (ed.) (1981), *Tanner Lectures on Human Values*, Vol. II, Cambridge: Cambridge University Press.

Stiglitz, Joseph P. (1988), "Economic Organization, Information, and Development", in Hollis B. Chenery and T.N. Srinivasan, *Handbook of Development Economics*, Vol. 1, New York: Elsevier Science Publishers.

___________ (1991), "Another Century of Economic Science", *The Economic Journal*, 101:404, 134-141.

Streeten, Paul (1953), "Appendix: Recent Controversies", In *The Political Element in the Development of Economic Theory*, by Gunnar Myrdal, (translated by Paul Streeten), London: Routledge & Kegan Paul (pp. 208-217).

Sugden, Robert (1993), "Welfare, Resources and Capabilities: A Review of *Inequality Re-examined* by Amartya Sen", *Journal of Economic Literature*, 31 (Dec.), 1947-1962.

Taleghani, Ayatullah Sayyid Mahmud (1982), *Society and Economics in Islam* (Persian), Translated by R. Campbell, with annotations and introduction by Hamid Algar, Berkeley, California: Mizan Press.

Tawney, R.H. (1937), *Religion and the Rise of Capitalism*, Harmondsworth, England: Penguin Books (First published in 1926).

The Economist (2001), "Righting Wrongs", *The Economist*, London, August 18th – 24th, pp. 18-12; and the Leader ("Politics of Human Rights"), p. 9.

__________ (2002), "Time Travellers", in *The Economist* (March 23rd – 29th), pp. 3-18.

Tinbergen, Jan (1958), *The Design of Development*, Baltimore: The Johns Hopkins University Press.

__________ (1985), *Production, Income and Welfare: The Search for an Optimal Order*, Great Britain: Wheatsheaf Books Ltd.

Tobin, James (1985), "Unemployment, Poverty and Economic Policy", *America*, 4 May, 359-362.

UNDP's (1990 – 2000), *Human Development Reports*, New York: Oxford University Press.

__________ (2001), *Human Development Report*, New York: Oxford University Press.

Vaughan, Robert (1843), *The Age of Great Cities; or, Modern Society Viewed in its Relation to Intelligence, Morals and Religion*, London: Jackson & Walford.

Vickery, William (1960), "Utility, Strategy and Social Decision Rules", *The Quarterly Journal of Economics*, 74 (Nov.), 507-535.

Viner, Jacob (1978), "Protestantism and the Rise of Capitalism", *History of Political Economy*, 10:1, 10-189 (The article is also published in author's own work, *Religious Thought and Economic Society*, 1978, North Carolina: Duke University Press).

Watt, Montgomery, M. (1948), *Free Will and Predestination in Early Islam*, London: Luzac & Company Ltd.

__________ (1960), "Al-Ash'arī, Abū al-Ḥasan, 'Alī B. Islamā'īl", in B. Lewis, Ch. Pellat and J. Schacht (eds.), *The Encyclopaedia of Islam (new edition)*, (Vol. 1), Leiden: E.J. Brill.

Weber, Max (1905), *The Protestant Ethic and the Spirit of Capitalism*, (English Translation) London: Allen and Unwin and Scribners (1930).

Wensinck, A.J. (1932), *The Muslim Creed*, London: Frank Cass.

Wicksell, Knut (1896), "A New Principle of Just Taxation", Reprinted in Richard Musgrave and Alan Peacock (1958) (ed.) *Classics in the Theory of Public Finance*, New York: St Martin's Press.

Wilson, Rodney (1997), *Economics, Ethics and Religion: Jewish, Christian and Muslim Thought*, New York: New York University Press.

World Bank (2000), *World Development Report: Attacking Poverty*, New York: Oxford University Press.

Young, Michael (1958), *The Rise of Meritocracy*, London: Thames & Hudson.

Index